MESSAGE OF THE FATHERS OF THE CHURCH

General Editor: Thomas Halton

Volume 15

MESSAGE OF THE FATHERS OF THE CHURCH

GRACE AND THE HUMAN CONDITION

by

Peter C. Phan

Michael Glazier
Wilmington, Delaware

About the Author

PETER C. PHAN graduated *summa cum laude* from the University of London where he read French, Latin, and philosophy. He holds an S.T.D. degree from the Salesian Pontifical University, Rome, and a Ph.D. degree from the University of London. Besides contributing numerous articles to learned and popular journals, he has written several books, including *Social Thought: Message of the Fathers of the Church; Culture and Eschatology: The Iconographical Vision of Paul Evdokimov,* and *Eternity in Time: A Study of Karl Rahner's Eschatology.* Formerly a professor of Theology at the University of Dallas, Texas, he presently teaches systematic theology at the Catholic University of America.

First published in 1988 by Michael Glazier, Inc., 1935 West Fourth Street, Wilmington, Delaware 19805.

Library of Congress Cataloging-in-Publication Data
Phan, Peter C., 1943 -
    Grace and the human condition.

    (Message of the fathers of the church; 15)
    Bibliography: p. 311
    Includes Index.
    1. Man (Christian theology)—History of doctrines—Early church, ca. 30-600. 2. Grace (Theology)—History of doctrines—Early church, ca 30-600. 3. Fathers of the church. I. Title. II. Series: Message of the fathers of the church; v. 15.
BT701.2.P443   1988   233'.09'015   88-82461
ISBN 0-89453-355-0
ISBN 0-89453-326-6 (pbk.)

Message of the Fathers of the Church series:
    ISBN 0-89453-340-1
    ISBN 0-89453-312-6 (pbk.)
Typography by Phyllis Boyd LeVane

Printed in the United States of America   SM

To
Achille Triacca, S.D.B.
Maestro dello spirito
with profound gratitude

Acknowledgments

Generous use has been made of the standard English translations of the Fathers in such series as *Ancient Christian Writers, Fathers of the Church, Ante-Nicene Fathers* and *Post-Nicene Fathers,* often with adaptations and sometimes with corrections. In all cases the translations were checked with the original Greek and Latin texts in the best editions available.

TABLE OF CONTENTS

Abbreviations

AAS	Acta Apostolicae Sedis
ACW	Ancient Christian Writers
ACO	Acta Conciliorum Oecumenicorum, ed. E. Schwartz
ANF	Ante-Nicene Fathers
CCL	Corpus Christianorum, Series latina
CSCO	Corpus Scriptorum Christianorum Orientalium
CSEL	Corpus Scriptorum Ecclesiasticorum Latinorum
FOTC	Fathers of the Church
GCS	Die griechischen christlichen Scriftsteller
NPNF	Nicene and Post-Nicene Fathers
OECT	Oxford Early Christian Texts
PG	Migne, Patrologia Graeca
PL	Migne, Patrologia Latina
PLS	Patrologia Latina, Supplementum
PSt	Patristic Studies, Washington, D.C.
SC	Sources chretiénnes
SCA	Studies in Christian Antiquity, Washington, D.C.
TU	Texte und Untersuchungen

EDITOR'S INTRODUCTION

The *Message of the Fathers of the Church* is a companion series to The *Old Testament Message* and The *New Testament Message*. It was conceived and planned in the belief that Scripture and Tradition worked hand in hand in the formation of the thought, life and worship of the primitive Church. Such a series, it was felt, would be a most effective way of opening up what has become virtually a closed book to present-day readers, and might serve to stimulate a revival in interest in Patristic studies in step with the recent, gratifying resurgence in Scriptural studies.

The term "Fathers" is usually reserved for Christian writers marked by orthodoxy of doctrine, holiness of life, ecclesiastical approval and antiquity. 'Antiquity' is generally understood to include writers down to Gregory the Great (+604) or Isidore of Seville (+636) in the West, and John Damascene (+749) in the East. In the present series, however, greater elasticity has been encouraged, and quotations from writers not noted for orthodoxy will sometimes be included in order to illustrate the evolution of the Message on particular doctrinal matters. Likewise, writers later than the mid-eighth century will sometimes be used to illustrate the continuity of tradition on matters like sacramental theology or liturgical practice.

An earnest attempt was made to select collaborators on a broad inter-disciplinary and inter-confessional basis, the chief consideration being to match scholars who could handle the Fathers in their original languages with subjects in which they had already demonstrated a special interest and competence.

About the only editorial directive given to the selected contributors was that the Fathers, for the most part, should be
allowed to speak for themselves and that they should speak in
readable, reliable modern English. Volumes on individual
themes were considered more suitable than volumes devoted
to individual Fathers; each theme, hopefully, contributing an
important segment to the total mosaic of the Early Church,
one, holy, catholic and apostolic. Each volume has an intro-
ductory essay outlining the historical and theological development of the theme, with the body of the work mainly occupied
with liberal citations from the Fathers in modern English
translation and a minimum of linking commentary. Short lists
of Suggested Further Readings are included; but dense, scholarly footnotes were actively discouraged on the pragmatic
grounds that such scholarly shorthand has other outlets and
tends to lose all but the most relentlessly esoteric reader in a
semi-popular series.

At the outset of his *Against Heresies* Irenaeus of Lyons
warns his readers 'not to expect from me any display of
rhetoric, which I have never learned, or any excellence of
composition, which I have never practised, or any beauty or
persuasiveness of style, to which I make no pretensions.'
Similarly, modest disclaimers can be found in many of the
Greek and Latin Fathers and all too often, unfortunately, they
have been taken at their word by an uninterested world. In
fact, however, they were often highly educated products of the
best rhetorical schools of their day in the Roman Empire, and
what they have to say is often as much a lesson in literary and
cultural, as well as in spiritual, edification.

St. Augustine, in *The City of God* (19.7), has interesting
reflections on the need for a common language in an expanding
world community; without a common language a man is more
at home with his dog than with a foreigner as far as inter-
communication goes, even in the Roman Empire, which
imposes on the nations it conquers the yoke of both law and
language with a resultant abundance of interpreters. It is hoped
that in the present world of continuing language barriers the
contributors to this series will prove opportune interpreters of
the perennial Christian message.

Thomas Halton

Preface

What does it mean to be human? This is the perennial question that has been raised in every age of human history, and perhaps at no other times more disturbingly and persistently than in our days. To that question contemporary world-views give a host of so diverse and even conflicting answers that the result is more darkness than light. So people continue to ask: What does it mean to be human? What is the meaning of suffering, evil, death, which technological progress, the modern god in whom we have placed our trust, has not been able to eliminate? Is there any hope of salvation from our alienation—economic, political, spiritual and otherwise? Will our yearning for total liberation ever be fulfilled?

The early Christian writers, in their own way, considered these fundamental issues on the basis of the Judeo-Christian tradition they inherited. Perhaps their categories of image of God, original sin, and grace may sound odd or hopelessly old-fashioned to modern ears. And perhaps we should invent a new language to express our peculiar experience of our human condition, of our bondage and our liberation. Nevertheless, patristic anthropology, despite the obsoleteness of some of its elements, contains profound and perennial insights into the human condition which we cannot afford to ignore.

The present book seeks to recover the anthropological insights of those whom we traditionally call Fathers of the Church and to present them in their own words. The highly selected bibliography given at the end of the book is not intended simply to provide suggestions for further readings, but also to acknowledge the works I have found most useful and from which I have learnt so much.

I would like to express my thanks to Professor Thomas Halton for his advice and help which he has generously given me in this book just as he had done in my first book in the series. My gratitude also goes to Michael Glazier, who under *force majeure* had to entrust me with the writing of this volume. Thanks, too, to Jeri Guadagnoli, who cheerfully and expertly typed the entire manuscript.

Finally, the work is dedicated to Professor Dr. Achille Triacca, my first *Doktorvater,* who has never ceased to encourage and support me.

Peter C. Phan
Catholic University of America

Introduction

If it is true, as Rahner claims, that "dogmatic theology today must be theological anthropology and that such an 'anthropocentric' view is necessary and useful,"[1] then speaking about God necessarily involves speaking about humanity and vice versa. Furthermore, if it is true, as Vatican II teaches, that "it is only in the mystery of the Word made flesh that the mystery of humanity truly becomes clear,"[2] then not only anthropology is theology but also christology. And finally, since it is only in Christ's Spirit that the whole human person is inwardly renewed,[3] anthropology is not only theology and christology but also pneumatology.

It is of paramount importance to perceive the "circumincession" among these theological treatises—theology, christology, pneumatology and anthropology—in order to appreciate the full significance of the early theological controversies and the

[1]"Theology and Anthropology," *Theological Investigations IX,* translated by Graham Harrison (New York: Seabury Press, 1972), 28.

[2]*Gaudium et Spes,* no. 22. The Council goes on to affirm: "For Adam, the first man, was a type of him who was to come, Christ the Lord. Christ the new Adam, in the very revelation of the mystery of the Father and of his love, fully reveals the human person to himself and brings to light his most high calling. It is no wonder, then, that all the truths mentioned so far should find in him their source and their most perfect embodiment." English translation, slightly emended, in Austin Flannery, general editor, *Vatican II .The Conciliar and Post Conciliar Document* (Northport, New York: Costello Publishing Co., 1977).

[3]See *ibid.,* 22: "Conformed to the image of the Son who is the firstborn of many brethren, the Christian receives the 'first fruits of the Spirit' (Rom. 8:23) by which he is able to fulfill the new law of love. By this Spirit, who is the 'pledge of our inheritance' (Eph. 1:14), the whole human being is inwardly renewed, right up to the 'redemption of the body' (Rom. 8:23). 'If the Spirit of him who raised Jesus from the dead dwells in you, he who raised Jesus from the dead will give life to your mortal bodies also through his Spirit who dwells in you'" (Rom. 8:11).

first seven ecumenical councils. It is true that these controversies and councils, from Nicaea I (325) to Nicaea II (787) deal with primarily trinitarian and christological issues; nevertheless because they deal with them not as abstract truths but as realities embodied in the economy of salvation, they necessarily, even though indirectly, exhibit their relevance for the eternal destiny of humanity. Thus, for example, if the early Church defended with extreme vigor the full humanity and divinity of Jesus, it did so because it believed that whatever in humanity that is not assumed by God is not saved and that, were Jesus not God, his life and death, however noble and praiseworthy they might be, would not be able to redeem humankind. In this sense it may be argued that theological anthropology—the theology of human existence, of sin and grace—was the underlying leitmotif of post-apostolic and patristic writings.

Of course the early Christian writers did not start their theological reflections on grace and the human condition from scratch nor did they do so in a kind of cultural vacuum. They derived their raw material, as it were, from the Scripture and reformulated the biblical teaching in the language and thought forms of their time. It is necessary, therefore, to examine briefly biblical anthropology and Greco-Roman culture insofar as these form the indispensable background for, and appreciation of, the development of patristic anthropology.

I. Background and Context

The earliest and the most basic biblical affirmation about human beings is found in Gen 1:26-27: "Then God said: 'Let us make humanity in our image and likeness to rule the fish in the sea, the birds of heaven, the cattle, all wild animals on earth, and all reptiles that crawl upon the earth.' So God created humanity in his own image; in the image of God he created it; male and female he created them." As we will see, this verse forms the cornerstone of patristic anthropology, and many Fathers draw a sharp distinction between image (*selem-eikōn-imago*) and likeness (*demut-homoiōsis-similitudo*). Whatever may be said about their interpretation, it is clear that for the Bible only humanity is made in God's image and likeness. Image means, ordinarily, an exact copy or reproduction, and its strong implication is attenuated by the addition of likeness, ordinarily meaning resemblance or similarity. Furthermore, Hebrew thought knows no dichotomy between body and soul in the human person; it is the whole person that is in God's image and likeness. As God's image, humanity is his representative on earth having dominion over other creatures. Finally, there is a conviction that the distinction of the sexes is of divine origin and therefore good.

The Yahwistic account of creation, more vivid, concrete, and anthropomorphic than the priestly one, presents the story of creation as a prelude to the story of the fall and the consequent story of humanity's gradual estrangement from God. The center of interest is the creation of the first human being *(Adam* in the collective sense) into whom God breathed his "breath of life." The creation of the woman out of the man's rib suggests that she is the complement of the man, a social being by nature, but not his mere appendage; rather she is his equal insofar as she has the same nature as his. The two accounts of creation will be interpreted allegorically by some Fathers as implying a double creation; the first creation is that of the human souls who then "grew cold" in their love for God, and the second creation is that of the material world into which the fallen souls were consigned.

The story of the temptation and the fall of humanity reveals, on the one hand, the intimacy which the first human beings enjoyed with God in the garden and, on the other, its disruption by their pride in transgressing the divine command. Their shame at being naked is a symbol of the change in their condition: from God's friends they turned into his enemies, from immortal they became subject to death.

The New Testament takes over the teachings of the Hebrew Bible regarding the creation of the world and of humanity as well as the fall. However, it transforms them in two directions: first, the center of creation is no longer the people of Israel but Christ and his disciples (Acts 4:24-30; 1 Pet 4:19) and secondly, the role of Christ in creation is made explicit (Col 1:15-20, Heb 1:1-4; Jn 1:1-17).

Most important, however, is the New Testament understanding of the human condition and divine grace. Humans are seen as subject to death, inclined to evil, and sinful (Rom 7:14-25). The cause of this situation of sin, death, and condemnation is traced back to the first sin of Adam (the *"peccatum originale originans,"* Rom 5:12-21). The New Testament declares, however, that this situation of sin, death, and condemnation caused by the first Adam has been destroyed by Christ, the second Adam, who brought grace, life, and acquittal in abundance. The effects of Christ's redemption on humanity are described in many different ways: reconciliation and peace with God (Rom 5:1-5; Eph 2:14-22; 2 Cor 5:18-21), friendship with God (Jn 15:13-14), indwelling of the Trinity (Eph 3:17; 1 Jn 2:6, 24, 27-28), adoptive sonship (Rom 8:15-23; Gal 4:5; Eph 1:3-14; Jn 1:13). Sometimes the effects are described in terms of a created reality in the justified, as an intrinsic transformation (Tit 3:4-2) as a rebirth (Tim 3:5; 1 Pet 1:3-5; Jn 3:3-8), as participation in the divine nature (2 Pet 1:3-7).

One of the key words that the New Testament uses to characterize the saving work of Christ is *charis,* grace. In the Hebrew Bible, grace (*hen*) means affection, good will, favor, or friendliness, particularly on the part of someone in a high place. The meaning of *hen* is extended to the object of this favor to imply charm, graciousness or beauty. The Hebrew Bible recognizes that divine grace, in the form either of good will or of a gift, is both freely bestowed on God's part and undeserved on humanity's part. In the New Testament, *charis* has a definitely soteriological connotation. It signified God's supreme and gratuitous will to save, decreed from eternity and carried out in history by Christ's act of redemption, and is now achieving its effects in us and in the world.

This is, in brief outline, the biblical teaching on grace and the human condition which the early Christian writers inherited, reflected upon, and communicated to their contemporaries. In so doing, of course, they had to use the categories and thought forms of their times. In order to understand their writings it will be useful to review, again in summary fashion, the various cultural movements operative in the patristic era.[4]

[4]For excellent brief surveys, see J.N.D. Kelly, *Early Christian Doctrines* (New

Christian Gnosticism, it is generally held today, had its roots in trends of thought already present in pagan religious circles and in Jewish wisdom theories. In Christianity, the movement appeared at first as a school or schools of thought within the Church, but by the end of the second century the Gnostics had mostly become separate sects. Gnosticism took many different forms, commonly associated with the names of particular teachers, e. g. Valentinus, Basilides, and Marcion. The basic issue for the Gnostics is the origin of evil. Gnosticism claims that the material world is fundamentally evil, not the work of God, the supreme and unknowable divine Being, but of an arrogant evil power, called the Demiurge or creator god. The Demiurge was derived from God by a series of emanations or 'aeons'; he it was who, through a fall among the higher aeons, created and ruled the material world which is, therefore, imperfect and antagonistic to the spirit. Nevertheless, into the constitution of some human beings there had entered a seed or spark of divine spiritual substance, and through the secret knowledge revealed by God (*gnōsis*) and the rites associated with it, this spiritual element might be rescued from its evil material environment and hence saved. Such people are called 'spiritual' (*pneumatikoi*) whereas others were merely 'fleshly' (*sarkikoi*) or 'material' (*hylikoi*), though some Gnostics added a third intermediate class, the 'psychic' (*psychikoi*). The function of Christ was to come as the emissary of the supreme God to reveal this 'gnosis.'

The principal anti-Gnostic writers, such as Irenaeus, Tertullian, and Hippolytus rejected the Gnostic teachings by appealing to the plain meanings of the Scripture as interpreted by the tradition of the Church, which had been publicly handed down by a chain of teachers reaching back to the Apostles. They insisted on the identity of the Creator and the Supreme God, on the goodness of the material creation, on the need to be redeemed from an evil will rather than an evil environment. Other Fathers, such as Clement of Alexandria, would be more sympathetic toward Gnosticism and agreed with the Gnostics that 'gnosis,' religious knowledge or illumi-

York: Harper and Row, 1960), pp. 3-28; J. Patout Burns, *Theological Anthropology* (Philadelphia: Fortress Press, 1985), pp. 1-10.

nation, was the chief element in Christian perfection. Nevertheless, Clement maintained that true 'gnosis' was given only by Christ, the Logos, the source of all human reason and the interpreter of God to humankind. This 'gnosis' is now found in the faith of the Church, apostolic in its foundation and possessing divine revelation.

The second philosophical movement that had far-reaching influence on the Fathers is Platonism, or more precisely Neo-Platonism, which flourished from the middle of the third century. Its most influential representative is Plotinus (205-270) whose *Enneads* was well known to the Fathers. A monist, Plotinus conceives reality as one vast hierarchical structure with grades descending from what is beyond being (God or the One) to what falls below being (matter). The One, or the highest hypostasis, is the ineffable and unchanging source from which all beings emanate and the goal to which they ever strive to return. Immediately below the One is the second hypostasis, Mind or Thought (*Nous*), which comprises the world of forms, which it contemplates in its effort to return to the One. It is the causal principle, and is identified with Plato's Demiurge. Below the Mind is the third hypostasis, the Soul (*Psychē*), which is divided into two: the higher soul, which is akin to the Mind and transcends the material order, and the lower soul or Nature (*physis*), which is the soul of the world. From this World-Soul individual human souls proceed, and, like the World-Soul, they are divided into two elements, a higher element which belongs to the sphere of the *nous,* and a lower element which is directly connected with the body. The soul pre-existed before its union with the body, which is represented as a fall, and survives the death of the body. Below the sphere of soul is that of the material world. Matter, though ultimately proceeding from the One, is the lowest stage of the universe and is the antithesis of the One as darkness is opposed to light. Devoid of quality, as the privation of being and light, matter is the principle of evil.

Plotinian neo-Platonism exercised a strong influence upon the Alexandrian Fathers, Origen in particular, and the Cappadocian Fathers, especially Gregory of Nyssa, and, in the West, Ambrose and Augustine. The reasons for this are many and vary from writers to writers. But, no doubt Plotinus' elevated concept of God's transcendence, his triadic view of reality and, above all, the basic religious orientation of his systems, are among the most important elements that attracted the Fathers to his ideas. Since whatever exists is an emanation from the One, there is in all reality an ardent longing to return to and be united with the One. The means to achieve this goal is, according to Plotinus, contemplation, which is the most perfect activity the soul can perform. Fired by the heavenly Eros, the soul begins its ascent toward the One. In this ascent the ethical element (*praxis*) is subservient to the theoretical or intellectual element (*theōria*). It is composed of three stages. The first stage is purification (*catharsis*) by which the soul frees itself from the dominion of the body and the senses and rises to the practice of the "political virtues," that is, the four cardinal virtues. In the second stage, the soul first rises above sense perception, turning toward the *nous* and occupying itself with science and philosophy. Next the soul moves beyond discursive thought to union with *nous*. The third and last stage is that of mystical union with God or the One in an ecstasy characterized by the absence of all duality.

Along Plotinian lines several Greek Fathers (e.g. Gregory of Nyssa with his notion of *epectasis*) and Augustine (e.g. in *The Confessions* 1, 1: "You have made us for yourself, and our heart is restless until it rests in you") develop an anthropology in which human existence is conceived as a dynamic desire for union with God in knowledge and love and as a participation in God's perfections. Of course, there is a fundamental difference between Plotinus' "natural mysticism" and the Fathers' notion of participation in God's life, insofar as in the former union with the One is achieved by the unaided effort of the soul, whereas for the latter, it is a gratuitous gift of God. Nevertheless, it is true that Plotinus exercised a great influence on the early Christian writers, and through them Dionysius the Areopagite and later theologians and mystics.

In contrast to Platonic idealism, Stoicism is a form of materialistic pantheism or monism. It rejects the Platonic distinction between the transcendent world of intelligible forms not perceptible by the senses and the ordinary world of sensible experience and teaches that the universe as a whole is material. God or Logos is a finer matter, a fiery vapor, immanent in the material universe. This God, Logos, Providence, Nature, or the soul of the universe is the "active principle" and permeates and organizes the unformed matter, which is the "passive principle." Each particular thing is as it were a microcosmos, composed of the material active principle (the Logos) and the passive principle (unformed matter). Indeed, the Stoics speak of the 'seminal logoi' (*logoi spermatikoi*), that is, seeds through the activity of which individual things come into existence. The human soul is a portion of the divine Logos; it is composed of the five senses, the power of self-expression, the reproductive capacity, and the ruling element, namely reason. The Stoics made an important distinction between the 'immanent logos' (*logos endiathetos*), which is reason considered merely as present in humans, and the 'expressed logos' (*logos prophorikos*), which is reason made known by means of the faculty of speech.

Though some Fathers used certain Stoic expressions to expound the Christian teachings, e.g. Justin's use of the *logoi spermatikoi,* Theophilus of Antioch's use of the *logos endiathetos* and *logos prophorikos* in his Logos christology, and the frequent description of reason as the ruling faculty (*to hēgemonikon*), the materialist monism of Stoic cosmology was repugnant to them. On the other hand, many Fathers (e.g. Ambrose and Augustine) found their ethical system very appealing. In contrast to Epicureanism which makes pleasure the end of life, Stoicism believes that the end of life or happiness (*eudaimonia*) consists in virtue, that is, the life according to nature, the agreement of human action with the law of nature, or of the human will with the divine will. Hence the famous Stoic maxim, "Live according to nature." Life according to nature is life conducted in accordance with the principle that is active in nature, the Logos, the principle shared in by the human soul. The ethical end, therefore, consists in submission to the divinely appointed order. Characteristic of Stoic ethics is its emphasis on the four cardinal virtues and on the achievement of *apatheia,* the state of moral conquest of the passions and affections.

This Stoic ethics was transformed by the Fathers in light of the Christian doctrine of sin and grace; unfortunately not all early Christian writers were fully aware of the basic naturalism inherent in Stoicism, and their emphasis on the need for asceticism and self-conquest at times ran counter to the Christian doctrines of the fall, the bondage of the human will to sin, and the absolute necessity of grace. The stories of Pelagius and his disciples and of the so-called Semi-Pelagian monks of Southern Gaul are cases in point.

II. Patristic Anthropology: Basic Themes

It was in the context of Gnosticism, Neo-Platonism and Stoicism (to mention only the most important and obvious philosophical currents) that the early Christian writers developed their anthropologies on the basis of the Jewish heritage and the Christian gospel. Their approaches, methods and themes are no doubt extremely varied and permit no easy systematization. Nevertheless, some basic and overarching themes must be found to guide us in our reading of their voluminous writings and to function as a coherent criterion for our selection of texts. There is, of course, no one single approach to patristic anthropology that can claim exclusive validity. Patristic theology of human existence is so rich and diverse that in principle any one method can disclose aspects of it that another may have neglected. I have chosen the theme of "image of God" as the architectonic principle with which to organize patristic anthropology; my hope is that such a choice is not entirely arbitrary.

On the basis of patristic writings, it may be said that human beings derive their unique dignity from the fact that they have been created in the image and likeness of God. Of course the expression "in the image and likeness of God" is anything but obvious, and different Fathers give different interpretations to it that can hardly be harmonized, as the selected texts will show. Nevertheless, the fact that humans are so created remains fundamental. As Epiphanius has said, somewhat impatiently: "Where the image is and in what part it consists, God alone knows. But we should admit the image in human beings, lest we appear to reject God's gifts and refuse to believe in him."[5] Indeed, the Fathers discussed and disagreed whether

[5] *Haereses* III, 1, PG 42, 341-345.

there is a distinction between image and likeness, what these terms mean, where the reality of image is located, in the body or the soul, or both. But no one doubted that being created in God's image is unique to humans and constitutes their special dignity. Some, such as Augustine, even discern an explicitly Trinitarian image in the human person.

This image and likeness, however, was stained or disfigured by sin. Those Fathers who maintain a distinction between image and likeness would contend that the likeness, which they identify with divine grace, was lost by sin, whereas the image remains as the basis for a potential restoration of the likeness with God. Because of the fall, the condition of humanity became worse. The Christian writers of the first three centuries recognize that humanity is affected by an inherited corruption, manifested chiefly in its subjection to death, which it receives as an effect of Adam's fall and which leads to the multiplication of sins and eternal death. The expression 'sin,' however, is as a rule reserved for personal sins and is not used to designate the human condition after the fall. Sometimes the early Fathers explicitly denied that babies are born with sins; they were in fact opposed to Origen's notion of a pre-cosmic fall. Nevertheless, insofar as Christ is said to be the liberator of humankind and the Savior of all human beings, the practice gradually emerged of describing the state of hereditary corruption as 'sin.'

The practice of baptizing babies contributed not a little to this view. It is not known with certainty when this practice began, but no doubt toward the year 200 it was considered as traditional. Cyprian suggests that baptism should be given also to children, not because they are guilty of their own sins, but of the sin of others (cfr. letter 64, 5). His view will be often repeated and developed by Western theology. Augustine plays an important part in the development of the dogma of original sin; in fact he is the first to use the term 'sin' to designate the situation of the person not united with Christ. His controversies with Pelagius, Caelestius, and Julian of Eclanum afforded him the opportunity to clarify this doctrine of original sin which will be canonized by the Council of Carthage in 418.

The image of God, stained and weakened by sin, is restored in us by Christ, the only perfect image of God, by uniting us to himself. This union with Christ is described by the Fathers as 'physical' union, insofar as Christ, in the Incarnation, assumed our human nature. It is also called 'fundamental' because in sharing in our nature, Christ shares with us his obedience, so that his obedience is ours just as Adam's disobedience is also ours. It is 'pneumatic,' too, because the Holy Spirit, given in baptism, imprints upon us the likeness of Christ. Further, this union impels us to action, both by knowing and loving Christ and by living in the grace of the Spirit. Finally, this union is achieved by the sacraments, in particular baptism and eucharist.

The Fathers, especially the Greek, speak of the presence of God in the just as a formally trinitarian indwelling. All the three divine Persons dwell in the just who possess a special relation to each of them and particularly to the Holy Spirit. This patristic doctrine of the just person's relation to the Holy Spirit is interpreted by some (e.g. P. Galtier) as meaning only an appropriation, and by others (e.g. Petavius) as a specifically different relation. Besides this indwelling Trinity, which is now called Uncreated Grace, the Fathers also speak of the divinization (*theōsis*) of the just, a radical renewal, a rebirth, a participation in the divine nature, or, to use a modern term, created grace.

Finally, in the West, the Pelagian and Semi-Pelagian crises forced Augustine to reflect more deeply on the relationship between divine grace and human freedom, on different kinds of grace (e.g. *adjutorium sine quo non* and *adjutorium quo,* on the difference between the grace in innocent humanity in paradise and in fallen humanity, on different aspects of grace (e.g. 'healing' and 'elevating'), on predestination and on final perseverance. Augustine's anthropology, in its moderate form, was officially accepted by the Latin Church in the *Indiculus Caelestini* and especially in the canons of the Council of Orange in 529.

Patristic anthropology, as any other human achievement, is time-bound and culturally conditioned. There are in it, no doubt, outmoded expressions, archaic conceptual frameworks, and one-sided emphases. There are, on the other hand, concepts and images, insights and reflections, that still echo deeply in our hearts as we attempt a more authentic self-understanding, and it would be a pity if they are no longer remembered or lost.

1

Pre-Irenean Anthropology

The earliest Christian writers from the end of the first century to the second half of the second century, often referred to as the Apostolic Fathers and the Apologists, did not set out to offer a comprehensive exposition of the Christian faith, much less a theological anthropology. Most of their works were occasional pieces, generally of a practical and parenetic nature, responding to the pressing needs of the community. These include, among other things, preserving Church unity (the first letter of Clement of Rome), defending the true faith against the contamination of heresies, especially by means of the episcopacy (the letters of Ignatius of Antioch), organizing community life and worship (the *Didache*), pleading for Christianity against the attacks of the Roman emperors, the philosophers, the pagan populace and the Jews (the apologies of Quadratus, Aristides, Justin, Tatian, Athenagoras of Athens, Theophilus of Antioch and the *Letter to Diognetus*).

Despite their occasional nature, these early writings, because they focus upon the redemption of humankind, cannot but touch upon, however indirectly, God's creative act, the beginning of the history of salvation, the origin and nature of human beings, their fall into sin and the gift of grace which Jesus' passion, death, and resurrection brought to the world— so many essential themes of Christian anthropology. In discussing these topics most of the early Christian writers mentioned above did no more than repeat and paraphase the teachings of the Scripture. Some Apologists, however, especially Justin, did attempt, though in a very rudimentary fashion, to build a bridge between the Christian faith and Greco-Roman culture. In what follows let us examine the anthropology of thinkers whom we have for convenience called pre-Irenean, even though they do not in any sense constitute a uniform school of thought.

I. Belief in God the Creator

The belief in God the Creator is, of course, a fundamental article of the Jewish-Christian faith and was already clearly affirmed in the Creed. Though the present text of the *Symbolum apostolicum*, in which God is confessed to be "the Father almighty, Creator of heaven and earth," did not appear before the beginning of the sixth century, all the doctrinal elements therein contained had already been asserted in the numerous and varied formulas of faith found in early Christian literature. It should be remembered that in the first centuries the title "almighty" connotes God's universal control and sovereignty over reality, just as "Father" refers primarily to his role as Creator and Author of all things.

The *Didache* (1, 2), the first part of which, according to the best current scholarship, was originally a Jewish work, probably of Essene origin, and later, perhaps about 140, found entrance into Christian circles and was enlarged to make up the present text as a work for the instruction of catechumens, and the so-called *Letter of Barnabas* (19, 2), which is actually a theological tract, probably of Alexandrian origin (ca. 70/79 or 117/132), call God "our maker." His omnipotence and sovereignty must be acknowledged because he is "the Lord almighty" (*Didache* 10, 3), "the Lord who governs the whole universe" (*Letter of Barnabas*, 21, 5). After introducing the doctrine of the two ways, the *Didache* describes the way of life as based upon the confession that God is our fatherly Creator (1, 2), whereas the way of death is shown to be taken by those who "know not their Creator" (5, 2). Thus Christian morality is ultimately grounded in the will of the divine Creator. Faith in the Creator is also beautifully expressed in the prayer the *Didache* instructs to be said in the Eucharist: "Almighty Master, you have created everything for the sake of your name and have given food and drink to humans for their enjoyment, so that they may thank you" (10, 3). A similar doctrine of the two ways, is also taught by the *Letter of Barnabas* (cc. 18-21). The first letter of Clement (ca. 90) contains a series of doxologies to the Creator, "the Father and Maker of the whole world" (19, 2). In words redolent of Stoic cosmology, Clement extols the beauty and purposeful order of the universe:

> The heavens move at his (God's) order and peacefully obey him. Day and night observe the course he appointed them, without disturbing each other. The sun, and the moon, and the choirs of stars move harmoniously in their appointed courses at his command and never deviate from them. By his will, and without dissension or changing anything he has decreed, the earth becomes fruitful at the proper seasons and brings forth abundant food for humans and beasts and every living creature on it. The unsearchable abyss and the indescribable regions of the underworld are subject to the same decrees ... The ocean, which humans cannot cross, and the worlds beyond it are governed by the same decrees of the Master. The seasons, spring, summer, fall, and winter, peacefully succeed each other. The winds from their different points perform their service at the proper time and without hindrance. Perennial springs, created for enjoyment and health, never fail to produce life-giving water. The tiniest creatures come together in harmony and peace. All these things the great Creator and Master of the universe ordained to exist in peace and harmony. Thus, he showered his benefits on them all, but most abundantly, on us who have taken refuge in this compassion through our Lord Jesus Christ, to whom be glory and majesty for ever and ever. Amen. (20, 1-12).[1]

Stoic influence is also evident in the names Clement uses to describe the Creator: *"ho dēmiurgos kai patēr tōn aiōnōn"* (19, 2) and *"ktistēs tou sympantos kosmou"* (20,11). Never-

---

[1]Text: SC 167.134; trans. of *The Apostolic Fathers*, vol. 2, ed. R.M. Grant and Holt H. Graham, 43

theless, Clement rejects the pagan belief in demiurges; for him, God and the author of the universe are one and the same being. Whereas Clement's doctrine of creation is basically still that of the Old Testament, the christological dimension of creation is clearly brought out by the so-called second letter of Clement (ca. 150) and Ignatius of Antioch (+ ca. 110). The former, which is in fact an anonymous homily, appealing for a due appreciation of our redemption by Christ, says: "... He called us when we were not, and willed us to come into existence out of nothingness" (1, 8). There is therefore an intimate unity between creation and redemption.

Ignatius of Antioch, following St. Paul, calls Christ "*ho kainos anthrōpos*" (Ephesians 20,1) and speaks of the divine plan of salvation through the man Christ, who "was with the Father before all ages" (*Magnesians*, 6, 1). The christological dimension of creation is implied too in Ignatius' doctrine of the eucharist, which he describes in the well-known phrase as the "the medicine of immortality and the antidote against death, enabling us to live for ever in union with Jesus Christ" (*Ephesians*, 20:2).

Christ's role in creation is less evident in the *Shepherd of Hermas* (ca. 140/155), a rather lengthy work belonging to the genre of Jewish-Christian apocalypses dealing with repentance after baptism. Nevertheless, in its teaching on the origin of the world, it exercised a great influence since it was the first document in Christian literature to affirm the doctrine of the *creatio ex nihilo*:

> First of all, believe that there is one God who has produced, perfected, and made all things out of nothing so that they might exist, who comprehends all things and who alone is incomprehensible (*Mand.*, 1, 1).[2]

This teaching on the creation of the world out of nothing, which is one of the fundamental doctrines of Christian anthropology, and which is in radical conflict with Greek cosmology, remains a constant theme of the early Fathers, e.g.,

[2]Text: SC 53.144; trans. ANF 2.20

Justin, Theophilus of Antioch, Irenaeus, Origen and Tertullian. While the Apostolic Fathers considered so far tended to focus their attention on problems arising within the Christian community, their successors, the Apologists, were more concerned with defending Christianity against external attacks and in demonstrating its superiority over pagan philosophies and religions. In anthropology, in particular, they attempted to refute Greek notions of the gods and of the created world. Of course, in order to do so, it was necessary for them to present Christian belief in creation in terms of Greek—mainly Platonic and Stoic— cosmology.

Thus it is to be expected that Aristides of Athens (ca. 140), one of the earliest Apologists, opens the first chapter of his *Apology* with arguments of natural philosophy, in the manner of Middle Platonism, a fusion of Platonic, Aristotelian and Stoic elements represented in particular by Albinos, to prove that an eternal, uncreated Being governs the universe and ensures its harmony:

> When I saw that the world and all that is in it is moved by a force, I understood that He who moves and maintains it is God; for whatever moves something is stronger than that which is moved, and whatever maintains something is stronger than that which is maintained. I call the One who constructed all things and maintains them *God*: He that is without beginning and eternal, immortal and lacking nothing, and who is above all passions and failings such as anger and forgetfulness and ignorance and the rest (*Apol.*, 1, 1).[3]

Influenced by Platonism, Aristides sharply contrasts the incomprehensible, infinite, transcendent Creator with the anthropomorphic deities of popular religions: "Let us proceed, then, O King, to the elements themselves, so that we may demonstrate concerning them that they are not gods, but corruptible and changeable things, produced out of the non-existent by him who is truly God, who is incorruptible and

[3]Text: TU 4, 3.1-6; trans. ANF 10.263

unchangeable and invisible, but who sees all things and changes them and alters them as he wills" (1, 4).

Aristides' reasoning in this matter is closely followed by Justin, Theophilus, Tatian, and the author of the *Letter to Diognetus*. Justin (ca. 100/110-ca. 165) expounds the Christian faith in God the Creator as follows:

> ... We have also been taught that in the beginning God in his goodness formed all things that are for the sake of human beings out of unformed matter, and if they show themselves by their actions worthy of his plan, we have learned that they will be counted worthy of dwelling with him, reigning together and made free from corruption and suffering. For as he made us in the beginning when we were not, so do we hold that those who choose what is pleasing to him are, on account of their choice, deemed worthy of incorruption and of fellowship with him. For we did not bring ourselves into being on our own power; and in order that we may follow those things which please him, choosing them by means of the rational faculties he has himself endowed us with, he both persuades us and leads us to faith (*Apol.*, 10).[4]

Another work, attributed to Justin but without doubt spurious, *Cohortatio ad Graecos* (ca. 260/302) highlights the difference between the Greek and the Christian concepts of creation:

> And I think it necessary to attend to this also, that Plato never names him the Creator, but the *fashioner* of the gods *(dēmiurgos)*, although, in the opinion of Plato, there is considerable difference between these two. For the Creator creates the creature by his own capability and power, being in need of nothing else; the fashioner, on the other hand, frames his production when he has received from matter the wherewithal for his work (22).[5]

---

[4]Text: PG 6.341; trans. ANF 1.165
[5]Text: PG 6.281; trans. ANF 1.282.

Theophilus of Antioch (+ ca. 185/191) explicitly rejects the Platonist theory of eternity of matter in his apologetical work *To Autolycus* and argues strongly for the *creatio ex nihilo*:

> But Plato and those of his school acknowledge indeed that God is uncreated, and the Father and Maker of all things; but then they maintain that matter as well as God is uncreated, and aver that it is coeval with God. But if God is uncreated and matter uncreated, God is no longer, according to the Platonists, the Creator of all things, nor, so far as their opinions hold, is the monarchy of God established. And further, as God, because he is uncreated, is also unalterable, so if matter, too, were uncreated, it also would be unalterable and equal to God; for that which is created is mutable and alterable, but that which is uncreated is immutable and unalterable. And what great thing is it if God made the world out of existent materials? For even a human artist, when he gets material from some one, makes of it what he pleases. But the power of God is manifested in this, that out of things that are not he makes whatever he pleases; just as the bestowal of life and motion is the prerogative of no other than God alone (2, 4).[6]

Tatian the Syrian, whose fame rests on his harmony of the gospels (the *Diatessaron*, affirms in his *Address to the Greeks* (ca. 165/175) that matter is created:

> Matter is not without a beginning, like God; nor is it of equal power with God, through being without a beginning. It is created, and not produced by any other being; it is brought into existence by God alone who is the Creator of all things (5).[7]

Lastly, the author of the *Letter to Diognetus* (ca. 125/200) emphasizes the role of Christ in creation:

---

[6]Text: PG 6.1052; trans. ANF 2.95
[7]Text: PG 6.817; trans. ANF 2.67

It was truly the almighty, all-creating, and invisible God himself who established among humans the Truth from heaven and the holy and incomprehensible Word, and set him firmly in their hearts. Nor did he do this, contrary to what one might suppose, by sending to them some minister, or an angel or a ruler, or one of those in charge of earthly things, or one of those entrusted with the administration of heavenly things. Rather, God sent the very designer and creator of all things himself (*ton technitē kai dēmiurgon ton holōn*), through whom he had made the heavens, and by whom he had enclosed the sea within its own bounds; whose mysteries all the elements of nature faithfully guard; from whom the sun received the schedule of its daily flight; whose command the moon obeys in lighting up the night; to whom the stars give heed in following the path of the moon; by whom all things were ordered and bounded and placed in subjection; the heavens and the things in the heavens, the earth and the things on the earth, the sea and the things in the sea; fire, air, and the abyss; the things in the heights, the things in the depths, the things between —yes, he it was that God sent to humans (7, 2).[8]

Another aspect of creation was also well taught by the Apologists, namely God's freedom to create or not to create, and hence the personal character of creation. Tatian writes:

The heavenly Word, who is Spirit begotten by the Father, and Word from the rational potency, made humans an image of immortality in imitation of the Father who begot him .... Indeed, the Word, before humans were ever made, was the creator of the angels. Each of these species of creatures was created free, not having the nature of good, which pertains only to God, and which is brought to perfection by humans through their freedom of choice ... (*Address to the Greeks*, 7).[9]

[8]Text: SC 33.66; trans. LCL II, *The Apostolic Fathers*, 363, K. Lake tr.
[9]Text: PG 6.820; trans ANF 2.67

In summary, the Apologists put up a vigorous and effective defense of the Christian belief in God the Creator and, except in the case of Justin, of the *creatio ex nihilo*. They stoutly opposed the Hellenistic tendency toward dualism which made belief in creation impossible. Thanks to their effort, the truth of the *creatio ex nihilo* is so firmly anchored in Christian theology that Irenaeus and Tertullian will be able to take it for granted as part of the faith.

Of course this does not mean that the Apologists fully succeeded in preserving all the aspects of the Christian faith in creation. For one thing, God's transcendence over the world was so emphasized that it was necessary for the Apologists to introduce the mediation of the Logos which they, for the most part, interpreted in accordance with Philo's doctrine of creation. The result is christological subordinationism. Justin, for instance, has the Logos, the Father's intellect, proceed from him solely for the purpose of creation. Before creation the Logos is immanent in the Father. He proceeds *ad extra* only by generation, which, being ordered to creation, must depend on the Father's will. Though the Logos is not reduced to the status of a creature, since he is still called divine, nevertheless he remains subordinate to the Father even as a divine Person. This is clearly implied in Justin's description of the Logos as "another God and Lord subject to (besides?) the Maker of all things" (*theos kai kurios heteros hupo ton poiētēn tōn holōn* [*Dialogue with Trypho*, 56, 4]).

For Theophilus of Antioch too, the Logos is a sort of intermediate being, proceeding from God only for the purpose of creation and revelation (cfr. *To Autolycus*, 2, 22). This is clear from his distinction between *logos endiathetos* and *logos prophorikos* (2, 10 and 22). Thus the generation of the Logos is not an eternal process but one bound up with creation.

Athenagoras softens Theophilus' celebrated distinction by stressing the uncreatedness of the Logos and interpreting his procession at creation as his manifestation *ad extra* (cfr. *Supplication for the Christians*, 24). Nevertheless he, too, felt the need of mediation in the creation of matter which for him was carried out by the angels.

Besides christological subordinationism, the excessive emphasis on God's transcendence also obscures other aspects of the biblical doctrine of creation as well, in particular the problem of the purpose of creation and the character of divine providence. As regards the purpose of creation, the Apologists tended to think that the world must have been created for human beings' sake, *di'anthrōpous* (Justin, *Apol.*, 1, 10), thus opening the door to Stoic anthropocentrism. Theophilus writes:

> For the sake of humans, therefore, God prepared the world; for that which is created is by the same token in need, while the uncreated is in need of nothing (*To Autolycus*, II, 10).

The same opinion is espoused by Aristides (*Apol.*, 1, 3), the *Letter to Diognetus*, 4, 2, and Tatian (*Address to the Greeks*, 4). Apart from the fact that the relation between the primary and the secondary ends of creation (that is, God's glory and the benefit of humankind) remains obscure, this approach leaves out of consideration the christological purpose of creation as envisaged by the New Testament.

Concerning the notion of divine providence, the Apologists correctly rejected fatalism and daemonism and defended God's solicitude for his creatures, great and small (cfr. *To Autolycus*, 1, 5; Aristides' *Apol.*, 13; Justin's 1st *Apol.*, 1, 28; *Address to the Greeks*, 8, 1; 10, 1). Nevertheless, their concept of divine providence does not encompass the richness of the New Testament concept of God's involvement in history and is still too akin to the Stoic impersonal *pronoia*, which is seen to be at work in nature rather than in history.

Despite their shortcomings, however, it must be admitted that the Apostolic Fathers, and in particular the Apologists, succeeded in defeating pagan cosmologies and expounding the Christian faith in God the Creator, *archē tōn holōn*, (*Address to the Greeks*, 5, 1), who freely creates all things out of nothing (the *creatio ex nihilo*).

II. Human Beings in God's Image and Likeness

So far we have discussed early patristic teaching on creation in general. The most distinctive biblical teaching on humans, however, is not simply that they are God's creatures but that they are created in God's image and likeness (Gen 1:26-27, 5:1-3 and 9:5-6). And since the early Fathers were wont to make abundant use of the Bible, it is inevitable that one major element of second-century anthropology was the exegesis of the passages of Genesis relating to the creation of the first human beings.

There is little to detain us in the writings of the Apostolic Fathers. The text from Genesis does not appear in the *Shepherd of Hermas*, the authentic letters of Ignatius, nor in Polycarp. A passing reference to part of the text appears in the *Letter to Diognetus* (10, 2) and the complete text in Clement's *Letter to the Corinthians* (33). In neither place, however, is the text given any special consideration.

Nor did the earliest Apologists have much to say on the theme of the creation of humans in God's image and likeness. In Justin, it is connected with his doctrine of the Logos, briefly alluded to above. According to him, God created all things, especially the human race, through his Logos. In fact, although the divine Logos appeared in his fullness only in Christ, "a seed of the Logos" was scattered among the whole of humankind long before Christ. For every human being possesses in his reason a seed (*sperma*) of the Logos, and if he lives according to reason, he is a Christian:

> We have been taught that Christ is the first born of God, and we have declared that he is the Logos, of whom every race of humankind were partakers, and those who lived according to the Logos are Christians, even though they have been thought atheists, as among the Greeks, Socrates and Heraclitus, and people like them (1 *Apol.*, 1, 46).[10]

Furthermore, for Justin, the human being is made up of the unity of body and soul. In a fragment of his now lost work *On the Resurrection*, 8, he asks:

> For what is man but the rational animal composed of body and soul? Is the soul by itself man? No, but the soul of man.

[10]Text: PG 6.397; trans. ANF 1.178

Would the body be called man? No, but it is called the body of man. If, then, neither of these is by itself man, but that which is made up of the two together is called man, and God has called man to life and resurrection, he has called not a part but the whole, which is the soul and the body.[11]

Finally, against the Stoic doctrine of fate (*kath' eimarmenēs anankēn*), Justin develops the idea of human freedom and responsibility. We had no choice in being born, argues Justin, but we have a choice, in virtue of the rational powers God has given us, whether to live in a fashion acceptable to him or not (cfr. 1 *Apol.*, 10, 4). Even the Christian belief in prophecy, with its premise of divine foreknowledge, does not do away with human freedom since God does not so much predetermine the actions of human persons as foresee how by their own volitions they are going to act, and so announces it beforehand through his prophets (cfr. 1 *Apol.*, 44, 11; *Dialogue with Trypho*, 142, 2).

It is however only with Justin's disciple, Tatian, and Theophilus of Antioch that a somewhat detailed discussion of the nature of human beings as God's image and likeness was first encountered. Incidentally, in these two thinkers one can already find two main anthropologies which will be adopted by their successors. For Theophilus, the first Adam was, as it were, an imperfect sketch to be gradually perfected through the exercise of his freedom and education. This conception will be followed by Irenaeus, Clement, Tertullian, and Methodius. On the other hand, for Tatian, Adam was given perfection at the beginning which he then lost through his fall, and consequently salvation consists in the recovery of that which has been lost. This view is much akin to the speculations of Philo, the Gnostics, and the Hermetic writings. Let us examine each of these views in turn.

For Theophilus, the three days which preceded the creation of light and the luminous heavenly bodies are "types of the Trinity" (*typoi triados*), that is, of "God, the Word, Wisdom" (*To Autolycus*, 2, 15). He takes the words "let us make humanity" as addressed by God to "his Word and Wisdom,"

---

[11]Text: PG 6. 1585; trans. ANF 1.297

an idea later adopted by Irenaeus. This deliberation indicates a special dignity of human beings who alone are "worthy of his hands" (2, 19). In a suggestive analogy Theophilus compares God to the sun, and humans, his image and reflection, to the moon (cfr. 2, 15). He sees the image in the human being as something like an image or a mirror, and, if the mirror is kept without rust, without moral stain, then God can be beheld here. He makes bold to say to his pagan friends, "Show me your man, and I will show you my God" (1, 2).

Theophilus' exegesis of the accounts of creation is devoid of allegory. The two trees, the rivers, the paradise garden are all taken in the most literal sense. As to the creation of the human body, Theophilus follows the description in Gen 2:7. God forms the man from the dust of the ground and breathes into him a breath of life which makes him a living soul. God then places him in Paradise in which there are the tree of the knowledge of good and evil and the tree of life. The tree of the knowledge of good and evil is good for the man, but he is forbidden to eat its fruit before the time willed by God.

What is implied here is that for Theophilus human beings are not created already perfect but rather in a state of imperfection from which they are to grow into perfection. Paradise was an intermediate state between heaven and earth. Adam was still an infant, and that is why he was not yet fit to eat from the tree of the knowledge of good and evil. His condition is that of a child who must first be fed on milk before he can take bread. Thus humans possess within themselves "a principle of progress, in order that by developing themselves and becoming perfect, nay more, by being proclaimed god, they should then ascend to heaven, being possessed of immortality" (*To Autolycus*, 2, 24). Theophilus goes on to say:

> Humans had been created in an intermediate state, neither wholly mortal nor entirely immortal, but capable of either (2, 24). . . .
> Someone, however, will say to us, "Were humans made mortal by nature?" Certainly not. "Were they, then, immortal?" Neither do we say that. But someone will say, "Were they, then, made nothing?" Not so, I reply. By nature, in fact, they were made neither mortal nor immortal.

For if God had made them immortal from the beginning, he would have made them God. Again, if he had made them mortal, it would seem as if God were the cause of their death. He made them, then, neither mortal nor immortal, but, as we have said above, capable of either. Thus, if they should incline to the ways of immortality, keeping the command of God, they would receive from God the reward of immortality, and become God. If, however, they should turn aside to the ways of death, disobeying God, they would become for themselves the cause of death. For God made humans free and self-determining (2, 27).[12]

God wished, therefore, to test Adam's obedience and to preserve him in the "simplicity" (*haplotēs*) and "innocence" (*akakia*) of childhood. The theme of Adam as a child will be adopted by Irenaeus and Clement. It fits well with the conception of human life as *paideusis*, an educational process, in which punishment, even death, is God's benevolent means of correction.

Tatian's view of the human soul is somewhat similar to Theophilus': "The human soul is not in itself immortal, you Greeks, but mortal. But it is also possible for it not to die. If it does not know the truth, it dies and is dissolved along with the body, and rises again with the body at the consummation of the world, to be punished by receiving death in deathlessness. Otherwise, however, if it acquires the knowledge of God, it does not die, although it is dissolved for a time" (*Address to the Greeks,* 13). Humans are intrinsically neither mortal nor immortal; what they become depends on what they do with their freedom.

What is characteristic about Tatian's anthropology is, however, not his view of human immortality but his distinction between two kinds of spirit in the human person: "We know that there are two kinds of spirit (*pneuma*), one of which is called the soul (*psychē*) and the other is superior to the soul; it is this which is the image and likeness of God. In the first man both kinds were found, with the result that they were partly material and partly superior to matter" (*Address to the*

---

[12]Text: PG 6.1089; trans. ANF 2.104, 105

Greeks, 12). For Tatian, then, there are two principles in humans. One is the *pneuma*, common to all living creatures, including the human soul, and therefore material. The other is the divine *pneuma*, corresponding to the Old Testament spirit of Yahweh (*ruah yhwy*) and the Pauline concept of the divine life in which humans share through Christ (the *pneuma* as opposed to *sarx*). Now, it is the latter alone which is the image and likeness of God.

> Of itself the soul is but darkness, and no light is in it.... Hence it is not the soul which saves the spirit; on the contrary, the soul has been saved by the spirit.... That is why the soul which is abandoned to itself plunges into matter and dies with the flesh. But if it is conjoined with the divine Spirit, it no longer lacks assistance; it ascends toward the heights, whither the Spirit guides it. For its dwelling is above, just as its origin is from below. Indeed, in the beginning, the Spirit was a companion to the soul; but the Spirit abandoned it because the soul was not willing to follow the Spirit. The soul, however, retained as it were a spark (*enausma*) of the Spirit's power; but, once separated from the Spirit it could not perceive what was perfect, and in error fashioned for itself many gods, following the sophistries of the devils (*Address to the Greeks*, 13).[13]

It is to be noted that here Tatian maintains a dualism not between body and soul or between matter and spirit but between soul and spirit. The soul is darkness; it comes from below and belongs to matter, whereas the spirit is light and comes from above. In this sense, Tatian rejects the definition, classic for Middle Platonism, of human, as "a rational being, capable of intellection and knowledge," since for him not only humans but also animals are capable of these activities insofar as they too have soul. Tatian's dualism is never a philosophical dualism either of the Platonist version between the sensible and the intelligible orders of reality nor of the Gnostic kind between the *Plērōma*, the transcendent world of the supreme God and the *kenoma*, the material universe made by the

[13]Text: OECT, 26; trans. ANF 2.70

Demiurge and dominated by the evil powers. Despite some noticeable similarities between Tatian's anthropology on the one hand and Platonist and Gnostic (especially that of Valentinus and Theodotus) on the other, there are profound differences between them. For Tatian, God's "image and likeness," which are peculiar to humans, consist in their participation in the life of God (their "spirit") and in no sense are the faculties of the soul, whereas for the Gnostics (e.g. Theodotus) the 'image' is identified with the 'hylic' soul, and distinguished from 'likeness,' which corresponds to the 'breath of life' and denotes the 'psychic' soul, different from the 'hylic' and consubstantial with the Demiurge, an inferior god responsible for the creation of matter. Tatian's dualism is a religious one which contrasts life opposed to God (the Pauline *sarx*) with life in obedience to and union with God (the Pauline *pneuma*).

III. The Fall and Redemption

In discussing Theophilus and Tatian we have already hinted at the fall of humanity into sin. We will now examine more closely the teachings of the early Fathers on this topic. It is important to remember at the outset that for the Christians of the first centuries, original sin, both in the sense of *peccatum originale originans* (the sin of Adam) and *peccatum originale originatum* (the state of "sin" in us), was not in the foreground; on the contrary, Christ's redemption was the fundamental assertion. Moreover, redemption did not have for them such a close link with original sin as it will have later with Augustine and Anselm. It is not surprising, then, that, though the early writers did speak of God's grace and salvation, they did not mention original sin.

Clement's *Letter to the Corinthians* contains certain allusions to the Genesis account of man's creation (33: 4-5) but mentions neither the original fall nor the idea of solidarity with Adam. Clement, however, did speak fairly extensively of the work of Christ who gave his blood for us, his flesh for our flesh, his soul for our souls, and who has redeemed us (49, 6). In the *Letter of Barnabas* some references to the first chapters of Genesis are found but are of no significance. The episode of the bronze serpent gives occasion to recall the seduction of the first woman, but still more does it conjure up the figure of Christ raised upon the cross (12, 5-8). *Barnabas* does speak of the sacrifice of Christ (5, 2; 6, 7; 7, 9), but neither in Clement nor in *Barnabas* is there any linking between Christ's redemption and the original transgression. *Hermas* frequently recalls that sin leads to death (*Vis.* 1, 1, 8; *Mand.*, 12, 1-2; *Sim.*, 6, 5-7), and insists upon the part played by temptation and the devil (*Mand.*, 6, 3, 4; *Sim.*, 8, 3, 6), but it does not occur to him to speak of Adam and Eve.

In Ignatius, we find the first attempt at formulating a theology of salvation at the center of which is Christ, true God and true man. Against the Docetists, Ignatius insists on the reality of Christ's flesh "which has suffered for us and which by its death has delivered us from death." (*Smyrn*, 1-2). Elsewhere he writes:

> There is only one physician—of flesh yet spiritual, born yet unbegotten, God incarnate, genuine life in the midst of death, sprung from Mary as well as God, first subject to suffering then beyond it—Jesus Christ our Lord (*Ephesians*: 7: 2).[14]

In a beautiful image, Ignatius describes the role of the Trinity in salvation: "Like stones of God's Temple, ready for a building of God the Father, you are being hoisted up by Jesus Christ, as with a crane (that's the cross!), while the rope you use is the Holy Spirit" (*Ephesians*: 9: 1).

Manuals of theology often quote a text from Justin's *First Apology* (61) on the necessity of baptism as an indication of his belief in original sin. It must be admitted, however, that the text, though affirming that we are born with wayward inclinations, says nothing about the source of this evil. Adam and Eve are not even mentioned. In the *Apology*, only the devil is connected with the universality of sin (cfr. 54, 56). In his *Dialogue with Trypho*, Justin does affirm that "since the sin of Adam, the human race had fallen under the serpent's power of

---

[14]Text: SC 10.64; trans. *The Apostolic Fathers* LCL, tr. K. Lake, 1.180

death and error" (88, 4), but this allusion is not further exploited. Elsewhere, the tree of life is mentioned, but only to emphasize that it was a symbol of the tree of the cross, as were the staff of Moses and the bronze serpent (*Dialogue with Trypho*, 91, 4; 92, 2). In sum, in Justin's soteriology, original sin has scarcely any place.

There is, however, a beautiful text in the *Dialogue* in which Justin develops a striking parallel between the old and the new Eve, a theme brilliantly exploited later by Irenaeus:

> The Word became man by a virgin so that the disobedience that had come from the serpent might come to an end in the same way as it had begun. Eve was an undefiled virgin, and on conceiving the serpent's word she brought forth disobedience and death.... The Virgin Mary conceived faith and joy and she brought forth him by whom God destroys the serpent ... and delivers from death those who do penance for their evil deeds (100, 4-5).[15]

As we have seen, Justin's disciple, Tatian, held that the human soul, in the beginning, abandoned the divine Spirit, and that ever since humankind has been beset by suffering and death. He went on to elaborate the nature of humanity's fall in two curious passages in which the first human sin is connected with the fall of the angels:

> When human beings had followed him who, in his capacity of first born, had more intelligence than the others, when they had made a god of him who had rebelled against God's law, then did the power of the Logos exclude from his friendship the originator of that mad defection and all those who followed him. And he who had been made in God's image became mortal when the all-powerful spirit withdrew from him. The first born became a devil, and those who imitated him and his prodigies formed the army of devils; and since they acted freely, they were abandoned to their foolishness (*Address to the Greeks*, 7).[16]

[15]Text: PG 6.700; trans. ANF 1.249
[16]Text: PG 6.820; trans. ANF 2.67

Again, using the image of the wings of the soul that recalls Plato's *Phaedrus*, he continues:

> It is the perfect spirit which gives wings to the soul. The latter, having torn them off by sin fell to earth like a fledgling and cowered there in fear. The demons were driven from their first dwelling, and the first humans from theirs. The former were hurled from heaven, the latter from earth—not this earth, but another more fair (*Address to the Greeks*, 20).[17]

The devils next corrupted human beings, teaching them fatalism and astrology. Tatian delights in describing human misery as the consequence of a free human choice:

> We are not born for death, but we die through our own fault. It is our free will that has ruined us. We were free, but we have become slaves; it is on account of our sins that we have been sold. No evil thing is a work of God. It is we ourselves who have produced moral evil, and having produced it, we are capable of renouncing it (*Address to the Greeks*, 11).[18]

Salvation for humans, in Tatian's view, consists in their recovery of what they have lost, namely union of their souls with the divine spirit:

> And now, if we desired to rediscover our ancient state, we must know how to reject everything that would hinder us.... Heaven is not infinite; above it are better worlds which do not know the changes of the seasons, and which behold a day that never ends and a light inaccessible to human beings of this world.... And it is possible for all who have been unclothed to be adorned once more and to return to their ancient kinship (*Address to the Greeks*, 20).[19]

[17]Text: PG 6.852; trans. ANF 2.73
[18]Text: PG 6.829; trans. ANF 2.69
[19]Text: PG 6.852; trans. ANF 2.74

Theophilus of Antioch took a different view of human nature and the original fall. As has been said above, Adam, for Theophilus, was but an infant who had still to grow into perfection. He was capable of attaining knowledge, but only in degrees, which was providential:

> When a child is born, he does not yet eat bread, but first of all feeds on milk. Successively, according to his development, he progresses to solid food. So it was with Adam: it was not through jealousy, as some imagine, that God commanded him not to eat of the tree of knowledge. What he wished to do was to test his obedience to the divine instructions. He wished too that man should prolong his state of simplicity and integrity by remaining a child. It is not only a divine law but also a human law that one should be subject to one's parents in simplicity and innocence. If children should be subject to their parents, should they not all the more be subject to the God and Father of all things? Furthermore, it is not normal that little children should have ideas beyond their age: age advances, and with it, ideas (*To Autolycus*, 2, 25).[20]

Hence, for Theophilus, Adam's fall, though producing serious consequences for him and his descendants, was excused by his ignorance and immaturity. And even the punishments for this original fall, Theophilus suggests, were a mark of God's benevolence, for Adam was given sufficient time to expiate his sin and was trained to the point where it was possible for God to call him anew. Death itself is a benefit, because it puts an end to human misery and gives us the chance to be wholly restored by a new creation. What appears as God's just punishment is in fact his kindness and mercy, a theme extensively developed by Irenaeus later:

> In their disobedience, humans experienced weariness, pain, grief, and at last fell into the power of death. That was, on God's part, a great mercy toward them: not to keep them always in a state of sin, but in some way to inflict on them a

[20]Text: PG 6.1092; trans. ANF 2.104

banishment by expelling them from paradise. The chastisement would permit humans to expiate their fault within a set time and, once they have been chastised, they would be called home. This is why, after the creation of humans in this world, Genesis, not without a certain mystery, tells us that they were twice placed in paradise. The first time was when they were originally placed there, the second will be after the resurrection and judgment. Just as a vase whose workmanship shows some defect is recast or remodelled in order to become new and perfect, so it is with the person who undergoes death: he is broken, so to speak, so that at the resurrection he may be found unblemished; that he may be found stainless, righteous and immortal, is what I mean to say (*To Autolycus*, 2, 25, 26).[21]

In Theophilus, as in other Apologists, demons play an extensive role in human affairs, and for them the one chiefly responsible for evil is not Adam but Satan. The devil is the apostate, the one who flees from God. Having failed to bring about the death of Adam and Eve he concentrates on their posterity. It is he who drove Cain to murder his brother, and so, Theophilus tells us, death entered into the world and spread throughout the human species (cfr. *To Autolycus*, 2, 29). Here, also, the responsibility for death lies with Satan.

At the end of this survey of pre-Irenaean anthropology one may judge that it is rather meager and primitive. In a sense such a judgment is justified since the Apologists, and *a fortiori* their predecessors, did not attempt a general exposition of the Christian faith and they still lacked sophisticated theological categories with which to express their thoughts. Nevertheless, one cannot but admire their firm defense of the Christian faith in God the Creator, their bold speculations on the nature of the human person, their vivid awareness of universal sinfulness, and their eloquent exposition of the work of redemption by God in Christ.

Furthermore, it would be well to remember that Christian anthropology was expounded not only in theological texts but also in early liturgies, especially baptism and eucharist, and the

[21]Text: PG 6.1092; trans. ANF 2.104

creeds. In all of these we keep finding the same doctrine confessed and celebrated: The Father created us, and the Word became flesh in order to save us and give us the Spirit who sanctifies us. The gift of the Holy Spirit is the notion that governed the whole theology of grace in the early days of Christianity. The Christians of the first centuries were aware of living a new life that had not been available to them before. The rites of baptism, the imposition of hands, the anointing, absolution, the partaking in the Supper of the Lord—all these acts bestow and strengthen the gift of the Holy Spirit which we later call justification and sanctifying grace.

2

Irenaeus and the Struggle
Against Gnosticism

Irenaeus (ca. 140-ca. 202), the second bishop of Lyons, was a native of Asia Minor, probably of Smyrna, where as a boy he had been a disciple of St. Polycarp. Ecclesiastically, he is famous for his efforts at reconciling Pope Victor of Rome (189-198) and Polycrates of Ephesus in the Quartodeciman controversy. Theologically, Irenaeus' greatest contribution was his attack upon Gnosticism, especially the system of Valentinus. His *magnum opus* is the five-book work entitled *Detection and Overthrow of the Pretended but False Knowledge*, usually called *Adversus Haereses*. His other important writing is called *The Demonstration of the Apostolic Teaching*, an apologetic treatise.

Irenaeus is certainly the most important theologian of the second century. Not only did he succeed in unmasking the pseudo-Christian character of Gnosticism but he also was the first to offer a rather comprehensive exposition of the Christian doctrine. His teachings on Scripture, tradition, the apostolic succession, the "potentior principalitas" of the Church of Rome, and the universal restoration (*recapitulatio*) remain the permanent legacies of Western theology.

As far as anthropology is concerned, Irenaeus elaborated his own in conscious opposition to the dualism of Gnosticism. Whereas the Apologists had been principally concerned with the external threat of Judaism and paganism, Irenaeus had to contend with the enemy from within, namely Gnosticism. Originally a religious movement of pre-Christian matrix, and an amalgam of Oriental mythology, magical rites and Greek philosophical speculation, Gnosticism made use of some Christian doctrines to develop a dualistic anthropology and an anti-cosmic theory of salvation inimical to the Christian teaching on creation and redemption.

In the first book of *Adversus Haereses,* Irenaeus attempts a "detection" of the Gnostic heresy by giving a detailed description of the doctrine of the Valentinians. He then relates the beginning of Gnosticism by speaking of Simon Magus and Menander and by citing other leaders or schools, such as Satornil, Basilides, Carpocrates, Cerinthus, the Ebionites, the Nicolaites, Cerdon, Marcion, Tatian and the Encratites. In the remaining books he proceeds to "overthrow" the gnosis of the Valentinians and the Marcionites from reason (Book II), from the teaching of the Church on God and Christ (Book III), from the sayings of Jesus (Book IV), and the last book is devoted to a discussion of the resurrection of the flesh, which was denied by all the Gnostics.

In what follows we will summarize Irenaeus' teachings on creation, the nature of the human person, his original fall, and God's redemptive grace with illustrative quotations from his writings.

I. The One God Creator and Savior

One of the fundamental elements of Gnostic teaching was the distinction between the Demiurge, or creator god, and the supreme transcendent and remote God. The Demiurge was derived from God by a series of emanations or "aeons." Through some fall among the higher aeons, it was the Demiurge, and not God, the divine being himself, who was the immediate source of creation and ruled the world, which was therefore imperfect and antagonistic to what was truly spiritual.

To this metaphysical dualism, Irenaeus opposes a conception of creation and saving history based on Scripture and tradition. First of all, he vigorously rejects the Gnostic idea of a God who has nothing to do with creation:

The Church, though dispersed throughout the whole world, even to the ends of the earth, has received from the apostles and their disciples its faith in one God, the Father Almighty, who made the heaven, and the earth, and the seas, and all that is in them . . . . (*Adv. haer.*, I, 10).[1]

It is proper, then, that I should begin with the first and most important head, that is, God the Creator, who made the heaven and the earth, and all things that are therein (whom these blasphemers [i.e. the Gnostics] claim to be the fruit of a defect), and to demonstrate that there is nothing either above him or after him; and that, not influenced by any one, but of his own free will, he created all things, since he is the only God, the only Lord, the only Creator, the only Father, alone containing all things, and himself commanding all things into existence (*Adv. haer.* II, 1,1).[2]

Irenaeus decisively affirms the *creatio ex nihilo* against the doctrine of eternity of matter. God's omnipotence is most obvious from the fact that he depends on no material for his works. His sovereignty also rules out the notion of a lesser aeon's being the intermediate agent of creation.

While humans, indeed, cannot make anything out of nothing, but only out of matter already existing, God is in this aspect preeminently superior to humans. He himself called into being the substance of his creation, when previously it had no existence. The assertion that matter was produced from the Enthymesis of an Aeon going astray, and that this Aeon was far separated from her Enthymesis, and that, again, her passion and feeling, apart from herself, became matter — is incredible, fatuous, impossible, and untenable (*Adv. haer.*, II, 10, 4).[3]

As regards his greatness, therefore, it is not possible to know God, for it is impossible to measure the Father. But as regards his love . . ., when we obey him, we always learn that there is so great a God, and that it is he who by himself

---

[1]Text: SC 264.154; trans. ANF 1.330
[2]Text: SC 294.26; trans. ANF 1.359
[3]Text: SC 294.90; trans. ANF 1.370

has established, selected, adorned and contains all things, among which ourselves and this our world. He also made us, along with those things which are contained in it. And this is he of whom the Scripture says, "And God formed the human being, taking clay of the earth, and breathed into his face the breath of life." It was not angels, therefore, who made us, nor who formed us; neither had angels power to make an image of God, nor any one else, except the true God, nor any Power remotely distant from the Father of all things. For God did not stand in need of these beings in order to accomplish what he had himself determined to do, as if he did not possess his own hands. For with him were always present the Word and Wisdom, the Son and the Spirit, by whom and in whom, freely and spontaneously he made all thingss . . . .(*Adv. haer.*, IV, 20 1).[4]

Since creation is the work of God with his two "hands," that is the Son and the Spirit, Irenaeus rejects the Gnostic idea that creation was occasioned by an aboriginal fall. Rather, creation is interpreted as a blessing from God; nay, in Irenaeus' view, there is a strict connection between creation and redemption, or better still, the world was created for the sake of the Redeemer and redemption. This link becomes explicit when the Creator and the Redeemer are identified with the person of Christ. The Son, or the Word in whom all things are created, is recognized as Jesus the Redeemer.

And then, [speaking of his] baptism, Matthew says, "The heavens were opened, and he saw the Spirit of God, as a dove, coming upon him: and, behold, a voice from heaven, saying: This is my beloved Son, in whom I am well pleased" (Matt 3:16-17). Christ did not at that time descend upon Jesus, neither were Christ and Jesus different persons. Rather, the Word of God who is the Savior of all and the ruler of heaven and earth, who is Jesus, and who, as I have already pointed out, did also take upon himself flesh, and was anointed by the Spirit of the Father—was made Jesus

Christ. . .(*Adv. haer.,* III, 9, 3).[5]

All, therefore, are outside of the Christian dispensation, who, under the pretext of knowledge, claim that Jesus was one, and Christ another, and the Only-begotten another. . ., and the Savior another, whom these disciples of error allege to be a production of those who were made Aeons in a state of degeneracy. Such people are to outward appearance sheep; for they appear to be like us, by what they say in public, repeating the same word as we do. Inwardly, however, they are wolves. Their doctrine is homicidal, conjuring up, as it does, a number of gods, and simulating many Fathers, but chopping up and dividing the Son of God in many ways (*Adv. haer.,* III, 16, 8).[6]

Irenaeus firmly confessed that "[God's] only-begotten Word, who is always present with the human race, united to and mingled with his own creation, according to the Father's pleasure, and who became flesh, is himself Jesus Christ our Lord, who did also suffer for us and rose again on our behalf, and who will come again in the glory of his Father, to raise up all flesh, and for the manifestation of salvation, and to apply the rule of just judgment to all who were made by him" (*Adv. haer.,* III, 16, 6). For Irenaeus, then, creation and redemption become one in the love of God, the latter being the purpose of the former. As he puts it tersely: "Since indeed he [Christ] preexists as the Savior, it was necessary that what should be saved should also be called into existence, in order that the Savior should not exist in vain (*Adv. haer.,* III, 22, 3).

If creation leads to redemption, then the latter must be the perfection and consummation of the former. This idea of growth is exemplified not only in the world but above all, according to Irenaeus, in human beings.

[5]Text: SC 211.106; trans. ANF 1.423
[6]Text: SC 211.318; trans. ANF 1.443

II. In God's Image and Likeness

In Gnostic cosmology three kinds of substance came into existence: the material, the psychic, and the spiritual. Corresponding to these were three classes of human beings, represented by the three sons of Adam—Cain, Abel, and Seth. The truly spiritual people (the *pneumatikoi*) are not in need of salvation, and the material (the *hylikoi* or *sarkikoi,* mostly Jews and pagans) are incapable of it; but the psychic (the *psychikoi*) are both vulnerable to the fall and capable of redemption. These three types of humans correspond to the Platonist tripartite division of human beings understood as composed of flesh, soul, and spirit.

To this basically dualistic anthropology, Irenaeus replies that there is not a natural person and a spiritual person, but that human beings are at one and the same time carnal and spiritual. It is the *one* human being, composed of flesh, soul, and spirit, that God created in the beginning with his two hands, the Son and the Spirit. Irenaeus vigorously emphasizes the unity of the human person:

> If one takes away the reality of the flesh (*caro*), that is to say, of the material form (*plasma*), and considers the spirit (*spiritus*) in isolation, what is left is not a spiritual person but the spirit of man or the Spirit of God. But when this spirit, mingled with the soul, is united to the material form, then, because of the outpouring of the Spirit, the human person becomes spiritual and perfect. It is such a human being who is made in the image and likeness of God. If, on the other hand, the Spirit is missing from the soul, then what we have is certainly an animate being, but one who remains carnal and imperfect; he indeed possesses the image in the material form, but he does not acquire the likeness which comes from the Spirit. In the same way, therefore, as this being is imperfect, so, if we take away the image, and despise the material form, we can no longer speak of a human person, but only of a part of him or something other than him (*Adv. haer.*, V, 6, 1).[7]

[7]Text: SC 153.74; trans. ANF 1.531

This passage leads us into the heart of Irenaeus' anthropology. Not only does it show clearly how, for this fighter against Gnostic dualism, the human person is composed of body, soul and spirit, all the three elements being necessary to him as God made him and meant him to be, but also it introduces the important distinction Irenaeus makes between image and likeness of God. Image (*eikōn, imago*) he takes to be constituted by the human body and soul, whereas the likeness (*homoiōsis, similitudo*), the supreme gift of the Spirit. Irenaeus' use of these two terms, derived from Gen 1: 26, is not always consistent. There are a number of passages in which at first sight it would appear that Irenaeus is using the terms 'image' and 'likeness' as synonymous (e.g. *Adv. haer.,* III, 18, 1; 23, 1; 23, 2; IV, 38, 3; 38, 4; V, 1, 3). Nevertheless, it is generally true to say that for him 'image,' which denotes bodiliness, rationality and freedom, is distinguished from 'likeness,' which is the supernatural gift of God. The latter, Irenaeus will say, was lost at the Fall and must be restored by Christ, whereas the former remains even today in all human beings. The same distinction is maintained in another text:

> But humans he [God] fashioned with his own hands, taking of the purest and finest of earth, in measured wise mingling with the earth his own power, for he gave their frame the outline of his own form, that the visible appearance too should be godlike—for it was as an image of God that humans were fashioned and set on earth—and that they might come to life, he breathed into them the breath of life, so that they became like God in inspiration as well as in frame (*Demonstration,* 11).[8]

At this point another aspect of Irenaeus' anthropology must be introduced which will entail profound consequences for his theology as a whole. According to Irenaeus humans are not created in a perfect state. Of course, in a certain sense there is 'perfection' in the beginning: God did give humans his spirit which makes them similar to him. They are created both as 'image' (the 'natural' gifts) and as 'likeness' (the 'supernatural'

[8]Text: SC 62.48; trans. ACW 16.54, tr Joseph P. Smith, S.J.

gifts) of God. Any progress there may be, therefore, is not a movement from the natural to the supernatural. Nevertheless, in words that recall Theophilus of Antioch, Irenaeus reminds us that Adam was but a child that still had to grow into maturity. Consequently, only as much Spirit was given him as his abilities as a child allowed him to receive, and what he received he could very easily lose. Furthermore, in God's economy, only Christ, who is to come as the second Adam, possesses the perfect likeness of God. Before him, everything, though part of the same plan, was but rough drafts, inchoate and tentative. It is in Christ alone that God's design is perfectly realized; it is in the risen Christ alone that the Spirit lays hold once for all upon all the flesh in order to bestow upon it incorruptibility and so to fashion the perfect humanity. Perfection comes at the end, not at the beginning. Several important extracts must be given:

> If someone says, Why? Could not God have created humans perfect from the beginning?—let him know that for God, being immutable and unbegotten, all things are possible as regards himself. But created things are bound to be inferior to him who created them by the very fact of their later beginning. It was not possible for things recently created to be unbegotten; and inasmuch as they are not uncreated, to that extent they fall short of perfection. And insofar as they are recent, they are also but babes; and to the extent they are babes, they are unaccustomed to and unpracticed in perfect conduct. Just as a mother may well give grown-up food to an infant, but the infant itself is not yet able to take food that is too strong for it, so God was certainly capable of giving humans perfection from the beginning, but they were incapable of receiving it, because they were still infants. That is why our Lord in recent times, recapitulating all things in himself, came to us, not in such ways as he was able to do, but as we were able to see him. For he could have come to us in his immortal glory, but we could never have borne the greatness of his glory. That is why he who is the perfect bread of the Father offered himself to us in the form of milk, because we were babes. He did this when he appeared as a man so that we, nourished, as

it were, from the breast of his flesh and having, by such milk-feeding, become accustomed to eat and drink the Word of God, may be able also to contain in ourselves the Bread of immortality, which is the Spirit of the Father (*Adv. haer.,* IV, 38, 1).[9]

God created an infant humanity and asked of it only what it could bear. Then he set out to educate it, in an orderly fashion and in successive stages, to bear more:

> God could indeed have given humans perfection from the beginning; but humanity, being only recently created, was incapable of receiving it or holding it once received, or preserving it once held.... That is why the Son of God, though himself fully perfect, became a child, accepting limitation, not for his own sake, but for the sake of humans who were still infants, in such a way that they could receive him.... Humanity was created and formed in the image and likeness of the uncreated God. It was the Father who approved and commanded this, the Son who did the work and fashioned humans, the Spirit who nourished and increased them, so that they slowly made progress and moved toward perfection, that is, came near to the uncreated.... But it was necessary that humans should first be created, then grow, then come to adulthood, then multiply, then become strong, then be glorified, and then finally behold their Master.... Therefore, people who do not wait for the period of growth, who attribute weakness of their nature to God, are totally unreasonable. Knowing neither God nor themselves, insatiable and ungrateful, unwilling first to be that which they were made...they transgress the law of human nature; they already want to be like God before they even become human beings. They want to do away with all the differences between the uncreated God and created humans (*Adv. haer.,* IV, 38, 2-4).[10]

[9]Text: SC 100.942; trans. ANF 1.521
[10]Text: SC 100.950; trans. ANF 1.521

Human perfection, Irenaeus reminds us, comes only at the end of time and by the grace of God:

> Just as, from the beginning of our formation in Adam, the breath of life which was from God, united to the material form, animated humans and showed them to be endowed with reason, so also, in the end, the Word of the Father and the Spirit of God, having become united with the ancient substance from which Adam was formed, rendered them living and perfect, receptive of the perfection of the Father, in order that, as in the physical (*psychikos*) Adam we were all dead, so in the spiritual (*pneumatikos*) Adam we shall all be made alive. For Adam never escaped from the hands of God, to whom the Father addressed these words: "Let us make humanity in our image and likeness." And for this reason, at the end, not by the will of the flesh, nor by the will of human beings, but by the good pleasure of the Father, his hands perfected the human being, so that Adam should be in the image and likeness of God (*Adv. haer.*, V, 1, 3).[11]

Again, it is the eschatological events of Christ's incarnation, death, and resurrection that perfected the image and likeness of God in us:

> For the breath of life, which makes humans animated beings, is one thing, and the life-giving Spirit, which perfects them as spiritual, is another. For this reason Isaiah says: "Thus says the Lord, who made heaven and established it, who founded the earth and the things therein, and gave breath to the people upon it, and Spirit to those walking on it": (Is 42: 5). Thus, it is said that the breath of life is given in common to all people upon the earth, but the Spirit is given only to those who tread down earthly desires. And hence Isaiah himself, distinguishing the things already mentioned, exclaims: "For the Spirit shall go forth from me and I have made every breath of life" (Is 57: 16). Thus Isaiah attributes the Spirit exclusively to God, who pours it out in the last

[11]Text: SC 153.26; trans. ANF 1.527

days upon the human race by the adoption of sons and daughters; but the breath of life he links with the creation, declaring it to be a thing made. Now something which is made is different from the one who made it. Therefore, the breath of life is temporal, but the Spirit is eternal. Further, the breath increases in strength for a short period and continues for a while; after that it departs, leaving its former abode destitute of breath. But when the Spirit pervades a human person within and without, inasmuch as he continues there, he never leaves him. "But," says the Apostle, "it is not the spiritual which is first, rather what is first is animal, and then that which is spiritual" (1 Cor. 15: 46). For it was necessary first that humans should be formed, and that having been formed they should receive a soul; and only then that they should in this way share in the Spirit. That is why "the first Adam was made" by the Lord, "a living soul, the second Adam a life-giving Spirit" (1 Cor. 15: 45) (*Adv. haer.*, V, 12, 2).[12]

Finally, the role of Christ in the restoration of the image and likeness of God in us is made clear in the following passage:

God has no other hand than that which from beginning to end forms us, fits us for life, and is present to the creature he had formed, and perfects him in the image and likeness of God. And this Word revealed himself, when the Word of God was made man, assimilating himself to humanity and humanity to himself, with the result that by virtue of its likeness to the Son, humanity becomes precious to God. For in times past it was asserted, indeed, that humans were made in the image of God, but it was not demonstrated. For the Word was at that time still invisible, he in whose image humans had been made; and that is why they easily lost their likeness. But when the Word of God was made flesh, he established both the one and the other. He manifested the true image by becoming that which was his image; and he restored the likeness by consolidating it, making humans

12Text: SC 153.142; trans. ANF 1.537

like the Father by means of the visible Word (*Adv. haer.*, V, 16, 1-2).[13]

Here, Irenaeus' anthropology marvellously interlocks with his christology and Trinitarian theology. We are made in God the Father's image and likeness; but since the Logos is the Father's image, or better still, since the incarnate Logos is the Father's perfect visible image, we may be said to be made in the image of the Logos incarnate. Moreover, since we cannot be transformed fully into the image of the Logos, except by the Father's other hand, the Spirit, our perfect status as God's image and likeness is the fruit of the Spirit. Anthropology necessarily includes pneumatology and vice versa.

III. A Radical Evil or An Excusable Sin?

Does Irenaeus' conception of Adam as a child and of human history as a process of training (*paideia*) make original sin an impossibility or at least an excusable weakness?

If by original sin one understands the fall of Adam, the *peccatum originale originans,* then it must be admitted that Irenaeus presents it as extremely excusable. The following texts gives ample reasons:

> So, having made the man lord of the earth and everything in it, God made him in secret lord also of the servants in it. They, however, were in their full development, while the lord, that is, the man was a little one. He was a child and had need to grow so as to come to his full perfection. And in order that he might have nourishment and grow up in luxury, a place was prepared for him better than this world, well-favored in climate, beauty, light, things good to eat, plants, fruit, water, and all other necessities of life. Its name is the Garden. And so fair and enjoyable was the Garden that the Word of God was constantly walking in it. He would walk round and talk with the man, prefiguring what

---

[13]Text: SC 153.214; trans. ANF 1.544

was to happen in the future, how he would become the man's fellow, and talk with him, and come among humankind, teaching them justice. But the man was a little one, and his discretion still undeveloped, wherefore he also was easily misled by the deceiver (*Demonstration,* 12).[14]

The image of God in the man was not yet firmly established, it could very easily be lost (*Adv. haer.,* V, 16, 2). Furthermore, responsibility for the sin falls much more on the devil than on the man. Making use of the doctrine that Satan was the angel who became jealous of the honors of the first man, Irenaeus described the role played by him in the fall of humanity:

> But so that the man should not have thoughts of pride and become puffed up, as if he had no lord, on account of the dominion that has been given him and his freedom, so that he should not fall into sin against God his Creator, overstepping his bounds and take up an attitude of self-conceited arrogance toward God, a law was given him by God, that he might realize that he had for lord the Lord of all. And God laid down for him certain conditions, so that, if he kept the commandment of God, then he would remain always as he was, that is, immortal; but if he did not, he would become mortal, melting into earth, whence his frame had been taken....
> This commandment the man did not keep, but disobeyed God, being misled by the angel, who, becoming jealous of the man and looking on him with envy because of God's many favors which had been bestowed on the man, both ruined himself and made the man a sinner, persuading him to disobey God's commandment. The source and instigation of sin was this angel and his deceit. And because he had rebelled, he was called by the Hebrew name Satan, that is, Rebel (*Demonstration,* 15-16).[15]

Such speculations will be found later in Methodius of Olympus and Gregory of Nyssa. But not only is Adam's sin

[14]Text: SC 62.50; trans.ACW 16.55
[15]Text: SC 62.54; trans. ACW 16.56-57

excusable because of his immaturity and the deceit of Satan, but also, Irenaeus suggests, because of the very nature of human freedom. Against the Gnostics who maintained that people are good or bad by nature, he argues that such a disposition would be morally unacceptable: "If some are by nature good and others by nature bad, neither are the good worthy of praise nor the bad of blame" (*Adv. haer.,* IV, 37, 2). Rather, God endowed humans with freedom so that they might voluntarily seek good and shun evil and enjoy happiness:

> For they (that is, humans) were made capable of reason and deliberation and judgment, and not—like irrational or inanimate things, which can do nothing of their own will, but are drawn to the good by force and necessity, having but one idea and one pattern of behavior—inflexible and without judgment, able to be nothing except that which they were made. In such circumstances neither would what is good be pleasant to them, nor would the gift of God be precious, nor would the good be something to be greatly sought after, if it came about without any effort, or care, or zeal of their own, but innately of its own accord and without effort. . . . In that case they would neither understand that the good is beautiful, nor would they enjoy it. For what enjoyment of the good can there be in those who are ignorant of the good? Or what glory can there be for those who have not sought it with zeal? (*Adv. haer.,* IV, 37,6).[16]

But Irenaeus goes farther than this. He appears to say that humans would not be able to appreciate the value of the good without actually experiencing hardship and sin:

> How would people have learned that they are weak and mortal by nature, and God powerful and immortal, if they had not learned by experience (*experimentum=peira*) the meaning of both these conditions? For to learn one's own weakness by patient endurance is not an evil—nay rather it is a good not to be mistaken about one's own nature. That

---

[16]Text: SC 100.934; trans. ANF 1.520

which brought great evil upon humans was their being exalted against God and becoming presumptuous on the grounds of their own glory, thus making them ungrateful (*Adv. haer.*, V, 3, 1).[17]

What Irenaeus is driving at is not that sin is a necessity or that one must sin in order to know the good, a sort of "sin mystique" (cfr. Rom 6: 1-2). Rather, given the created and finite nature of human freedom and the immaturity in which humanity found itself, it was *inevitable* that an actual experience of sin was the way to grow in self-knowledge:

> It was necessary first that human nature should be made apparent, and then afterwards that what is mortal should be conquered and swallowed up by immortality, and what is corruptible by incorruptibility, and that humans should be made in the image and likeness of God after they had acquired the knowledge of good and evil. But humans have received the knowledge of good and evil...they have learned both the good of obedience and the evil of disobedience in such a way that the eye of their mind, acquiring experience of both, may make its choice of the better with judgment.... But how could they have received instruction in what is good, if they were ignorant of its opposite...? For just as the tongue acquires experience of sweet and bitter by taste ... so too the mind, receiving instruction in the good by the experience of both good and evil, is made more steadfast to maintain the good in obedience to God, first indeed by penitence and by rejecting disobedience, since that is bitter and evil (*Adv. haer.*, IV, 38, 4-39, 1).[18]

Consequently, the punishment for the first sin seems to Irenaeus more the sign of God's compassion than of his anger. The experience of evil is salutary for us; it makes us doubly esteem God's kindness:

[17]Text: SC 153.42; trans. ANF 1.529
[18]Text: SC 100.960; trans. ANF 1.522

God was magnanimous when, before humanity's failure, he foresaw the victory that he would give it through the Word. Because, while virtue proved itself in infirmity (2 Cor 12: 9), it threw into relief the kindness of God and the great splendor of his power. Hence, just as God patiently tolerated Jonah's being consumed by a sea monster, not that he should be swallowed and utterly perish, but that, when he had been thrown up, he should be still more subject to God, that he should still more glorify the one who had given him unexpected deliverance in order to lead the Ninivites to firm repentance and to turn them to the Lord who would deliver them from death ... so too from the beginning God tolerated that humanity should be consumed by the great monster, the originator of disloyalty, not that it should be swallowed and utterly perish, but because he had in advance established and prepared the means of deliverance, a deliverance carried out by the Word in accordance with the sign of Jonah, for those who had the same attitude toward the Lord as had Jonah.... Such, then, was the magnanimity of God. He ordained that humans should pass through all the stages; that they should receive knowledge of the Law governing their actions; that they should come through it to the resurrection of the dead; that they should learn by experience the evil from which he had been delivered, in order that they should always be grateful to the Lord, and that, having been endowed by him with incorruptibility, they should give evidence of it to him by all the more love (*Adv. haer.*, III, 20, 1-2).[19]

The expulsion from the Garden far away from the tree of life was seen by Irenaeus as a blessing in disguise, because the tree of life would have made humans immortal and therefore their misery would never end. As it is, death is an act of divine grace, which sets a limit to the life of sin and allows God to recreate human beings in the resurrection.

---

[19]Text: SC 34.338; trans. ANF 1.449

For this reason also God cast Adam out of paradise, and set
him far away from the tree of life—not in order to deprive
him of that tree through jealousy, but in pity toward him, so
that he should not continue forever as a transgressor, and
that the sin which surrounded him should not be immortal,
an interminable and incurable evil. Instead he checked his
transgression by interposing death and causing sin to cease,
putting an end to it by the dissolution of the flesh (*Adv.
haer.,* III, 23, 6).[20]

It is this conviction that leads Irenaeus to insist at some length
against Tatian that Adam was saved. Contrasting Adam with
his son Cain, he points out how Adam repented of his sin and
how God gave him the "coats of skins," a theme followed but
interpreted quite differently later by Origen:

Immediately after his transgression, Cain was seized with
fear. He hid himself, not imagining that he would be able to
escape from God, but filled with shame at the thought that
the breach of the precept had rendered him unfit to appear
in God's presence or to speak with him. . . . Adam gives
good evidence of his repentance by the belt of fig leaves with
which he covers himself. While there were many other types
of leaves that would have been less uncomfortable to his
body, he wishes to make for himself a garment in keeping
with his disobedience.
Terrified as he was by fear of God, and repressing the
insolent ardor of his flesh (for he had lost his childlike
nature and sensitivity, and as a result of this had come to the
awareness of evil), he encircled himself and his wife with a
girdle of restraint, living henceforth in the fear of God and in
the expectation of his coming. It was as if he wished to
say: "Because my disobedience has lost for me the garment
which I received from the spirit of holiness, I now
acknowledge that I deserve such a covering as this." It
certainly affords him no pleasure, but pricks and wounds
him. He would have kept this garment always, to humble

[20]Text: SC 34.390; trans. ANF 1.457

himself, if the merciful Lord had not clothed him with coats
of skins in place of the fig leaves (*Adv. haer.,* III, 23, 5).[21]

Irenaeus' anthropology contains a theology of history in which
sin and its consequences enter as integral components. The
Law, the pedagogue leading humans to Christ, brings sin to
light. God, as it were, has enclosed all the human race in a
voluntary disobedience in order that he may show mercy to all.

IV. Grace as Participation in God

The first to formulate a synthesis of the Pauline and
Johannine theologies of grace, Irenaeus makes soteriology the
heart of his theology. As we have seen, for him, the Redeemer
and redemption are the purpose of creation itself. Christ came
to "recapitulate" all humanity in himself (*anakephalaiōsis*), to
restore the likeness of God destroyed by sin, to give humanity
the Holy Spirit in abundance. The Christian possesses the
Spirit, lives in him and is united with him. This participation in
the Spirit makes him a perfect and spiritual being. The Spirit
makes him a child of God, renders him similar to the Son and
the Father, and allows him to participate in the gift of
immortality.

Some of Irenaeus' lapidary and pregnant formulas to
describe our life of grace have become the treasure of Christian
anthropology. The Son of God was given to humanity, says
Irenaeus, "so that humanity might partake of God" (*"ut homo
fieret particeps Dei"*[*Adv. haer.,* IV, 28, 2]). Again, "the glory
of God is the life of humanity, and the life of humanity is the
vision of God" (*"Gloria Dei vivens homo, vita autem hominis
visio Dei"*[*Adv. haer.,* IV, 20, 7]). The following extracts will
give a glimpse of the richness of Irenaeus' soteriology, in
particular his grand vision of the final recapitulation in Christ.

> For in what way could we be partakers of the adoption of
> sons and daughters, unless we had received from him

---

[21]Text: SC 34.390; trans. ANF 1.457

through the Son that fellowship which refers to himself, unless his Word, having been made flesh, had entered into communion with us? Wherefore also he passed through every stage of life, restoring to all communion with God.... But what he did appear, that he also was: God recapitulated in himself the ancient formation of humanity, that he might kill sin, deprive death of its power and vivify human beings....(*Adv. haer.,* III, 18, 7).[22]

For this is why the Word of God became man, and this is why the Son of God became the Son of man, that humans might possess the Word, receive adoption and become children of God. In no other way could we receive incorruptibility and immortality except by being united with incorruptibility and immortality. But how could we be united with incorruptibility and immortality, unless incorruptibility and immortality had first become what we are, in order that what is corruptible might be absorbed by incorruptibility and what is mortal by immortality, that so we might be adopted as children? (*Adv. haer.,* III, 19, 1).[23]

But as the engrafted wild olive does not certainly lose the substance of its wood, but changes the quality of its fruit and receives another name, being now not a wild olive, but a fruit-bearing olive and is called thus, so also when humans are grafted in by faith and receive the Spirit of God, they certainly do not lose the substance of flesh, but change the quality of the fruit of their works and receive another name, showing that they have become changed for the better, being now not mere flesh and blood but spiritual beings and are called such (*Adv. haer.,* V, 10, 1-2).[24]

So the Lord now manifestly came to his own, and, borne by his own created order which he himself bears, he by his obedience on the tree recapitulated what was done by disobedience in connection with a tree; and the power of that seduction by which the virgin Eve, already betrothed to a man, had been wickedly seduced, was broken when the

---

[22]Text: SC 34.326-328; trans. ANF 1.448
[23]Text: SC 34.332; trans. ANF 1.448
[24]Text: SC 153.122; trans. ANF 1.536

angel in truth brought good tidings to the Virgin Mary, who already by her betrothal belonged to a man. For as Eve was seduced by the word of an angel to flee from God, having rebelled against his Word, so Mary by the word of an angel received the glad tidings that she would bear God by obeying his Word. The former was seduced to disobey God and so fell, but the latter was persuaded to obey God, so that the Virgin Mary might become the advocate of the virgin Eve. As the human race was subjected to death through the act of a virgin, so it was saved by a Virgin, and thus the disobedience of one virgin was precisely balanced by the obedience of another. Then indeed the sin of the first-formed man was amended by the chastisement of the First-begotten, the wisdom of the serpent was conquered by the simplicity of the dove, and the chains were broken by which we were in bondage to death (*Adv. haer.*, V, 19, 1).[25]

Therefore, Christ recapitulates these things in himself, uniting humans to the Spirit; and placing the Spirit in humans, he himself is made the head of the Spirit, and gives the Spirit to be the head of humanity, for by him we see and hear and speak. He therefore completely recapitulated all things in himself, both taking up the battle against our enemy, and crushing him who had at the beginning led us captive in Adam, trampling on his head, as you find in Genesis that God said to the serpent, "And I will put enmity between you and the woman, and between your seed and her seed; he will be on the watch for your head, and you will be on the watch for his heel" (Gen 3: 15). From then on it was proclaimed that he who was to be born of a Virgin, after the likeness of Adam, would be on the watch for the serpent's head. . . . The enemy would not have been justly conquered unless it had been a man born of woman who conquered him. For it was by a woman that he had power over humans from the beginning, setting himself up in opposition to them. Because of this the Lord also declares himself to be the Son of Man, so recapitulating in himself that primal man from whom the formation of humanity by

[25]Text: SC 153.248; trans. ANF 1.547

woman began, that as our race went down to death by a
man who was conquered, we might ascend again to life by a
man who overcame; and as death won the palm of victory
over us by a man, so we might by a man receive the palm of
victory over death (*Adv. haer.,* V, 20, 21.1).[26]

3

Alexandrian Anthropology:
Clement and Origen

The two authors whose anthropology is studied in this chapter are often spoken of as belonging to the Alexandrian school. Toward the end of the second century a catechetical school was founded at Alexandria in Egypt, with the mission of propagating the Christian faith among the more cultured classes. Its first known teacher was Pantaenus (died ca. 190); it attained its apogee under his successors Clement (ca. 150-ca. 215) and Origen (ca. 202-231). Other influential theologians of this school include Dionysius, Pierius, Peter, Athanasius, Didymus and Cyril.

Alexandrian theology, in contrast to its counterpart in Antioch, received from its cultural environment distinctive characteristics: a heavy leaning toward Platonic philosophy with its strong appreciation for the spiritual world and its dualistic cosmology, the use of allegory in biblical exegesis, and a penchant for theological speculation. In their doctrines of God and Christ, the Alexandrians tended to emphasize the transcendence of God, the distinction between the three divine persons (sometimes to the point of tritheism) and the divinity of the incarnate Logos (sometimes to the denial of his humanity as in monophysitism and monothelitism).

I. Clement of Alexandria (ca. 150-ca. 215)

Probably an Athenian by birth, Clement, after studying Christianity and philosophy in several places, settled in Alexandria and became the disciple and then associate of Pantaenus whom he finally succeeded as head of the famous catechetical school, most probably in the year 200. Two or three of his main works are: *The Exhortation to the Greeks* (the *Protrepticus*), basically an apologetics for the superiority of Christianity over pagan myths and mysteries; *The Tutor (Paidagogos),* which consists of three books and continues the theme of the *Exhortation;* and lastly the *Stromata,* a miscellany on various topics woven together without any logical connection.

More an Apologist, and indeed a kind of Christian philosopher, than an exegete or a systematic theologian, Clement was as strongly opposed to paganism and Gnosticism as any other Apologist of his times. Nevertheless, like Justin, he knew that one can mount a convincing defense for Christianity, not by ridiculing or heaping invectives against its enemies (as Tatian had done, for example), but by constructing a positive synthesis of its doctrine in terms understandable to its opponents. Thus he endeavors to show to the Gnostics that Christianity leads to true wisdom or religious knowledge or illumination (*"gnōsis").* True gnosis, for him, is given only by the Logos. Christ, the Logos, is the true Teacher, the source of all human reason and the interpreter of God to his mankind. Such gnosis is now contained in the faith of the Church. The Christian is the perfect Gnostic. Clement was not so much concerned with demonstrating the errors of Gnosticism as with establishing points of contact between it and Christianity and with interpreting the Gnostic doctrine as far as possible in a Christian sense.

THE LOGOS AS CREATOR

The influence of Platonism, especially as mediated by Philo, upon Alexandrian theology is particularly evident in Clement's doctrine of creation. Like the Jewish philosopher, he assumes that there are two worlds: the world of sense (*kosmos aisthētos*) and the world of thought (*kosmos noetos* or *archetypos*). Indeed, he argues that such a cosmology was plagiarized by Greek philosophers from the Old Testament:

> Again the barbarian philosophy knows the world of thought and the world of sense—the former archetypal, and the latter the image of that which is called the model. It assigns the former to the Monad as being perceived by the mind, and the latter to the number six. For six is called by the Pythagoreans marriage, as being the genital number. And in the Monad are placed the invisible heaven and the holy earth, and intellectual light. For "in the beginning," it is said, "God made the heaven and the earth; and the earth was invisible." And it is added, "And God said, 'Let there be light'; and there was light" (Gen 1: 1-3). And in the material cosmogony God creates a solid heaven (and what is solid is capable of being perceived by sense), and a visible earth, and a visible light. Does not Plato hence appear to have left the ideas of living creatures in the intelligible world, and to make intelligible objects into sensible species according to their genera? Rightly, then, does Moses say that the body, which Plato calls "the earthly tabernacle," was formed of the earth, but that the rational soul was breathed by God into the man's face (*Stromata,* V, 14, 93).[1]

Clement, therefore, takes Gen 1: 1 to refer to the creation of Platonic ideas. Here Clement reveals another characteristic feature of the Alexandrian doctrine of creation, namely a spiritual interpretation of the story of creation and paradise. Based on an allegorical exegesis of the number six, he suggests that the creation account should not be understood literally as implying God's creative act in six days; rather creation, he believes with Philo, is a simultaneous, timeless, and eternal act that still goes on (*creatio continua*):

> . . . Thus the Lord himself is called "Alpha and Omega, the beginning and the end" (Rev 21: 6), "by whom all things

[1]Text: SC 278.178; trans. ANF 2.466

were made, and without whom not even one thing was made" (Jn 1: 3). God's resting is not then, as some think, that God ceased from creating. For, being good, if he should ever cease from doing good, he would cease from being God, which it is sacrilege even to say. God's resting is, therefore, his ordering that the order of created things should be preserved inviolate, and that each of the creatures should cease from the ancient disorder. For the creation of things on the different days followed in a most important succession, so that all things brought into existence might have honor from priority; though they were created together in thought, they are not of equal worth. Nor was the creation of each thing signified by the voice inasmuch as the creative work is said to have made them at once. For it is necessary that something should have been named first. Those things were announced first from which came those that were second, though all things were originated together from the one essence by the one power. For the will of God was one, in one identity. And how could creation take place in time, if the time itself was born along with things which exist (*Stromata,* VI, 16)?[2]

The influence of Greek philosophy would have been even more apparent if it is true, as Photius says, that Clement had upheld the eternity of matter, an opinion he later rejected (cfr. *The Tutor,* I, 62). Despite this undoubted influence of Greek philosophy, it remains true that Clement had a genuinely Christian understanding of the role of the Logos in creation. The Logos is a personal being, the Creator of the world, and the Teacher of authentic *"gnōsis":*

... We define wisdom to be certain knowledge, a sure and indisputable apprehension of things divine and human, comprehending the past, present, and future, which the Lord has taught us, both by his advent and by his prophets.... This wisdom, then—rectitude of soul and of reason, and purity of life—is the object of the desire of

[2]Text: PG 9.369; trans. ANF 2.513

philosophy, which is kindly and lovingly disposed toward
wisdom, and does its best to attain it. Among us, those are
called philosophers who love Wisdom, the Creator and
Teacher of all things, that is, who know the Son of God....
The unoriginated Being, the omnipotent God, is one; one,
too, is the First-begotten, "by whom all things were made,
and without whom not one thing ever was made" (Jn
1: 3).... And he is called Wisdom by all the prophets. This
is he who is the Teacher of all created beings, the Fellow-
counsellor of God, who foreknew all things. He from above,
from the first foundation of the world, "in many ways and
many times" (Heb 1: 1), trains and perfects; whence it is
rightly said, "Call no man your teacher on earth" (Mt
23: 10) (*Stromata,* VI, 7).[3]

HUMAN BEINGS AS IMAGE AND LIKENESS OF GOD

Among creatures human beings occupy a privileged position
on account of their being created in the image and likeness of
God. As will be recalled, these two terms are used by Irenaeus
in a distinct way. Clement's usage of the words *eikōn* and
homoiōsis is not consistent and they may denote very different
things at different times. In some passages *eikōn* is almost
synonymous with *homoiōsis* and indicates the human person
in his resemblance to Christ.

> For being pure and separated from all wickedness the mind
> begins to be receptive of the power of God, the divine image
> (*eikōn)* being set up in it, as it is said: "Everyone that has
> this hope in the Lord purifies himself even as he is pure" (Jn
> 3: 3) (*Stromata,* III, 5).
> The perfect inheritance is given to him who attains to the
> perfect humanity in the image of the Lord (*Stromata,* VI,
> 14).[4]

---

[3]Text: PG 9.277; trans. ANF 2.492
[4]Text: PG 8.1145; PG 9.337; trans. ANF 2.506

In other passages, the two terms are used in different senses, "eikōn" referring to that rationality which is universal in humans, the power of reasoning, and "homoiōsis" to a more perfect resemblance to God, something over and above the formal resemblance of the image. Christ was the first man to possess the likeness, which has in it no physical element, but is a spiritual similarity of the soul to God. The task of the Logos is to educate humankind and to conform it to this likeness, which he possesses first in himself. And the whole of human history may be considered as the story of the creation, the development and the perfecting of the new image of God in humans, a process which will be terminated only in heaven. Believers, says Clement, are to be "made like (*exomoiousthai*) to the Lord as much as they can" (*Stromata,* III, 5). "Assimilation (*exomoiōsis*) to God to the utmost of one's ability" (*Stromata,* IV, 22) is the duty of a true Gnostic:

> The person of understanding and perspicacity is, then, a Gnostic. His business is not merely abstinence from what is evil (for this is but a step to the highest perfection), or the doing of good out of fear. . . . This, then, is the perfect human's first form of doing good, namely when it is done not for any advantage in what pertains to him, but because he judges it right to do good; and having exerted himself vigorously in all things, he becomes himself good in the very process, and not simply good in some things and bad in others. He hereby acquires the habit of doing good, neither for glory, nor, as the philosophers say, for reputation, nor for reward either from man or God, but so as to pass life after the image and likeness of the Lord (*Stromata,* IV, 22).[5]

The distinction between "image" and "likeness" is even clearer when Clement says that whereas all humans are in the image of God, only the Christians exhibit an image that is truly like God:

> It is time then for us to say that the pious Christian alone is rich, and wise, and of noble birth and thus call and believe

[5]Text: PG 8.1345; trans. ANF 2.434

him to be God's image, and also his likeness, having become righteous and holy and wise by Jesus Christ, and so far already like God (*Exhortation,* 12).[6]

Now, O you, my children, our Instructor is like his Father God, whose Son he is, sinless, blameless, and with a soul devoid of passion; he is God in the form of man, stainless, the minister of his Father's will, the Word who is God, who is in the Father, who is at the Father's right hand, and with the form of God is God. He is to us a spotless image; to him we are to try with all our might to assimilate our soul (*The Tutor,* I, 1, 2, 4).[7]

The view I take is that Christ himself formed humans of the dust, and regenerated them by water, and made them grow by his Spirit, and trained them by his Word to adoption and salvation, directing them by sacred precepts. All this he did in order that, transforming earth-born humans into holy and heavenly beings by his advent, he might fulfill to the utmost that divine utterance, "Let us make humanity in our own image and likeness" (Gen 1:26). And, in truth, Christ became the perfect realization of what God spoke, whereas the rest of humankind is conceived as being created merely in his image" (*The Tutor,* I, 12).[8]

As far as the ontological make-up of human beings is concerned, Clement is rather eclectic, employing different systems in different contexts. Sometimes he uses the Platonic triad of *epithumia* (desire), *thumos* (soul), and *logismos* (reason) and at other times the Scriptural one of *sarx* (flesh), *psychē* (soul) and *pneuma* (spirit). At other times he follows the Stoic triple division of body, the animal soul (psychē), which is the subordinate spirit (*hypokeimenon*) animating the body, and the rational soul (*nous*), which is the superior controlling spirit (*hēgemonikon*). To this triple composition he adds the gift of the Holy Spirit.

---

[6]Text: SC 2.192; trans. ANF 2.206
[7]Text: SC 70.114; trans. ANF 2.209
[8]Text: SC 70.284; trans. ANF 2.234

There is, therefore, a kind of union of ten elements in humans: the five senses, the voice, the sexual instinct, and, in the eighth place, the spiritual principle communicated at their creation; and the ninth, the ruling faculty of the soul (*hēgemonikon*), and the tenth, the distinctive characteristic of the Holy Spirit which comes to them through faith (*Stromata,* VI, 16).[9]

Against the Gnostics Clement attached a high value to the body:

Those, then, who attack that which was formed, and vilify the body, are wrong. They do not see that the human body was formed erect so as to contemplate heaven, and that the organization of the senses tends to knowledge, and that the members and parts are arranged for good, not pleasure. Whence this abode becomes the receptacle of the soul which is most precious to God, and is dignified with the Holy Spirit through the sanctification of soul and body, perfected with the perfection of the Savior. . . . The soul is confessedly the better part of human beings, and the body the inferior. But neither is the soul good by nature, nor, on the other hand, is the body bad by nature. Nor is that which is not good *ipso facto* bad. For there are things which occupy a middle place, and among them are things to be preferred, and things to be rejected. The constitution of humans, then, which has its place among things of sense, was necessarily composed of things diverse, but not opposite—body and soul (*Stromata,* IV, 26).[10]

Though he recognizes the goodness of the body, Clement believes that it is the mind (*nous*) that gives humans their real dignity. Contrary to Irenaeus, Clement does not think that the human body is part of God's image. Rather, the image is constituted by the human "mind," the *Nous* or *Logos:*

[9]Text: PG 9.360; trans. ANF 2.511
[10]Text: PG 8.1372; trans. ANF 2.439

Are not humans rightly said "to have been made in the image of God?"—I reply, not in the form of their bodily structure, but, inasmuch as God creates all things by the Word (*Logos*), the person who has become a Gnostic performs good actions by the faculty of reason (*to logico*) (*Stromata,* VI, 16).[11]

The superiority of the "Nous" over the body is clearly affirmed in the following passage:

Besides, in addition to these ten human parts, the Law appears to give its injunctions to sight, hearing, smell, touch, taste and to the organs subservient to these, which are double, namely the hands and the feet. For such is the formation of humans. And the soul is introduced, and previous to it the ruling faculty, by which we reason, not produced in procreation, so that without it there is made up the number ten, of the faculties by which all human activities are performed. For, immediately upon its creation, in an orderly fashion human life begins with sensations. Accordingly, we assert that the rational and ruling power is the cause of the constitution of the living creature, and that the irrational part is animated by it and is a part of it. Now the vital force, which comprises the power of nutrition, growth and motion, is assigned to the carnal spirit, which has great susceptibility of motion, and passes in all directions through the senses and the rest of the body, and through the body is the primary subject of sensations. But the power of choice, in which investigation, study and knowledge reside, belongs to the ruling faculty. But all the faculties are placed in relation to one—the ruling faculty. By means of it humans live and live in a certain way. Through the corporeal spirit, then, humans perceive, desire, rejoice, are angry, are nourished and grow. It is by it, too, that thoughts and conceptions advance to actions. And when it masters the desires, the ruling faculty reigns (*Stromata,* VI, 16).[12]

[11]Text: PG 9.561; trans. ANF 2.512
[12]Text: PG 9.360; trans. ANF 2.511

Beyond the body, the soul, and the mind, Clement believes that a fourth element is required to have a perfect human being, namely the *pneuma,* the Holy Spirit. This is, as we have seen above, the tenth element in human beings which sanctified both their body and soul and which is known only in Christian revelation:

> It is far from correct to say that humans do not participate in the divine thought, since it is written that at their creation they partook of the breath, receiving a substance purer than any given to other living creatures. Hence the Pythagoreans say that mind comes to humans by divine providence, as Plato and Aristotle also acknowledge. But, whereas the Platonists make the mind (*nous*) dwell in the soul as an emanation (*aporroia*) from a divine endowment, and the soul (*psychē*) in the body, we say in addition that the Holy Spirit has been breathed (*prosepipneisthai*) into the believer (*Stromata,* V, 13, 87).[13]

This gift of the Spirit, by which a human being is made perfectly human, is linked with the coming of Christ. It is bestowed only on Christian believers in their baptismal regeneration. Hence, it is not something naturally innate in human beings. Humanity is not, according to Clement, divine by nature and has somehow fallen from perfection. Rather it is created as capable of achieving perfection through the exercise of freedom:

> You must know that we are disposed to virtue by nature, but that we do not possess it from birth, we are merely capable of acquiring it. .12. It is this which resolves the problem posed by heretics: was Adam created perfect or imperfect? If he was created imperfect, how could a perfect God have created an imperfect work, and especially an imperfect human being? But if he was created perfect, how did he come to violate the commandments? They must understand that Adam was not perfect from his creation,

[13]Text: SC 278.168; trans. ANF 2.465

but only fitted to acquire virtue. For it is of great importance that virtue be made attainable. And it is intended that we should be saved by ourselves. It is the nature of the soul to move of itself.... Now an aptitude is a movement toward virtue, not virtue itself. All human beings, then, are naturally constituted for the acquisition of virtue. But one person applies more, another less, to learning and training. Some have been able to attain to perfect virtue, others to a degree of it, and still others, through negligence, have turned to the opposite, even though they may be of good disposition in other respects (*Stromata,* VI, 11, 12).[14]

Thus, for Clement, the root of spiritual progress for each individual is the exercise of his freedom. Unlike Irenaeus, Clement does not entertain a progressive notion of the collective development of human history in which sin would be no more than a disturbance to the evolutionary process. Rather, he focuses on the individual who through a good or bad act of choice promotes or retards or even destroys his growth toward perfection.

THE FIRST SIN AS DISOBEDIENCE

The first bad act of choice, according to Clement, consists in an act of disobedience by which the first parents had sexual intercourse before the appointed time, being drawn to this by the passion of youth:

The Savior came to us who had gone astray in our thoughts, which had been corrupted by disobedience to the commandments, we being lovers of pleasure, possibly because the first man anticipated the right time and sinned by a desire for the good gift of marriage before the appointed time.... When, therefore, the Apostle says, "Put on the new man, created according to God" (Eph 4: 24), he is not speaking of the old order of the creation and the new of the

14Text: PG 9.517; trans. ANF 2.502

regeneration, but of life in disobedience and in obedience (*Stromata,* III, 14).[15]

This act of disobedience introduced a serious disorder into human life. The passions, in particular anger and desire, are no longer controlled by the higher part of the soul, the *nous,* and consequently humans are no longer "logical" and become like the animals:

> Everything that is contrary to right reason is sin. Accordingly, the philosophers think fit to define the most generic passions thus: lust as desire disobedient to reason; fear as weakness disobedient to reason; pleasure as an elation of the spirit disobedient to reason. If, then, disobedience to reason is the cause of sin, how shall we escape the conclusion that obedience to reason—the Word—which we call faith, will of necessity be the efficacious cause of duty? For virtue itself is a state of the soul rendered harmonious by reason in respect to the whole life.... Therefore, as soon as the first man sinned and disobeyed God, it is said of him that he "became like the animals" (Ps 49: 12), lacking reason. It is natural that he should be regarded from then on as irrational (*alogikos*) and likened to animals (*The Tutor,* I, 13).[16]

Does this state of unruly passions constitute for Clement what is called original sin (*peccatum originale originatum*)? Emphasizing human responsibility and freedom against the Gnostics, Clement says that, sin being necessarily an act of the will, the infant who has done no evil cannot be regarded as involved in the sin of Adam:

> Let them (the Gnostics) tell us how the newborn babe has committed fornication, or how one who has as yet done nothing at all have fallen under the curse of Adam. They have, as I see it, no other course open to them except to

[15]Text: PG 8.1196; trans. LCC 2.84
[16]Text: SC 70.290

draw the logical conclusion that the very process of generation is evil, not only the generation of the body, but also that of the soul, from which that of the body flows (*Stromata*, III, 16).[17]

But to say so, of course, would be blasphemous since it would mean that God himself is the author of evil. But does Clement then deny that the sin Adam rebounds on his descendants at all? He continues:

When David said: "I was conceived in wickedness, and in sin my mother brought me forth" (Ps 50: 7), his words were prophetic, and refer to Eve. In Eve was "the mother of all living" (Gen 3: 70). But even though he was conceived in sin, he is not himself in sin, nor is he yet without sin. It is simply that every human person who is converted must be converted to life from his solidarity (*sunētheia*) with a mother who is in some respect a sinner. . . . (*Stromata*, III, 16).[18]

Though Clement's thought is less than transparently clear here, it seems correct to say that he does not deny original sin as such but rather understands our disorderly condition as sinful in an analogous sense. On the one hand, it is not sinful in the sense that it is not the result of our free choice; on the other hand, it is "sinful" insofar as it is connected with the first sin of disobedience.

SALVATION AS KNOWLEDGE

Clement's apologetic method led him to highlight the function of the Logos as teacher. It is through his teaching that the Logos divinises. In an eloquent passage Clement makes Christ address people of all races thus:

---

[17]Text: PG 8. 1200; trans. LCC 2.87
[18]Text: PG 8.1201; trans. LCC 2.87

Hear, you myriad tribes, rather whoever among humans are endowed with reason, both barbarians and Greeks. I call on the whole human race, whose Creator I am, by the will of the Father. Come to me, that you may be put in your due rank under the one God and the one Word of God. Do not enjoy only the advantage of the irrational creatures in the possession of reason: for to you of all mortals I grant the gift of immortality. I want to impart to you this grace, bestowing on you the perfect boon of immortality, and I confer on you both the Word and the knowledge of God, my complete self. This I am, this God wills, this is symphony, this the harmony of the Father, this is the Son, this is the Christ, this is the Word of God, the arm of the Lord, the power of the universe, the will of the Father; of which things there were images of old, but not all adequate. I desire to restore you according to the original model, that you may become also like me. I anoint you with the oil of faith, by which you throw off corruption, and show you the naked form of righteousness by which you ascend to God (*Exhortation,* 1, 12).[19]

Adopting the Gnostics' division of the human race into three groups, Clement suggests that the *hylics* are the pagans, living a natural and material existence, vaguely aware of a higher knowledge. Yet, contrary to the Gnostics, Clement believes that they too are called by God to follow the divine Teacher and the higher knowledge he reveals. The *psychics* are the Christians of simple faith, who are still immersed in a material approach to God and who accept a literal interpretation of the Scriptures. The *pneumatics* are the Christian Gnostics who, through conversion and ascetical purification, understand the higher teaching of the Logos, penetrate into the spiritual meaning of the Scripture, and finally arrive at the state of "apatheia":

He is the Gnostic, who is after the image and likeness of God, who imitates God as far as possible, deficient in none

---

[19]Text: SC 2.190; trans. ANF 2.205

of the things which contribute to the likeness as far as possible, practicing self-restraint and endurance, living righteously, controlling the passions, bestowing of what he has as far as possible, and doing good both by word and deed (*Stromata*, 2, 19).[20]

The Gnostic is such that he is subject only to the affections that exist for the maintenance of the body, such as hunger, thirst and the like....Christ was entirely impassible (*apathes*), inaccessible to any movement of feeling, either of pleasure or pain. While the apostles, having most gnostically mastered, through the Lord's teaching, anger and fear and lust, were not liable even to such of the movements of feeling as seem good, courage, zeal, joy, desire through a steady condition of mind, not changing in the least, but ever continuing unvarying in a state of training after the resurrection of the Lord (*Stromata*, 6, 9).[21]

...a divine power of goodness clinging to the righteous soul in contemplation and prophecy, and in the exercise of the function of governing, impresses on it something, as it were, of intellectual radiance, like the solar ray, as a visible sign of righteousness, uniting the soul with light, through unbroken love, which is God-bearing and God-borne. Thence assimilation to God the Savior comes to the Gnostic as far as permitted to human nature, he being made perfect "as the Father who is in heaven" (Mt 5: 48) (*Stromata*, 6, 12).[22]

Clement's overemphasis on knowledge (*gnōsis*), contemplation (*theōria*), and passionlessness (*apatheia*) as the characteristics of a true Christian Gnostic makes his soteriology elitist and excessively dependent on Greek philosophy.

II. Origen (ca. 185-253/254)

Certainly the most brilliant and controversial theologian of the East, Origen had quite a checkered career. Born into a

[20]Text: SC 38.109; trans. ANF 2.369
[21]Text: PG 9.292; trans. ANF 2.496
[22]Text: PG 9.325; trans. ANF 2.504

Christian family, probably at Alexandria, he studied in the catechetical school under Clement. During the persecution in 202 in which his father, Leonidas, was killed, he was prevented from suffering martyrdom by the ruse of his mother, who hid his clothes. After peace was restored, Bishop Demetrius, in recognition of his scholarly gifts, made him the head of the catechetical school as successor to Clement, in spite of his being barely nineteen years old. Soon after, he turned the school over to Heraclas and devoted his energies to studying pagan philosophy, probably under the famous Ammonius Saccas, who was also the teacher of Plotinus. He quickly became known throughout the Church and travelled about the Empire. He visited Rome and Arabia, preached in Caesarea as a layman, expounded the Christian doctrine at the imperial court. In 230 he visited Caesarea again, where he was ordained a priest, without the knowledge and consent of his bishop Demetrius. The latter took offense, deprived him of his chair, deposed him from the priesthood, which he contended to be invalid because Origen had castrated himself, and sent him into exile. Origen took refuge at Caesarea (231), where he established a school which soon became famous, and where he continued to teach, write and preach. In 250, in the persecution of Decius, he was imprisoned and subjected to prolonged torture, from which he died four years later.

An extremely prolific author, he wrote on a wide variety of topics. He did textual criticism of the Old Testament (the *Hexapla*), wrote exegetical works on all the books of the Bible (scholia, homilies and commentaries), apologetical treatises (in particular *Against Celsus*), dogmatic treatises (in particular *De Principiis*) and ascetical and mystical works (especially *Exhortation to Martyrdom* and *On Prayer*). Unfortunately, many of his writings have perished and most of the others survived only in fragments or in loosely done Latin translations. The main reason for this almost complete loss of the originals is the later condemnations of his teachings.

Origen, like any original thinker, had both fierce opponents and enthusiastic supporters. Already at the beginning of the fourth century, Methodius of Olympus attacked Origen's exegetical method, his view of the resurrection, and his doctrine of the pre-existence of souls. On the other hand,

Eusebius of Caesarea, who wrote an account of Origen's life, and Pamphilus, who composed an *Apology for Origen,* took up arms for him. About 375, Epiphanius of Salamis mounted a fierce opposition to Origenism, especially its Trinitarian and christological doctrines, in addition to its doctrine of the transmigration of souls and its allegorical exegesis. Epiphanius succeeded in persuading Jerome to join his ranks. In 398, Rufinus' Latin translation of the *De Principiis* added fuel to the fire. In 400, Theophilus, the patriarch of Alexandria, condemned Origen and Origenism. Finally, in the sixth century, a synod of Constantinople (543) officially condemned Origen and his views, and the condemnation was ratified by the Fifth General Council of 553. On the other hand, Origen remained influential with Athanasius, the Cappadocians, fourth-century monasticism, Evagrius Ponticus, Pseudo-Dionysius, John Cassian, Gregory the Great, Maximus the Confessor and many others. Through them Origen's theological legacy has become a perennial part of the Christian tradition. Perhaps it is well to remember that in these heated controversies on Origenism, Origen's teachings have often been misrepresented; no sufficient care was taken to distinguish between the teachings of Origen himself and their developments by his disciples, between what Origen presented as secure doctrines and what he boldly proposed as working hypotheses. Unfortunately, owing to the loss of the originals of most of his works, a satisfactory reconstruction of his authentic thought is not always possible.

THE CREATION OF TWO WORLDS:
THE PRE-EXISTENT WORLD OF
SPIRITS AND THE WORLD OF MATTER

The influence of Platonic philosophy, which we have seen in Clement's anthropology, is even more extensive in Origen's. Origen was the first to compose a complete exposition on Genesis, a forerunner of so many later accounts of the Hexaemeron (Basil, Gregory of Nyssa, Victorinus of Pettau, Ambrose and Augustine), and to attempt to relate Genesis to the cosmology of the commentaries of *Timaeus.* For Origen, the traditional rule of faith is the norm for theological speculation. This is made clear in the preface to his *magnum opus,* the *Peri Archōn* or *De Principiis:* "We maintain that that only is to be believed as the truth which in no way conflicts with the tradition of the Church and the apostles"(I, praef. 2). In this sense, Origen is a Christian theologian.

On the other hand, Origen is no less a committed Platonist, and together with Plotinus, he must be regarded as one of the founders of Neoplatonism. This is indisputable in his view of creation. In Platonic fashion, God is conceived as existing absolutely apart from time and space, absolutely transcendent and immutable, transcending mind and being itself. This is, in Christian terminology, God the Father, who alone is God in the strict sense (*autotheos*), the unbegotten (*agennētos*). Being absolute goodness and power, he must always have had objects on which to exercise them. Hence he has brought into existence a world of spiritual beings, or souls, coeternal with himself (cfr. *De Princ.,* 1, 2, 10; 1, 4, 3; 2, 9 1). To mediate, however, between his absolute unity and their multiplicity, he has his Son, the Logos, his express image, the meeting place of a plurality of "ideas" (*epinoiai,* the Platonic 'forms') which explain his twofold relation to his Father and the world (cfr. *C. Cels.,* 2, 64). Being outside of time and space, the Father begets the Son by an eternal act (*aeterna ac sempiterna generatio, De Princ.,* 1, 2, 4), so that there was not when he was not. In this context Origen coins the word *homoousios* (consubstantial), which would become famous in the Arian controversy. Nevertheless, the divinity of the Son is derivative; he is the "secondary God" (*deuteros theos, C. Cels.,* 5, 39). Thus, Origen is accused of subordinationism. Finally, Origen, following Christian revelation, parts company with Greek philosophy and introduces a third hypostasis, namely, the Holy Spirit, whom he calls "the most honorable of all the beings brought into existence through the Word, the chief in rank of all the beings originated by the Father through Christ" (*In Ioh.,* 2, 10, 75).

As was mentioned above, Origen believes that God eternally creates a single world of rational beings (*ta logika*) or souls. These are created equal and free. This is Origen's famous doctrine of the pre-existence of souls which would be fiercely attacked by his opponents:

> ... God the Creator of the universe is both good and just
> and omnipotent. Now when "in the beginning" (Gen 1: 1)
> he created what he wished to create, that is, rational beings
> (*ta logika*), he had no other reason for creating them except
> himself, that is, his own goodness. As therefore he himself,
> in whom was neither variation, nor change, nor lack of
> power, was the cause of all that was to be created, he created
> all his creatures equal and alike, for the simple reason that
> there was in him no cause that could give rise to variety and
> diversity. But since these rational creatures ... were
> endowed with power of free will, it was this freedom which
> induced each one by his own voluntary choice either to
> make progress through the imitation of God or to deteriorate
> through negligence. This...was the cause of the diversity
> among rational creatures, a cause that takes its origin, not
> from the will or judgment of the Creator, but from the
> decision of the creature's own freedom. God, however, who
> then felt it just to arrange his creation according to merit,
> gathered the diversities of minds into the harmony of a
> single world, so as to furnish, as it were, out of these diverse
> vessels or souls or minds, one house, in which there must be
> "not only vessels of gold and silver, but also of wood and of
> earth, and some unto honor and some unto dishonor" (2
> Tim 2: 20) (*De Princ.*, 2, 9, 6).[23]

Origen, then, transforms the story recorded in Genesis, which
Theophilus, Irenaeus and Clement had accepted as historical
fact, into a cosmic myth. Creation is not in time but eternal and
the fall of humankind is projected into the transcendent realm.
The created spirits are free, but freedom implies instability and
mutability:

> The rational creatures which were made in the beginning
> were created, not having existed beforehand. Since, there-
> fore, they once were not, but had a beginning of their

---

[23]Text: SC 252.364; trans. ANF 4.291

existence, they are of necessity changeable and must abide, because, whatever may be the virtue communicated to their substance, it does not belong to it by nature, but was given by God. That what they are, then, they derive not from themselves but from the gift of God. Now, anything which has been given can also be taken away and withdrawn. The reason for such withdrawal will be that the movement of the soul is not directed aright, as it ought to be. For the Creator has of himself granted to created spirits the power of free and voluntary movement, by means of which they might make the good their own, and keep it by their own will. But sloth and weariness of taking trouble to preserve the good, coupled with disregard and neglect of better things, began the process of withdrawal from the good. Now to withdraw from the good is nothing else than to be immersed in evil; for it is certain that to be evil means to be lacking in good. Hence it is that in whatever degree one declines from the good, one descends into an equal degree of evil (*De Princ.,* 2, 9, 2).[24]

With the unique exception of Christ's pre-existent soul, all these rational beings opted in varying degrees to depart from the good; the result was their fall, which gave rise to the manifold and unequal gradations of spiritual existence. In this way Origen hoped to account for the justice of God: all differences between the condition of one individual and another in this world had their sources in the merits or demerits of the person concerned in a prior existence. To punish the fallen souls, God created the material world, including the bodies, to which the souls are tied.

Before the ages all the intellectual beings were pure, demons, souls, angels, offering service to God and keeping his commandments. But the devil, who was one of them, since he possessed free will, willed to oppose God, and God rejected him. With him all the other powers revolted. Some sinned deeply and became demons, others less and became

[24]Text: SC 252.354; trans. ANF 4.290

angels, others still less and became archangels. Thus, each in turn received his reward proportionate to his sin. There remained souls, who had neither sinned so seriously as to become demons, nor so lightly as to become angels. God therefore made the present world and tied the soul to the body as punishment. For it was not from favoritism that God made, of all the spiritual creatures who had been of a single nature, one a demon, another an angel, and another a soul. Rather it is clear that God made one a demon, one an angel, one a soul as a means of punishing each in proportion to his sin. For if this were not so, and souls had no pre-existence, why do we find some new-born babes to be blind, when they have committed no sin, while others are born with no defect at all? But it is clear that certain sins existed before the souls, and as a result of these sins each soul receives a recompense in accord to its deserts (*De Princ.*, I, 8, 1).[25]

There are then three main categories of being: the *caelestia,* the angels and the heavenly bodies whom God associates with himself in his work; the *terrestria,* the human race who receives help from the angels and who can through this help be restored to blessedness; and lastly, the *inferna,* the evil angels or demons, for whom there is, at least in this world, no cure and who continue to trouble humankind. These three groups are not totally separated from each other; they represent different degrees of fallenness. Origen contemplates the possibility that a member of one group, through his imitation or through the rejection of the Logos, may ascend to the higher or descend to the lower group, as the case may be.

It is also clear that in Origen's cosmology the body does not form part of the first primordial creation; rather it is created by God in the second phase as a means of punishment for the fallen soul. Nevertheless, Origen, contrary to Plato and Plotinus, does not consider the body as evil. Matter is not created by the Demiurge as an evil order; rather it is a secondary order created by God himself as a means of

[25]Text: SC 252; trans. ANF 4

restoration of the souls to a higher level of being. Evil is in the will alone; matter is not connected with evil but with diversity.

> In regard then to this matter, which is so great, and so wonderful as to be sufficient for all the bodies in the world, which God willed to exist, and to be at the call and service of the Creator in all things for the fashioning of whatever forms and species he wished, receiving into itself the qualities which he had willed to bestow upon it, I cannot understand how so many distinguished men have supposed it to be uncreated, that is, not made by God himself, the Creator of all things, but in its nature and power the result of chance (*De Princ.*, 2, 1, 4).[26]

The body will be transformed together with the soul:

> When, therefore, all rational souls have been restored to a condition like this (i. e., immortality and spirituality), then also the nature of this body of ours will develop into the glory of a 'spiritual body' (1 Cor 14: 44). For just as in the case of rational creatures we see that there is not one kind which on account of its sins has lived in dishonor and another kind which on account of its merits has been summoned to blessedness, but that these are the same natures, which were formerly sinful and afterwards, through being converted and reconciled to God, were recalled to blessedness; so, too, in regard to our bodily nature, we must understand that there is not one body which we now use for lowliness, and corruption, and weakness, and a different one which we are to use hereafter in incorruption, and power, and glory, but that this same body, having cast off the weakness of its present existence, will be transformed into a thing of glory and made spiritual, with the result that what was a vessel of dishonor shall itself be purified and become a vessel of honor and a habitation of blessedness (*De Princ.*, 3, 6, 6).[27]

[26]Text: SC 252.242; trans. ANF 4.269
[27]Text: SC 268.246; trans. ANF 4.347

HUMANITY IN THE IMAGE AND LIKENESS OF GOD

Origen strongly underlines the difference between the Logos and human beings in terms of their being the image of God. Only the Logos can be called the image of God, whereas humans are only "according to the image" or "image of the image," the mediate image of God and the immediate image of the Logos who is the intermediary between the Father and humanity. The Logos' participation in, or better still, possession in common (*metochē*) of the divine nature is total, whereas humankind's participation is partial; the former's participation is substantial, that is, immutable, whereas the latter's is accidental, that is, susceptible of increase or decrease. Whereas the Logos is the "filial image" of the Father which reproduces faithfully all the features of the model, humans are the "plastic image" which reproduces the model only in an imperfect way.

> Let us now see what we ought to understand by the expression 'image of the invisible God,' in order that we may learn therefrom how God can rightly be called the Father of his Son. Let us first of all consider what things are called images in ordinary human speech. Sometimes the term 'image' is applied to an object painted or sculptured on some material, such as wood or stone. Sometimes a child is said to be the image of its parents, when the likeness of the parent's features is in every respect faithfully reproduced in the child. Now I think that the first of these illustrations may be fitly applied to him who was made 'in the image and likeness of God,' that is, the human being.... But in regard to the Son of God ... the image may be compared to our second illustration; for this reason, that he is the invisible image of the invisible God, just as, according to the Scripture narrative, we say that the image of Adam was his son Seth (*De Princ.,* 1, 2, 6).[28]

As regards the divine image in humans, Origen, following Philo's exegesis of the two accounts of creation in Genesis (cfr.

---

[28]Text: SC 252.120; trans. ANF 4.247

De opificio, 134), speaks of a double creation. The first creation is that of the soul which is made in the image of God; the second is that of the body, in which the image does not reside (cfr. *In Jo.,* 20, 22; *In Rom.,* 2, 13; *Hom. on Gen.,* 1, 13; *In Mt.,* 14, 16; *Hom. on Jer.,* 1, 10).Again, following Philo, Origen uses the verb *poiein* for the making of the soul and *plattein* for the fashioning of the body. Origen places the image in the soul and not in the body: it is not the fashioned body which contains the image. Corporeal humans are not said to have been made but fashioned, as it is in effect implied in Genesis: "And God fashioned humankind from the slime of the earth. He who was made according to the image is our interior self, invisible, incorporeal, incorruptible and immortal" (*Hom. in Gen.,* 1, 13).[29]

Because humans are the image of the Logos, it is natural that the "according to the image of God" be situated in the "logical" part of human nature. This higher part is called *"Logos," "nous,"* or *"hēgemonikon,"* the Stoic term for the ruling part of the soul. It is the subject of an intellectual life and is equivalent as the intellect (*dianoētikon*), mind (*nous*), intellectual soul (*psychē noera*); it is opposed to sensation (*aisthēsis*), the imaginative or passionate soul (*psychē phantastikē* or *hormētikē*, the source of bodily passions. It is also the seat of free and moral activities. Finally, it is the principle of spiritual senses, that is, of spiritual sight, hearing, touch, smell, and taste that enable us to perceive supernatural realities.

Being made "according to the image of God" humans share in the nature of God and become in some way (*quodammodo*) "consubstantial" with him. Consequently, they become immortal:

> It will certainly not, I think, appear contrary to the plan of this work of ours if we repeat as briefly as possible the arguments concerning the immortality of rational creatures. Everyone who shares in anything is undoubtedly of one substance and one nature with him who shares in the same

[29]Text: PG 12.81; trans. FOTC 71.193, R.E. Heine

thing. For example, all eyes share in the light, and therefore all eyes, which share in the light, are of one nature. But though every eye shares in the light, yet since one eye sees clearly and another dimly, every eye does not share equally in the light. Again, all hearing receives the voice and sound, and therefore all hearing is of one nature; but each person is quick or slow to hear in proportion to the pure and healthy condition of his hearing organ. Now let us move from these illustrations drawn from the senses to the consideration of intellectual things.

Every mind which shares in intellectual light must undoubtedly be of one nature with every other mind which shares similarly in this light. If then the heavenly spirits receive a share of intellectual light, that is, of the divine nature, in virtue of the fact that they share in wisdom and sanctification, and if the soul of human beings receives a share of the same light and wisdom, then these beings will be of one nature and one substance. But the heavenly spirits are incorruptible and immortal; undoubtedly, therefore, the substance of the human soul will also be incorruptible and immortal. Furthermore, since the nature of Father, Son and Holy Spirit, to whom alone belongs the intellectual light in which the universal creation has a share, is incorruptible and eternal, it follows logically and of necessity that every being which has a share in that eternal nature must itself also remain forever incorruptible and eternal, in order that the eternity of the divine goodness may be revealed in the fact that they who obtain its blessings are eternal too. Nevertheless, just as in our illustration we acknowledge some diversity in the reception of the light, when we described the individual power of light as being either dim or keen, so also we must acknowledge a diversity of participation in the Father, Son and Holy Spirit, varying in proportion to the earnestness of the soul and the capacity of the mind (*De Princ.*, 4, 1, 36).[30]

[30]Text: SC 268.423; trans. ANF 4.380

Not only does Origen describe the creation of humans "according to the image" in terms of participation in the divine nature, but also, to the scandal of Jerome later, in terms of kinship with God, an image of no less Platonic origin than that of participation:

> ... Moreover, the marks of the divine image in humans may be clearly discerned, not in the form of their body, which will suffer corruption, but in the prudence of their mind, in their righteousness, their self-control, their courage, their wisdom, their discipline, in fact, in the whole complex of virtues, which exist in God essentially, and may exist in us as a result of our own efforts and our imitation of God.... We see, therefore, that humans have a kind of blood-relationship with God; and since God knows all things and not a single intellectual truth escapes his notice ... it is possible that a rational mind, too, by advancing from a knowledge of small to a knowledge of greater things and from things visible to things invisible, may attain to an increasingly perfect understanding (*De Princ.*, 4, 4, 10).[31]

But, as has already been said above, for Origen humans are not the image of God directly; indeed, only the Logos is the image of God. Humans are the image of God insofar as they are made after the Logos; that is why they are said to be "according to the image." Hence, participation in God means first of all participation in the Logos.

> It is clear that the source of that life which is pure and unmixed with anything else resides in him who is "the first-born of all creation" (Col 1: 15). Drawing from this source, those who have a share in Christ truly live that life. But those who try to live apart from him, just as they do not have the true light, also do not possess the true life (*In Jo.*, 1, 28).[32]
> For, since he is the invisible "image of the invisible God" (Col 1: 15), he himself grants participation in himself to all

[31]Text: SC 268.426; trans. ANF 4.381
[32]Text: SC 290.278; trans. ANF 10

rational creatures in such a way that the participation each
of them receives from him is proportionate to the passionate
love with which they cling to him (*De Princ.*, 2, 6, 3).[33]

In virtue of this participation, human beings receive the power
to become children of God (cfr. *De Princ.*, 4, 4, 5) by sharing in
the Sonship of the Only-Begotten. Further, because Christ is
truth, wisdom, and light, those who participate in the Logos
are "logical" (*logika*), that is, share in the characteristics of the
Logos. This sharing, it must be pointed out, is understood by
Origen, not as "natural" but as "supernatural," even though he
does not use such terminology. Finally, such participation
admits of degrees (which establishes a hierarchy of beings) and
can be lost. "Logical" beings can become "a-logical" by
sinning.

THE FALL: DISTORTION OF THE IMAGE

We have already seen that Origen postulated a pre-cosmic fall
of the spirits to explain the hierarchy of beings and the
different lots human beings receive at birth and that the human
souls are united to bodies as a punishment for their sins.
Beyond this, does Origen believe that humanity as a whole is
affected by sin and depravity that is the result of Adam's sin? In
other words, does he believe in original sin?

When treating Adam as a historical person and not as a
symbol of humanity, Origen grants that he was in a condition
superior to ours. He possessed gifts of immortality and
incorruptibility, i.e., divine life (cfr. *In Rom.*, 10, 14). He
possessed as distinct both the image and the likeness of God.
By reason of his intellectual soul (*nous*), he was made
"according to the image" (*kat'eikōna*) of God (*Hom. in Gen.*,
7: 13). He possessed the likeness (*homoiōsis*), not as a static
perfection, but as a dynamic orientation to a greater likeness of
God by assimilation to his nature through "imitation of God"
(*De Princ.*, 3, 6, 1). By sinning, Adam lost all these privileges.

Elsewhere (*C. Cels.*, 4, 37-40), Origen regards the story of

---

[33]Text: SC 252.314; trans. ANF 4.287

the garden and Adam's expulsion from it as an allegory of the pre-cosmic fall, pointing out that where Moses seems to be speaking of an individual he really has human nature as a whole in mind. As a result, Origen seems to deny any doctrine of corporate sinfulness, for his allegorical interpretation of Genesis suggests that if human beings are sinful from birth, their wickedness is the legacy of their own misguided choices in the transcendental world, and has nothing to do with the disobedience of any one first man.

> . . . the subjects of Adam and his son will be philosophically dealt with by those who are aware that in the Hebrew language Adam signifies humanity; and that in those parts of the narrative which appear to refer to Adam as an individual, Moses is discoursing upon human nature in general. For "in Adam" (as the Scripture says) "all are," and were condemned in the likeness of Adam's transgression, the word of God asserting this not so much of the one particular individual as of the whole human race. For in the connected series of statements which appear to apply as to one particular individual, the curse pronounced upon Adam is regarded as common to all the members of the race, and what was spoken with reference to the woman, is spoken of every woman without exception. And the expulsion of the man and woman in paradise and their being clothed with tunics of skins (which God, because of their transgression, made for those who had sinned), contain a certain secret and mystical doctrine (far transcending that of Plato) of the soul's losing its wings, and being borne downwards to earth, until it can lay hold of some stable resting-place (*C. Cels.*, 4, 40).[34]

Further, in his *Commentary on Romans*, Origen seems to have taken *eph'o* in Rom 5: 12 in the causal sense, i.e., death has befallen all human beings *because* they all have sinned, notwithstanding Rufinus' Latin translation which interprets it as *in whom*, implying the doctrine of "corporate guilt."

[34]Text: SC 136.288; trans. ANF 4.516

Other texts, however, seem to indicate that Origen believes that humanity suffered from a state of moral pollution. Commenting on the legal purifications prescribed by *Leviticus* for a woman after childbirth, Origen says that they could not be applied to the Virgin Mary who had not conceived from human insemination. But why is the woman declared unclean? Why must the infant be redeemed? There seems to be a great mystery:

> It seems that the simple fact of having cooperated in bringing a child into this world demands an atonement, a purification. As the Scripture says, "the priest shall make an atonement for her and she shall be clean." I scarcely dare to say anything about this. I feel there are hidden mysteries here, that there are deep secrets in this statement that a woman who becomes a mother with the assistance of a man, is unclean and must offer a victim for sin, must cleanse herself as if she were guilty. Her child, too, boy or girl, even though only one day old, is not exempt from stain, Scripture tells us. It is necessary that you know: there is in this something so important that not one of the saints ever doubted it; not one of them even marked his birthday by a feast or a great banquet; not one of them experienced joy on the birthday of a son or daughter. The sinners are alone in so doing. Thus we see it is Pharaoh, king of Egypt, in the Old Testament, Herod in the New, who celebrated their birthday with festivities.... Not merely did the saints not celebrate their birthday, they held it in horror. Jeremiah, so great that from his mother's womb he was sanctified and consecrated a prophet for the nations (cf. Jer 1: 5), and whose books must last forever, would have uttered vain words, did they not contain great and difficult mysteries, as for example, "Cursed be the day of my birth and the night when it was said, 'It is a boy!'" Would this prophet have uttered such a vehement denunciation if he had not known that the birth of the body is something that calls down a curse on itself, the same thing that impels the legislator to prescribe purifications....? Job, too, inspired by the Holy Spirit, cursed the day of his birth: "Cursed be the day on which I was born, the night when it was said: 'It is a boy'...!" Do you

still wish to hear what other saints thought of their birth? Listen to David: "In guilt I was born, a sinner I was conceived." He thus shows that by its birth in the flesh every soul contracts a stain of sin and iniquity. Hence that other utterance which we have already recalled: "No one is exempt from stain, not even the day-old child." One more thing must be added: Why should baptism for remission of sins be administered, as is the practice of the Church, even to little children? Undoubtedly, if in little children there were nothing that needs forbearance and pardon, the grace of baptism would be superfluous (*In Lev.*, 8, 2-3).[35]

THE RETURN TO GOD: LIFE IN THE SPIRIT

Human beings were created "according to the image of God." In them was placed a seed (*sperma*), which if nurtured and well taken care of, will grow and transform them into children of God, when the image is changed into the likeness of God. Unfortunately, by sinning, humans take on, Origen suggests, the image of the devil.

> No human being who wants to fulfill the desires of the devil has God as father, but becomes the child of the devil. Because he wants to execute the desires of the evil one, he receives the form and image of his bad father. It is from the evil one that are born those who are called images of the Earthly and receive their characteristics; indeed he is the first earthly one (*In Jo.*, 20, 22, 181).[36]

However, for Origen, sinners do not lose their "according to the image," which is sullied but not destroyed; rather they lose their "likeness" to God:

> The Son of God is the painter of this image. The work of such a great artist, it can be darkened through negligence, but not destroyed by malice. The image of God remains

[35]Text: SC 287.14-20
[36]Text: PG 290.246

always present, though it is covered up by that of the earthly one. Of this second picture, it is you who are the author. . . . When Christ has wiped away these taints made up of colors of malice, then the image of God created in you will shine (*Hom. in Gen.*, 13, 3-4).[37]

The work of restoration of the image into the likeness of God is carried out by the Logos and the Spirit. Origen interprets the redemptive work of the Logos in three ways: as our teacher, lawgiver and model; as the conqueror of the devil in his death and resurrection; and as a propitiatory sacrifice offered to God the Father. The goal of human existence is to become more like the Logos, and through him, more like God the Father.

> The highest good, toward which all rational nature is progressing, and which is also called the end of all things, is defined by very many, even among philosophers, in the following way, namely, that the highest good is to become as far as possible like God (*Theaetetus*, 176 B). But it is not so much, I think, a discovery of their own as something taken by them out of the divine books. For Moses, before all others, points to it when in recording the first creation of humans he says, "And God said, 'Let us make humanity in our own image and likeness.'" Then he adds afterward: "And God made humanity; in the image of God he made humanity; male and female he made them, and he blessed them."
>
> Now the fact that he said, "He made humanity in the image of God," and was silent about the likeness, points to nothing else but this, that humans received the honor of God's image in the first creation, whereas the perfection of God's likeness was reserved for them at the consummation. The purpose of this was that humans should acquire it for themselves by their own earnest efforts to imitate God, so that while the possibility of attaining perfection was given to them in the beginning through the honor of the "image," they should

---

[37]Text: PG 12.234; trans. FOTC 71.192-193

obtain for themselves the perfect "likeness" (*De Princ.*, 3, 6, 1).[38]

The souls became like God by sharing in the Logos:

> "He was the true light that enlightens every human being who comes into the world"(Jn 1: 9). Whatever is of rational nature has a nature in the true light; and every human being is of rational nature. But while all human beings share in the word, the power of the Logos increases in some and decreases in others. If you see a soul full of passion and sin, you will see there the power of the Logos decreasing. If you see a holy and just soul, you will see the power of the Logos bearing fruit day by day, and what was said of Jesus will apply to the just. For it was not just for him that it was said: "Jesus increased in wisdom and in age, and in favor with God and man" (Lk 2: 52) (*Hom. in Jer.*, 14, 10).[39]

The Holy Spirit, too, is active in this work of transformation:

> I am of the opinion, then, that the activity of the Father and the Son is to be seen both in saints and sinners, in rational humans and in dumb animals, yes, and even in lifeless things and in absolutely everything that exists. But the activity of the Holy Spirit does not extend at all either to lifeless things or to things that have life but yet are dumb, nor is it to be found in those who, though rational, still live in wickedness and are not at all converted to better things. Only in those who are already turning to better things, and walking in the ways of Jesus Christ, that is, who are engaged in good deeds and who abide in God, is the work of the Holy Spirit, I think, to be found (*De Princ.*, 1, 3, 5).[40]

Unlike Augustine who had to battle against the Pelagians, and therefore had to emphasize divine grace, Origen, in his struggle

[38]Text: SC 268.234; trans. ANF 4.344
[39]Text: SC 238.84
[40]Text: SC 252.152; trans. ANF 4.253

against naturalistic gnosticism, which transferred good and evil into the nature created by God, had to defend and emphasize human freedom and human collaboration.

> ...Since the nature of this reason in humans includes a faculty of distinguishing between good and evil, and when they have done this, they possess also the power of choosing that which they have approved of, they are rightly deemed worthy of praise when they choose what is good, and of blame when they follow what is base and evil (*De Princ.*, 3, 1, 3, Latin version).[41]
>
> Let us now also look at the statement of Ezekiel in which he says, "I will take away from them their stony heart, and I will put in them a heart of flesh, that they may walk in my judgments and keep my ordinances" (Ez 11: 19-20). Now if God, when he wills, takes away "the heart of stone" and puts in a "heart of flesh," so that humans may keep his ordinances and observe his commandments, it will be seen that it is neither in our power to put away wickedness . . . nor to insert a heart of flesh . . . . "
>
> If, then, God promises to do this, and if, before he takes away our "stony heart" we are not able of our own selves to lay it aside, it follows that it is not in our power to cast off wickedness, but in God's only. And again, if it is not by our own act that there comes into us the "heart of flesh," if it is the work of God alone, then to live a virtuous life will not be our work, but in all respects the work of God's grace.
>
> Now this is asserted by those who wish to prove by the authority of Scripture that nothing lies within our power. We shall reply to them that these words must not be understood in that sense, but as follows. It is as if our uneducated and uninstructed person, becoming conscious of his condition, whether by being stirred at the exhortation of another, or by a desire to rival those who are wise, should entrust himself to one by whom he is confident that he can be carefully trained and competently instructed. If, then, he, who had formerly hardened himself in ignorance, entrusts

[41]Text: SC 268.22; trans. ANF 4.303

himself, as we have said, with full purpose of mind to a master and promises to obey him in everything, the master, on seeing clearly his purpose and determination, will on his part undertake to take away from him his lack of education, not promising, however, to do this if the disciple withholds his assent and cooperation, but only if he offers and pledges himself to complete obedience.

So, too, the divine word promises to take away the "stony heart" from those who come to it, not, indeed, from those who do not listen to it, but from those who submit to the precepts of its teaching. . . . In this way also does the divine word promise to give instruction by taking away the stony heart, that is, by banishing wickedness, in order that humans may thus be able to walk in the divine ordinances and keep the commandments of the law (*De Princ.*, 3, 1, 15, Latin version).[42]

Though emphasizing the role of human freedom, Origen is in no way a Pelagian; he is convinced of the utter gratuitousness and necessity of grace.

Nothing which God gives to a created nature is given by way of obligation; instead he gives everything as grace. . . . In no way is eternal life a payment or any kind of debt on the part of God; instead it is his grace (*Co. on Rom., frag.*)

When the Apostle says, "To one who works, his wages are not reckoned as a gift but as his due; and to one who does not work but trusts him who justifies the ungodly, his faith is reckoned as righteousness" (Rom 4: 4-5), he seems to be indicating that the grace of the one justifying is as it were in the faith, but that the justice of the one making retribution is in the work. But when I consider the exalted status of this Logos, I can barely convince myself that there can be any work which would require payment from God as something owed, because even our ability to do anything at all, or to think, or to talk, we can do only as a result of his gift and generosity (*Co. on Rom.*, 4, 1).[43]

[42]Text: SC 268.88; trans. ANF 4.315-316
[43]Text: PG 14.965

4

African Anthropology

All the Fathers so far considered wrote in Greek, even though in some cases, e.g. Irenaeus and Origen, the originals of some of their important works are now lost and survive only in translations, chiefly in Latin. Greek, it should be remembered, was the official language of the primitive Church of Rome and of its liturgy. By the middle of the third century, however, Latin had emerged as the official language of the Church of Rome and by the middle of the fourth century, under the pontificate of Damasus (366-384), the language of the liturgy.

The Fathers under consideration in this chapter wrote mostly in Latin. They all belonged to the North African Church. The Church of Rome, of course, had its own theologians: Minucius Felix, Hippolytus, who still wrote in Greek, and Novatian, whose *De Trinitate* was perhaps the first theological treatise to be written in Latin. Nevertheless, the contribution of the North African Church to theology was far greater than Rome's. It gave to Latin Christianity the most original thinker of the ante-Nicene period, Tertullian; the great ecclesiologist and martyr, Cyprian; and two lay theologians, Arnobius and Lactantius. Of these, we shall treat only of the first and the last, since they alone have discussed anthropological issues to a significant extent.

I. Tertullian (ca. 155/160-ca. 240/250)

Born in Carthage of pagan parents, Quintus Septimius Florens Tertullianus became a lawyer. After his conversion (ca. 193), he made use of his legal expertise to defend Christianity, and from this period dates the majority of his Apologies (e.g. *Apologeticum, De praescriptione haereticorum*). For some ten years after his conversion (his "Catholic" period, from 195-206) his orthodoxy was above reproach. But about 206 his intemperate zeal and mysticism caused him to join the sect of Montanus, whose rigorist teaching he found suited to his temperament (his "semi-Montanist" period, from 206-212). After 213, Tertullian definitely broke with the Church and devoted his energy to combating the *psychicists*, that is to say, ordinary Catholics, whom he regarded as carnal and gross because they allegedly neglected the gifts of the Holy Spirit (his "Montanist" period from 213). The last period is marked by a considerable slowing down of his literary output. While he wrote twenty works in the first period and thirteen in the second, he only produced six from 213 to 222.

THE ONE GOD CREATOR AND REDEEMER

The struggle which Irenaeus had carried out against the Gnostics was taken up by Tertullian, who was greatly influenced by the author of *Adversus Haereses*, especially in his *Adversus Valentinianos*. Against Marcion, Tertullian firmly defends the unity of the one God, the God of the Old Testament and the God of Jesus Christ, who is both Creator and Redeemer. He fiercely attacks Marcion's dualism and presents an impassioned apology for the goodness and beauty of creation:

> The principal, and consequently the entire, contention lies in the point of number, whether it is permissible to maintain the existence of two gods, or, perhaps, by poets' or painters' license, and now by heretical license, of a third. But Christian truth has decisively asserted this principle: God is not, if he is not one; because it is more reasonable to admit the non-existence of that which does not exist in such a manner as it ought. If you want to know that God must be one only, ask what God is, and you will find that he cannot be otherwise than one. Insofar as human beings can form a

definition of God, I adduce one which all people possessed
of common sense will accept: God is the supremely great,
firmly established in eternity, unbegotten, uncreated, without beginning and without end. For this status, I say, must
be ascribed to that eternity in virtue of which God is
supremely great, and so are the other attributes besides: so
that God is the great Supreme both in form and in reason, in
might and in power. Now, since all are agreed on this
point— for no one can deny that God is the great Supreme,
except perhaps the one who holds the contrary opinion that
God is but some inferior being so as to reject his godhead by
stripping him of all that is characteristic of God—what then
must be the character of the great supreme being himself?
Surely he has nothing equal to himself, that is, there is no
other thing supremely great. For if there is, he will have an
equal, and if he has an equal, he can no longer be the
supremely great, except by a reversal of that condition and,
so to speak, of that law which precludes anything being
accounted equal to that which is supremely great (*Against
Marcion*, 1, 3, 1-5).[1]

Having proved the unicity of God, Tertullian went on to
defend the goodness of God in creating the world. The
Marcionites did not deny that God was the master of his
creation; rather they denied that the God of the Old Testament,
the God Creator, is good.

Since then, with the intention of making God known, the
goodness of God added this to his original notification that
he first prepared a dwelling-place for humankind, the vast
structure of the world to begin with, and then afterwards,
even a greater one, so that humans on a great as well as on a
smaller stage may practice and advance in their probation,
and to be promoted from the good thing God had given
them, that is, from their high position, to God's best, that is,
some higher dwelling-place. To this good work he also

[1]Text: OECT, ed. Ernest Evans, 8-10

appoints a supremely good agent and administration, his own Word. "My heart," he says, "has emitted my most excellent Word" (Ps 45: 1).

Let Marcion here take his first lesson on the noble fruit of this truly excellent tree. But like an utterly clumsy rustic, he has grafted a good branch on a bad stock. The sprout of his blasphemy, however, will never grow strong; it will wither with its planter, and thus will the nature of the good tree be made manifest. Look at the total result: how fruitful was the Word! "And God said, Let there be, and there was: and God saw it was good" (Gen 1:2). Not as if God did not know the good thing unless he saw it, but he saw it because it was good, and he honored and testified and consummated the goodness of his works by deigning to look at them. Thus God blessed what he made good, in order that he might commend himself to you as whole and perfect, good both in word and in act. As yet the Word knew no malediction because he was a stranger to malefaction. We shall see what reasons would require even this of God. Meanwhile the world consisted of nothing but good things, and gave indication enough of how great a good was in store for him for whom all this was being prepared. Who indeed was worthy to have his home among the works of God? Only God's own image and likeness. That image and likeness, too, was created by God's goodness, an even more effective goodness, not by an imperious word but by a kindly hand preceded by a persuasive word, "Let us make humanity in our image and likeness" (Gen 1: 26). It was God's goodness who spoke, it was God's goodness who formed the man out of the dust of the ground into so noble a substance of the flesh, built up out of one material with so many qualities. It was Goodness that breathed soul into him, not dead soul but living. Goodness gave him dominion over all things, to enjoy and to rule, and even to give them names. Furthermore, it was Goodness that gave the man additional delights, so that although possessing the whole world he had his dwelling place in the more salubrious part of it, that is, he was moved into paradise, and from there out of the world into the Church. That same Goodness also sought out a help for the man, so that no good thing might be lacking: "It is not good," God said, "that the man should be alone" (Gen 2: 18) (*Against Marcion*, 2, 4, 1-5).[2]

If God created everything out of goodness, did he create out of preexisting matter or *ex nihilo?* In an earlier work, Tertullian refuted the opinion of Hermogenes, who, influenced by the Middle-Platonism of his time, had upheld the eternity of matter. The first part of Tertullian's treatise, *Adversus Hermogenem*, consists of a philosophical reply to Hermogenes in which he exposes the absurdity of Hermogenes' theory by arguing that, if matter is eternal and if it is the principle of evil, evil itself would have to be equal to God.

> Hermogenes declares that his theory still preserves intact God's attributes, of being the only God, and the First and the Author of all things, the Lord of all things and his incomparableness—attributes which he straightaway ascribes to Matter also. He is God, to be sure. God shall also attest to the same; but he has also sworn sometimes by himself that there is no other God like him. Hermogenes, however, will make him a liar. For Matter will be such a God as he—being uncreated, unbegotten, without beginning and without end. God will say, "I am the First" (Is 41: 4). Yet, how is he first when Matter is co-eternal with him? Between co-eternals and contemporaries, there is no sequence of rank. Is Matter then, also the first? "I," says the Lord, "have stretched out the heavens alone" (Is 44:24). But indeed he would not be alone if that, of which he made the expanse, also stretched them out. When Hermogenes asserts that Matter is eternal, without any encroachment on the condition of God, let him see to it that we do not in ridicule turn the tables on him, that God similarly is eternal without any encroachment on the condition of Matter, the condition of both being still common to them. The position, therefore, remains unassailed both in the case of Matter, that it does itself exist, only along with God, and that God exists alone, but with Matter. Matter also is first with God,

[2]Text: OECT, 92-96

as God, too, is first with it; it is, however, not comparable with God, as God, too, is not comparable with God; with God also, Matter was the author of all things, and with God their Sovereign. In this way Hermogenes proposes that God has something, and yet not the whole, of Matter. Accordingly, he has reserved for God nothing which he had not equally conferred on Matter, so that it is not Matter which is compared with God, but rather God who is compared with Matter. Now, inasmuch as these qualities which we claim as peculiar to God—to have always existed, without a beginning, without an end, and to have been the First, and Alone, and the Author of all things—are also compatible to Matter, I want to know what property Matter possesses which is different and alien from God, and hence special to itself, by reason of which it is incapable of being compared with God? That Being, in which all the properties of God are alleged to exist, is sufficiently predetermined without any further comparison (*Against Hermogenes*, 6).[3]

Tertullian goes on to show that if Hermogenes' theory of the eternity of matter be true, one would have to conclude that not only is matter equal to God but also is superior to him and that God himself is the author of evil (chapters 8-16). To avoid these absurdities, Tertullian appeals to the teaching of the Scripture that God created everything out of nothing (*creatio ex nihilo*).

This rule (i.e. God creates out of nothing) is required by the nature of the unique God, who is unique in no other way than as the sole God, and in no other way than as having nothing else co-existing with him. So also he will be first, because all things are after him; and all things are after him, because all things are created by him; and all things are created by him, because they are of nothing. Reason, therefore, accords with Scripture which says, "Who has known the mind of the Lord? Or who has been his counsellor? Or with whom did he take counsel? Or who has

[3]Text: CCL 1.402; trans. ACW 24.; trans. J.H. Waszink

shown to him the way of wisdom and knowledge? Who has first given to him, and it will be recompensed to him again?" (Rom 11: 34-35). Surely none! Because there was present with him no power, no material, no nature which belonged to any other than himself. But if it was with some part of Matter that he effected his creation, he must have received from that Matter itself both the design and the treatment of its order, as being "the way of wisdom and knowledge." For he had to operate in conformity with the quality of the thing, and according to the nature of Matter, not according to his own will; in consequence of which he must have made even evil things suitably to the nature, not of himself, but of Matter (*Against Hermogenes*, 17).[4]

If any material was needed for God's creation, Tertullian suggests, it was not matter but the Word or Wisdom of God. Referring to the Genesis text ("*originale instrumentum Moysi*" [*Against Hermogenes*, 19, 1]), Tertullian argues that the words *in principio* means *in the Word* and not out of matter, in which case it would have been *ex principio*.

But in proof that the Greek word (*archē*) means nothing else than beginning, and that *beginning* admits of no other sense than the *initial* one, we have that being (i.e. Wisdom) acknowledging such a beginning, who says, "The Lord established (*condidit*) me, the beginning of his ways for the creation of his works" (Prov 8: 22). For since all things were made by the Wisdom of God, it follows that when God made both the heaven and the earth *in principio* —that is to say, in the beginning— he made them in his Wisdom. If, indeed, 'beginning' referred to *matter*, the Scripture would not have informed us that God made such and such *in principio* (at the beginning), but rather *ex principio* (out of the beginning); for he would not have created *in*, but *out of*, matter. When Wisdom was, however, referred to, it was quite appropriate to say: *in* the beginning. For it was in Wisdom that God made all things at first, because by

[4]Text: CCL 1.410; cf ACW 24.48; trans. J.H. Waszink

meditating and arranging his plans therein, he had in fact already done the work of creation. And if he had even intended to create out of Matter, he would yet have effected his creation when he was previously meditating on it and arranging it in his Wisdom. In fact, Wisdom was the beginning of his ways: this meditation and arrangement were the primal operation of Wisdom, opening as it does the way to the works by the acts of meditation and thought . . . (*Against Hermogenes*, 20).[5]

THE HUMAN SOUL

The opposition between paganism and Christianity is most evident in Tertullian's anthropology. He has already refuted the materialism of Hermogenes in his theology of creation, now he goes on to attack his conception of the soul. He does this in the treatise *De censu animae*, no longer extant. A summary of it, however, is found in the *De anima*. In this latter work, Tertullian extends the discussion by examining the views concerning the soul as held by Empedocles and Pythagoras, Plato and Aristotle, the Stoics and Epicurus.

Hermogenes had maintained that the soul consists rather "of the piling up of matter than of the breath of God" (*ex suggestu materiae quam ex Dei flatu* [On the Soul, 1, 1]). His argument seemed to be based upon his reading of Gen 2:7 as *spiritus* (*pneuma*) *vitae* rather than *flatus* (*pnoē*) *vitae*, that is, *spirit* of life rather than breath of life. Since *spiritus* is a divine principle and therefore cannot fall into sin, the source of sin in humans, Hermogenes argues, must be their material principle, which includes the soul. The spirit comprises their higher faculties and these are alien to the soul (cfr. *On the Soul*, 2).

Tertullian rejects Hermogenes' rendering of *spiritus* for *pnoē* and maintains that the correct translation is *flatus* (breath). Further, he affirms that the soul does not originate in matter, but in the breath of God.

[5]Text: CCL 1.114; cf ACW 24.53

We have already decided one point in our controversy with Hermogenes . . . when we claimed the soul to be formed by the breath (*flatu*) of God, and not out of matter. We relied even there on the clear direction of the inspired statement which informs us that "the Lord God breathed on the man's face the breath of life so that the man became a living soul" (Gen 2: 7), by that breath of God, of course (*On the Soul,* 3, 4.)[6]

There is another text in *Against Marcion* which is equally significant:

First and foremost we have to hold fast to the meaning of the Greek scripture, which says not 'spirit' but 'breath.' For some, when translating from the Greek, fail to reflect upon the difference: over looking the precise meaning of the words, they substitute 'spirit' for 'breath' (*afflatus*), afford the heretics the opportunity of tarnishing with sin the spirit of God, which means God himself. The question is by no means a new one. Note then that breath, though it comes from the spirit, is something less than spirit—as it might be an exhalation of spirit, not spirit itself. So a breeze is weaker than a wind; and even if a breeze derives from wind, a breeze is not a wind. One may even say that breath is an image or reflection of spirit: for it is in this sense that humans are the image of God, that is, of spirit, since God is Spirit. And so breath is an image or reflection of spirit. Yet the image cannot in every respect be equated with the reality behind it: for it is one thing to be like the reality and quite another to be the reality itself. Likewise, though breath is the image of spirit, it cannot be equated to the image of God in such a way that because the reality, namely the Spirit, which is God, is without sin, the breath, which is the image, is to be thought also incapable of sin. The image is less than the reality, and the breath inferior to the Spirit. The soul, admittedly, possesses those lineaments of divinity: immortality, freedom, mastery over its own choices, foreknowl-

[6]Text: CCL 2.785; trans. ANF 3

edge in many instances, reasonableness, capacity of understanding and knowledge; yet even in these, it is an image and
never attains to the actual power of divinity nor exemption
from sin, an attribute which is exclusive of God alone, that
is, of the reality, and not be affirmed of an image (*Against
Marcion*, 2, 9).[7]

The main point here is the idea of the *flatus Dei*, which
Tertullian contrasts with the *spiritus*. Whereas Middle
Platonism, as represented by the Valentinian Gnostics such as
Theodotus, maintains that the human soul (*psychē*) is made
from matter (*hylē*) and hence not radically different in humans
and in animals, and is therefore to be contrasted with the
pneuma, the spirit of God, Tertullian holds that the soul does
not have its origin in matter, but in the breath of God. In other
words, the *census* of the soul is different from that of the body.
On the other hand, whereas Hermogenes takes *spiritus* of
Gen 2: 27, that is, the divine principle in humans, to imply that
they are incapable of sinning and that it is only the material
soul in humans that sins, Tertullian affirms that the *flatus Dei*
does not belong to the divine order and therefore does not
make humans incapable of sinning. In interpreting the *pnoē* of
Gen 2: 27 not as the divine *pneuma*, but as the breath of life, in
such a way that humans are composed of the body, the breath
as the principle of the intellectual life, and the Holy Spirit,
Tertullian is without doubt following the teaching of Irenaeus
(see *Adv. haer.* 5, 12, 2).

Having discussed the origin of the soul, Tertullian gives a
concise definition of the soul:

> We define the soul as born of the breath of God (*Dei flatu
> natam*), immortal (*immortalem*), corporeal (*corporalem*),
> having shape (*effigiatam*), simple in substance (*substantia
> simplicem*), susceptible of the functions proper to it (*de suo
> sapientem*), developing in various ways (*varie procedentem*),
> having freedom of choice (*liberam arbitrii*), affected by
> external events (*accidentibus obnoxiam*), mutable in its

[7]Text: OECT, 110-112

faculties (*per ingenia mutabilem*), rational (*rationalem*),
dominant (*dominatricem*), capable of presentiment (*divi-natricem*), evolved out of one soul (*ex una redundantem*)
(*On the Soul*, 22).[8]

These epithets, not of equal importance, are difficult to
understand, and a few words of explanation may be in order.
For Tertullian, the soul is the *flatus Dei*, not, as the Platonists
think, some kind of uncreated god. Moreover, Tertullian
refuses to distinguish between the soul and intelligence, the
psychē and the *nous*. The *mens* of the Latins, the *nous* of the
Greeks, is the soul (*anima*) as he understands it. This soul is
immortal; it outlives the body. Yet it is said to be "corporeal":
corporalis is intended to indicate that the soul is a substance,
something real. It is *effigiata*, that is, the soul is a kind of a
duplicate of the body, a very subtle species of body penetrating
and animating all parts of the body, it is the Pauline "interior
self." The soul is *dominatrix*, which translates the Greek
hēgemonikos, the superior and ruling part of the soul. Above
all, the soul is free, and by its choices, it can be inclined toward
the good or toward the evil. Finally, the souls are said to
develop out of one soul.

Tertullian goes on to explain what he means by the origin of
all the souls from a single soul. First of all, he rejects the
doctrine of the pre-existence of the souls (chapters 23-24); he
equally rejects the doctrine that souls enter the bodies after
birth (chapter 25), the doctrine of transmigration of souls
(chapters 28-33). As regards the origin of the individual souls,
Tertullian holds that they are transmitted from the parents,
more precisely from the sperm of the father. This theory, called
traducianism, proved to be quite influential with Augustine:

> How, then, is a living being conceived? Is the substance of
> both body and soul formed together at one and the same
> time? Or does one of them precede the other in natural
> formation? We indeed maintain that both are conceived,
> and formed, and perfected simultaneously, as well as born

[8]Text: CCL 2.814; trans. ANF 3.202

together, and that not a moment's interval occurs in their conception, so that a prior place can be assigned to either Well now, in this usual function of the sexes which brings together the male and the female in their common intercourse, we know that both the soul and the body discharge a duty together: the soul supplies desire, the body contributes the gratification of it; the soul furnishes the instigation, the body affords the realization. The entire man, being excited by the common effort of both natures, discharges his semen, which derives its fluidity from the body and its warmth from the soul. Now if *the soul* in Greek is a word which is synonymous with *cold*, how does it happen that the body grows cold after the soul has quitted it? Indeed . . . I cannot help asking whether we do not, in that very heat of extreme pleasure produced by the ejaculation of semen, feel that something of our soul has come out of us? And do we not experience a faintness and prostration along with a dimness of sight? This, then, must be the soul-producing seed, which arises at once from the outdrip of the soul, just as that fluid is the body-producing seed, which proceeds from the drainage of the body. . . .

Therefore, as these two different and separate substances, the clay and the breath, combined at the first creation in forming the individual man (i.e. Adam), they then both amalgamated and mixed their proper seminal rudiments in one, and ever afterward communicated to the human race the normal mode of its propagation, so that even now the two substances, although diverse from each other, flow forth simultaneously into one united channel; and finding their way together into their appointed seed-plot, they fertilize with their combined vigor the human fruit out of their respective natures. . . . Accordingly, from the one primeval man comes the entire outflow and redundance of human souls, nature proving herself true to the commandment of God, "Be fruitful and multiply" (*On the Soul*, 27).[9]

For Tertullian, then, there is a real sense in which all souls, actual or potential, were contained in Adam, since they must

[9]Text: CCL 2.822; trans. ANF 3.207

all be ultimately detached portions of the original soul breathed into him by God. This common origin of all souls in the soul of Adam will serve as an argument for the existence of original sin. This thesis, which is at the antipodes of Hellenistic Christians, will weigh heavily upon Augustinian theology.

"EVERY SOUL IS UNCLEAN UNTIL BORN AGAIN IN CHRIST" (*On the Soul,* 40)

Against Marcion, Tertullian affirms that evil does not come from God, the good Creator, but from human freedom:

> From now on it is understood that when I maintain that the man had free power over his own choice, my intention is that the blame for what happened to him should be imputed to himself and not to God....(*Against Marcion*, 2, 6).[10]

Yet free will is not the only source of our misdeeds; account must be taken of the inclination toward sin in which Adam's transgression has involved humankind (cfr. *Against Marcion*, 1, 22). As the result of Adam's sin, all his children are sullied and under the power of the devil when they begin to exist.

> All these endowments of the soul, which are bestowed upon it at birth, are still obscured and depraved by the evil being who, in the beginning, regarded them with an envious eye, so that they are never seen in their spontaneous action, nor are they administered as they ought to be. For to what individuals of the human race will not the evil spirit cleave, ready to entrap their souls from the very portal of their birth, at which he is invited to be present in all those superstitious processes which accompany childbearing. . .? Hence in no case (I mean of the pagans, of course) is there any birth which is pure of idolatrous superstition. It was from this circumstance that the Apostle said that when either of the parents was sanctified, the children were holy (1 Cor 7: 14); and this as much by the prerogative of the

[10]Text: OECT, 100

Christian seed as by the discipline of the institution (i.e. by baptism and Christian education). "Else," says he, "the children would be unclean" by birth: he meant us to understand that the children of believers were destined for holiness, and thereby for salvation; by the pledge of such a hope, he gave support to marriage the integrity of which he had determined to defend. Besides, he had certainly not forgotten what the Lord had so definitively stated: "Except a man be born of water and of the Spirit, he cannot enter the Kingdom of God" (Jn 3: 5); in other words, he cannot be holy (*On the Soul*, 39).[11]

Only by the regeneration of Christ will such a state of defilement be wiped away:

Every soul, then, by reason of its birth, has its nature in Adam until it is born again in Christ; moreover, it is unclean so long as it remains without this regeneration; and because unclean, it is actively sinful and suffuses even the flesh, by reason of their conjunction, with its own shame (*On the Soul*, 40).[12]

The devil, Tertullian admits, was the tempter and exerted a baneful influence; nevertheless:

Besides the evil which comes to the soul from the intervention of the evil spirit, there exists another antecedent evil, which is derived from the fault of our origin (*ex originis vitio*) and has become in a way natural to us. For, as I have stated, the corruption of our nature is second nature (*alia natura*), having a god and a father of its own, namely the author of that corruption (*On the Soul*, 41).[13]

Deceived by Satan from the beginning, the first man "transgressed the commandment of God, and, having been given

---

[11]Text: CCL 2.842; trans. ANF 3.219
[12]Text: CCL 2.843; trans. ANF 3.220
[13]Text: CCL 2.844; trans. ANF 3.220

unto death, made the whole human race, which was infected by his seed, the transmitter (*traducem*) of condemnation" (*The Testimony of the Soul*, 3). For this reason even the children of the faithful must be reckoned impure until they have been reborn by water and the Holy Spirit.

In *On the Flesh of Christ*, Tertullian explains that Christ took a flesh similar to ours, but unmarked by the sin of Adam (*vitio Adae*). He loved this flesh of sin, the *carnem peccati,* but being the author of spiritual rebirth, he destroyed the sin of flesh (*peccatum carnis*), the ancient blemish from which he was exempt:

> This is the new birth; a man is born in God. And in this man God was born, taking the flesh of the ancient race, without the help, however, of the ancient seed, in order that he might reform it with a new seed, that is, in a spiritual manner, and cleanse it by removing all its ancient stains (*On the Flesh of Christ*, 17, 3).[14]

In the treatise *On the Resurrection*, Tertullian recalls that just as all die in Adam, so all are made alive in Christ. He is come to save that which was lost, not just one part of the human being, but the human being whole and entire, body and soul. We must bear the image of the second Adam after having borne the image of the first:

> We have indeed borne the image of the earthly, by our sharing in his transgression, by our participation in his death, by our banishment from Paradise. Now, although the image of Adam is here borne by us in the flesh, yet we are not exhorted to put off the flesh; but if not the flesh, it is the old dispensation in order that we may then bear the image of the heavenly in ourselves—no longer indeed the *image* of God, and no longer the *image* of a Being whose state is in heaven, but after the lineaments of Christ, by our walking here in holiness, righteousness and truth (*On the Resurrection of the Flesh*, 49).[15]

[14]Text: CCL 2.904; trans. ANF 3.536
[15]Text: CCL 2.991; trans. ANF 3.582

II. Lactantius (ca. 250-325)

Though theologically far less important than his fellow Africans, Tertullian and Cyprian, Lactantius, a rhetorician and a disciple of Arnobius, has the distinction of composing the first Latin summa of Christian thought, the *Divine Institutes*. Given the title of "Christian Cicero" by Pico della Mirandola, Lactantius earned his reputation not so much as an original and profound theologian as an eclectic apologist who attempted to win cultured pagans over to Christianity by presenting its doctrine in the most beautiful language possible.

The *Divine Institutes*, composed of seven books and written during the years 304-310, has the double purpose of refuting paganism and of expounding the true doctrine of Christianity. In what follows we will give some representative passages from this apologetic work dealing with the creation of humans, their fall and their way to salvation.

HUMAN BEINGS AS CREATURES OF GOD

Lactantius rejects his teacher Arnobius' opinion that creation was effected by subordinated powers. Rather he affirms that "the same God who made the world also created humans from the beginning" (2, 5, 31). God personally fashioned both spirit and flesh infusing the former into the latter so that the product is entirely his. The creation of humanity is presented in the larger context of the creation of the world. God begins by creating the world and the animals in view of the creation of humanity which comes after. Thus it is made clear that humanity is the goal of creation, whereas humanity itself is created for God. Lactantius, though not quoting verbatim the Genesis texts, clearly has these creation stories in mind in his *Divine Institutes:*

> When the world had been completed, God commanded the animals of various kinds and different species to come to existence, both great and small . . . to all of these, according to their kind, God gave sustenance from the earth, that they might be of use to humans; some for food, others for

clothing, and those of greatest strength for help in tilling the soil, whence they are called beasts of burden. And thus, when all things were disposed in a marvelous arrangement, he decided to prepare an eternal kingdom for himself and to create innumerable souls to whom to give immortality. He made a sensible and intelligent likeness to himself, that is, according to the form of his image, than which nothing can be more perfect. He fashioned the man from the clay of the earth, whence he was given the name 'man', which means made from the earth. So Plato says that the human form is of the divine image, and it is Sybil who says: "An image is man, not having a correct word..." (2, 10).

When God had made the male first in his likeness, he then also formed the woman for a counterpart for the man, so that by the union of the two sexes offspring may be propagated and people the whole earth. In making humanity of those two materials, which we said were contrary to each other—fire and water—God concluded and perfected a plan. And when the body was made, he breathed into it a soul of the living source of his everlasting Spirit, so that it might bear a likeness of the world itself from the contrary unchanging elements. Humans, then, consist of a soul and a body, of heaven and earth, as it were, inasmuch as the soul by which we live has its origin from God as though from heaven, and the body from the earth of whose clay we said it was formed...(2, 12).[16]

Lactantius emphasizes that creation has a purpose, namely to serve humans, who in turn must serve God:

The world, therefore, was certainly not made by God for its own sake, for it does not need the heat of the sun or the light of the moon or the blowing of the winds or the water of the rains or the produce of the crops, since it is without sense. Nor can it be said that God made the world on account of himself, since he can exist without the world, as he was before, and because God himself does not use all those

[16]Text: CSEL 19.146, 155; trans. FOTC 49.138-147

things that are in it and are generated in it.

It is clear, then, that the world was made for the sake of the living creatures in it, since these enjoy those things of which it consists. In order that these may live, that they may exist, all necessities are provided them at fixed times. Again, that the other animals were made for the sake of humans is clear from the fact that they serve them and have been given to their care and use, since whether they are of the land or of the water, they do not sense the plan and purpose of the world as humans do. . . .(7, 4, 17).[17]

Let us return now to the reason why God made human beings. If the philosophers had known this, or if they had defended those things which they had found out, they would not have fallen into the greatest errors. . . . Just as God did not make the world for himself, because he does not need its advantages, but because of humans who use it, so he made them on account of himself. "What usefulness is there in humans for God that he should make them for himself?" asks Epicurus. Surely, it was so that they might understand his works; that they might be able to admire with their senses and declare with their voice the providence of his arrangement, the plan of his accomplishment, and the greatness of his completion of the work. And, most of all, as the crown of all these acts, it was so that they might worship God. For those who understand these things worship him; those who measure the power of his majesty from the invention, inception, and completion of his works pay the Maker of all things, their true Father, due veneration.

What plainer argument can be brought forward to prove that God made the world for humans, and humans for himself, than the fact that humans alone of all living creatures have been so formed; that with their eyes directed toward heaven and their face gazing upon God, their countenance should be like to God their Father; and that God should seem to have lifted them from the earth and to have raised them in his right hand to the contemplation of himself (7, 5).[18]

[17]Text: CSEL 19.594; trans. FOTC 49.481
[18]Text: CSEL 19.596; trans. FOTC 49.483

Lactantius, following the biblical teaching, affirms that humans are made in the "image and likeness" of God. He uses words such as *imago, similitudo* (and *similis*), *simulacrum, figura, figmentum, sigillum*, and *templum* to describe the relationship between the human person and God. Lactantius, however, does not follow the distinction made between "image" and "likeness" found in Philo, Irenaeus, Clement and Origen. Further, differently from Tertullian, he affirms that the human body, and not only the soul, is made in the image of God. In a passage of the *Divine Institutes*, Lactantius, without explicit reference to Genesis, declares that "from reason itself and prudence it is understood that a certain likeness exists between humans and God" (7, 9). This likeness, which is given at creation as an ontological element of human nature, must be developed by means of a virtuous life. Lactantius even distinguishes three levels of virtuous life in the quest for the likeness to God.

> . . . . no one can be without fault as long he is burdened with the covering of the flesh. Its infirmity lies subject to the dominion of sins in the threefold manner: by deeds, by words, and by thought. Through these steps justice advances to the highest degree. The first step of justice is to refrain from evil deeds; the second, from evil words; and the third, from the consideration or thinking of evil thoughts. He who shall have ascended the first step is just in a sufficient or moderate degree; he who makes the second is already of perfect virtue, since he fails in neither words nor deeds; but he who reaches the third seems, in truth, to have attained a likeness to God. For it is almost beyond human nature to not even admit into one's thought what is evil in act or wicked in speech (6, 13).[19]

[19]Text: CSEL 19.533; trans. FOTC 49.431

HUMAN BEINGS IN GOD'S PLAN:
SIN AND SALVATION

What happened to the human beings once they had been created? Lactantius' answer to this question includes a discussion of the nature of original sin, the knowledge of God, and moral life.

> After this (i.e. the creation of the man and the woman), God placed them . . . in Paradise, that is, in the most fertile and most pleasant garden, in which he planted every kind of wood and tree in the orient, so that from their various fruits they might be nourished, and that free from all labors they might serve God the Father with the highest devotion. Then he gave them certain commands; if they observed these, they would remain immortal; and if they transgressed them, they would be punished with death. This was a precept; that of one tree which was in the middle of Paradise they should not eat. On that tree God had placed knowledge of good and evil. Then the evil one, envying the works of God, applied all his fallacies and clever deceits for the downfall of humans so that he might rob them of immortality. First, he enticed the woman with his trickery to eat the forbidden food, and through her he persuaded the man himself also to transgress the law of God. Then, when the knowledge of good and evil was experienced, the man and woman began to be ashamed of their nudity and they hid themselves from the face of God, something which they had not been wont to do. Then God passed the sentence upon the sinners and drove them out of Paradise so that they would have to gain their living by their own labor. He surrounded Paradise itself with a wall of fire, so that they could not approach until God holds upon the earth the final judgment and calls back to the same place the just, those who worship him, when death has been destroyed (2, 12).[20]

The immediate result of this sin of disobedience is death; sin, says Lactantius, is "the food of death" (4, 25, 7). Another

---

[20]Text: CSEL 19.157; trans. FOTC 49.148

consequence is the rebellion of the body against the soul which must conquer and guide its body. The dualism, which is manifest in the following passage and of which Lactantius had often been accused, is more ethical than ontological.

> Therefore, because God has proposed virtue to humans, though the soul and body be joined, they are, however, contrary to each other and fight against each other. The goods of the soul are evils of the body, namely, flight from wealth, ban on pleasure, contempt of pain and death. In the same way, the goods of the body are evils to the soul, desire and passion, with which both riches and the delights of various pleasures are sought after, and by which the soul is enervated and its life extinguished. It is necessary, then, for the good and wise people to be in all evils, since the conqueror of evils is fortitude; whereas the unjust are in riches, honor, power, which are bodily and earthly goods. These pass an earthly existence, nor can they attain immortality, since they have given themselves to pleasures which are the enemies of virtues. So this temporal life ought to be subject to that eternal one, as the body is to the soul (7, 5, 23)[21]

Does Lactantius expressly teach that this sinful condition is transmitted to all human beings? As we have seen, Tertullian seems to have affirmed the existence of an "original sin" in us, and his traducianist theory of the origin of the soul provides him with a ready argument. Lactantius, however, rejects traducianism; the soul is begotten through the efforts of neither the father nor the mother nor both together; rather it is created directly by God (cfr. *On the Workmanship of God*, 19, 1). Hence, Lactantius does not seem to have developed a doctrine of original sin as such; he simply affirms that human beings, because of their bodily constitution, experience a corruption of their nature.

Because of this corruption humans are often subjected to errors, especially in religious matters. Lactantius frequently

---

[21]Text: CSEL 19.600; trans. FOTC 49.487

attacks pagan philosophers, Socrates in particular, for their errors. To arrive at the truth, humans need revelation. It is the mission of Jesus to mediate the true knowledge of God. Lactantius views the role of Christ not so much as the Redeemer as the revealer of God and the model of salvation:

> Let all learn, therefore, and let them understand why Almighty God, when he sent his ambassador and messenger to teach humankind the precepts of his justice, wished him to be clothed with mortal flesh and to be afflicted with torture and to be condemned to death. For where there was no justice on the earth, he sent a teacher, a living law, as it were, to establish his name and a new temple, to sow the seeds of true and loving worship, throughout the whole earth, by his words and example. But, in order that it might be certain that he was sent from God, it was not necessary for him to be born in the common way in which a human person is born, i.e., from the union of two mortals, but that he might appear heavenly even in the human form, he was formed without the cooperation of a human father. He had a spiritual Father, God, and just as the Father of his Spirit is God, there being no mother, so the mother of his body is a virgin and there is no father. He was, therefore, both God and man, constituted midway between God and man (whence the Greeks call him Mediator), to be able to lead humanity to God, that is, to immortality. Because if he had been just God, as was said above, he could not have offered an example of virtue to humanity. If he were only human, he could not lead humanity to justice, unless authority and power greater than man's were added. For since humans consist of flesh and spirit, and since it is necessary for the spirit to merit by works of justice to become eternal, the flesh, because it is earthly and therefore mortal, draws the spirit, to which it is conjoined, and leads it away from immortality to death. Therefore a spirit, free of the flesh, was not able to lead humanity to immortality under any condition, for the flesh impeded the spirit from following God. The flesh is weak and subjected to sin, and sin is the food of death.
>
> For this reason, therefore, a mediator came, that is, God in

the flesh, so that the flesh could follow him, and that he might save humanity from death whose dominion is according to the flesh. And he clothed himself with humanity, the flesh, so as to show, by subduing the desires of the flesh, that sin was not necessary but the result of purpose and free will. We do have a great, outstanding struggle with the flesh, whose limitless desires press against the soul and do not allow it to retain the mastery, but manacled by pleasures and sweet enticements, they inflict it with everlasting death. But that we might be able to resist these also, God has opened up and shown us the way of overcoming the flesh. This perfect virtue, and absolute by any reckoning, imparts the crown and reward of immortality to the victors (4, 25).[22]

In conclusion, Lactantius' anthropology, though presented in an extremely pleasing style, is determined, it must be admitted, more by philosophy than Christian revelation. He speaks with great enthusiasm of divine creation and providence, of the dignity of human beings, and of the necessity of moral virtues; nevertheless, his ideal is basically that of *humanitas*, and he rarely mentions the supernatural gift of grace that enables us to realize that ideal. He discourses at length on the transformation of humans into incorruptible and immortal beings, but does not give sufficient attention to the redemption wrought by the death and resurrection of the divine Savior.

[22]Text: CSEL 19.375; trans. FOTC 49.307

5

Athanasius and Cyril of Alexandria

The two Fathers, Athanasius (ca 295-ca 373) and Cyril (d. 444), are studied together in this chapter, despite some seventy years that separate their deaths, not only because they were both patriarchs of one of the most illustrious sees of ancient Christianity, Alexandria in Egypt, not only because both played decisive roles in christological controversies against heretics, the former against Arius and the latter against Nestorius, but also because the latter was heavily influenced by the former (and by the Cappadocians, whom we will consider in the next chapter) in his systematic presentation of the doctrines of the Trinity and of the person of Christ. Even though chronologically Cyril should be treated after the Cappadocians, his connections with Athanasius justifies our consideration of their anthropologies together.

I. Athanasius

The name of Athanasius is indissolubly linked with the Church's struggle against Arianism. Five times banished from his see and more than seventeen years in exile, Athanasius was the undaunted champion of the divinity or the consubstantiality (*homoousios*) of the Logos with God the Father. Most of his writings are evidently connected with his defense of the faith of Nicaea, and the heart of his theology remains Trinitarian and christological doctrines. Nevertheless, because, in his famous words, "he (the Logos) was made man that we might be made

God (*theopoiēthomēn*)" (*On the Incarnation*, 54), it is impossible to separate his christology from anthropology.

THE LOGOS CREATOR

Athanasius, in his teaching on creation, was indebted to Origen, though fortunately untainted by the latter's subordinationism. For example, while defending the temporality of creation, he nevertheless admits an ideal pre-existence and simultaneous creation. Above all, like all Alexandrians, he emphasizes the role of the Logos in creating and preserving the world. The Logos is the creative principle, the archetype that sustains and vivifies the world. Further, Athanasius holds that the Logos, through whom the world was created, is also the Redeemer; once again creation and redemption are intimately linked together, even though he does not explicitly state, as Irenaeus did, that redemption is the purpose of creation.

Athanasius dedicates the last part of his *Against the Heathen* to prove that there is a Logos who, invisible in his nature, makes himself known through the order of the universe (n. 35), through instituting the natural laws and through forcing what is opposite into a peaceful harmony (nos. 36-37).

> God, who is good, and loves humans (*philanthrōpos*), and cares for the souls he has made, since he is by nature invisible and incomprehensible, being above all created things, and since humanity would fail to attain knowledge of him, being made from nothing while God is uncreated— for this reason, God so ordered creation through his Word that, although invisible by nature, he might be known to humans by his works. It is from his works that an artist is often known, even when he is not seen. . . . Similarly, from the order of the cosmos we must also think of its maker and Demiurge God, even if he cannot be seen with the eyes of the body. . . .(35).

Athanasius argues that the harmony of the opposites proves the existence of the Creator:

Who, seeing natural opposites united and keeping harmonious concord—for example, seeing fire mixed with cold, and the dry with the moist, not in hostility to each other but forming a unity like a single body—who would not consider that their binding agent was acting from outside them? And who, seeing winter give way to spring, spring to summer, and summer to autumn, and that these seasons are by nature opposed ... who would not think that there was someone superior to them who kept the balance between them all and governed them all, even if he could not see him? Seeing the clouds supported in the air, and the weight of the waters bound up in the clouds, who would not deduce some conception of the one who bound and ordered them...? (36)

So these discordant and naturally opposed entities would not have combined had there not been a superior being and master, who joined them together and to whom the elements themselves yield to and obey as slaves their lord. The elements no longer have regard to their individual nature nor fight among themselves, but, recognizing the Lord who has joined them, they are in harmony with each other, and though naturally opposites, yet by the will of their ruler they are reconciled....(37)

Furthermore, the oneness of the cosmos proves that there is only one Creator:

Nor must we think that the rulers and makers of creation are many, but for the sake of strict piety and truth we must believe that its Demiurge is one; and this is clearly revealed by creation itself. A sure indication that the maker of the universe is one is the fact that the world is not many but one. For if there were many gods, it would not be becoming that the many gods produced only one world nor that the one world were made by many gods, because that would entail many absurdities. In the first place, if the only world had been created by many, there would have been weakness on the part of its makers, because only one work had been produced by many. This would have been no insignificant indication of each one's lack of skill in creating. For if one were skillful enough, the many would not supplement their mutual shortcomings. But to say that in God there is a shortcoming is not only impious, but the limit of all godlessness. . . .

So since there is one creation, and one cosmos, and one order of this cosmos, one must conclude that its King and Lord Creator is one. It was for this reason that the Creator himself made the whole world one, but by the formation of many worlds it might be presumed that they had many creators, but rather, since there is only one creation, one must think that there is only one maker. And not because the Creator is one is the world one, for God could have made other worlds. But because the created world is one, we must believe that its Creator is also one (39).

Having asserted that there is a Creator of the world, Athanasius goes on to show that this Creator is no other than the Father of Jesus Christ. Jesus is the Word of the Father.

Who might this Creator be? That, too, is most necessary to indicate and make clear, lest anyone, led astray by ignorance about him, suppose him to be another and fall back into the same godlessness as before. But I think no one has any doubts about this. For if our argument has shown that the so-called gods in the writings of the poets are no gods, and if it has proved that those who deify creation err, and if, in general, it has shown that pagan idolatry is godlessness and impiety, then, as these have been overthrown, the orthodox religion must be ours, and he who is adored and announced by us, he alone, must be the true God, he who is both the Lord of creation and Maker of all that is. Who then is he, if not the most holy One, beyond all created substance, the Father of Christ, who as supreme pilot, through his own wisdom and his own Word, our Lord and Savior Christ, guides and orders the universe for our salvation, and acts as seems best to him. . .(40)?

Athanasius explains more clearly what he means by the Word of God and his role in creation:

By Word I do not mean the word involved and innate in every creature, which some also used to call seminal, which is lifeless and without power to reflect and think anything, but at work only by an extrinsic art according to the skill of him who applies it. Nor do I mean the word which humans use, composed of syllables and expressed in the air. I mean the living and acting God, the very Word of the good God of the universe, who is other than created things and all creation; he is rather the sole and individual Word of the good Father, who has ordered all this universe and illuminates it by his providence. For, being the good Word of the good Father, he established the order of all things, reconciling opposites and from them forming a single harmony. He, being the power of God and wisdom of God, turns the heaven, has suspended the earth, and by his own will has set it resting on nothing. Illuminated by him, the sun gives light to the world, the moon receives its measure of light. Through him water is suspended in the clouds, rains water the earth, the sea is confined, and the earth is covered with verdure in all kinds of vegetation. And, if somebody in unbelief inquired about what is being said, whether there is a Word of God at all, such a person would be mad to doubt the existence of the Word of God. But, from what he can see, he has proof that everything came into existence through the Word and Wisdom of God, and that nothing would subsist unless it had been created by a Word, the divine Word, as has been explained (40).[1]

IMAGE AND 'ACCORDING-TO-THE-IMAGE'

One of Athanasius' basic affirmations regarding the Logos is that "the Son is other in kind and in nature (*heterōgenēs kai heterophues*) than the creatures, or, rather, belongs to the Father's substance (*tēs tou patros ousias idios*)" (*I Discourse Against the Arians*, 1, 58). Hence, the Son is consubstantial with the Father (*homoousios tō patri*). To explain the Son's absolute equality in being with the Father, Athanasius makes

[1] Text: DECT, ed. R. W. Thomson, 94-112; trans. NPNF, ser. 2. 4. 22-26

abundant use of the biblical term "image" (*eikōn*). The Son is said to be the "image" of the Father. Now, in St. Paul at least, the term "image" denotes three things: resemblance, dependence or derivation, and manifestation (cf. Col 1: 15). It is of extreme importance to note that for Athanasius these three connotations of the term "image" must be very carefully qualified when it is applied to the Logos-Sun.

Certainly the Son, insofar as he is the image of the Father, is *similar* to the Father, but not any resemblance will do. Rather, by resemblance is meant absolute equality, a total and perfect possession of the being of the Father. In this sense, the Son does *not* "participate" in the Father. Being the Son, the Logos is derived *or* originated from the Father. But this derivation in no way implies the Son's subordination to the Father; rather it expresses the unity between the Father and the Son, who is begotten by nature, without division, from the essence (*ousia*) of the Father. Athanasius continually stresses the essential difference between generation and creation. Finally, as regards manifestation, whereas Paul speaks of Christ as the *visible* image of the Father, Athanasius refers to the Logos as the *invisible* image of the invisible Father. Of course Athanasius is well aware of the revelatory role of Christ, but he does not connect it with the notion of image. An important passage from *Against the Heathen* deserves notice:

> Being with him (i.e. God) as Wisdom and as Word seeing the Father, he created the universe, formed it and ordered it; and being the power of the Father, he gave all things the strength to come into existence.... His holy disciples teach that everything was created through him and for him, and that being the good offspring of the good Father and true Son, he is the power of the Father and his Wisdom and Word; not so by participation (*kata metochēn*), nor do these properties accrue to him from outside in the way of those who participate in him and are given wisdom by him, having their power and reason in him. Rather he is absolute Wisdom, very Word, and himself the Father's own power, absolute light, absolute truth, absolute justice, absolute virtue, and, indeed, stamp (*character*), effulgence (*apau-*

gasma) and image (*eikōn*). In short, he is the supremely perfect issue of the Father, and is alone Son, the express image (*eikōn aparallaktōs*) of the Father (46).[2]

These christological considerations are necessary preliminaries for a correct understanding of Athanasius' anthropology. One may recall that previous Fathers have used both terms 'image' and 'likeness' for humans, some distinguishing them (e.g. Irenaeus), some making the image reside in both body and soul (e.g. Irenaeus), others only in the soul (e.g. Clement, Origen). Athanasius does not seem to give much weight to the distinction between image (*eikōn*) and likeness (*homoiōsis* or *homoiotēs*). However, he is firm in maintaining that the term 'image of God' must be used *exclusively* of the Son, whereas humans are said to be '*according to the image*' of God (*kat' eikona*). Athanasius often speaks of the creation of humanity "according to the image"; the expression 'according to' (*kata*) indicates the relationship between humans and the Logos-Image, so that humans are made in the image of the Logos. Athanasius sometimes speaks simply of "humanity made according to the image" (*kat'eikona genomenos anthrōpos, On the Incarnation,* 6); of "the grace of the image" (*hē kat'eikona charis, ibid,* 12); finally, the expression is sometimes used as a substantive: *to kat'eikona* (*Against the Heathens,* 34; *On the Incarnation,* 13, 14, 20).

For God, the Creator of the universe and King of all, who is beyond all being and human thought, since he is good and bountiful, has made humankind according to his own image (*kat' idian eikona*) through his Word, our Savior Jesus Christ; and he also made humankind perceptive and understanding of reality through their similarity (*homoiōseōs*) to him, giving them also a conception and knowledge of his own eternity, so that as long as they kept this likeness (*tēn tautotēta sōzōn*), they might never abandon their concept of God or leave the company of the saints, but retaining the grace of him who bestowed it on them, and

[2]Text: OECT, 128; trans. NPNF 4.29

also the special power given them by the Father's Word, they might rejoice and converse with God, living on idyllic and truly blessed and immortal life. For, having no obstacle to the knowledge of the divine, they continuously contemplate by their purity the image of the Father, God the Word, in whose image they were made, and are filled with admiration when they grasp his providence toward the universe ... (*Against the Heathen*, 2).[3]

Athanasius' usage of the term "image" is therefore extremely precise; he never predicates it of a creature, not even of the angels, because, says he, "they are not images" (*On the Incarnation*, 13). He consistently uses the term "*to kat'eikona*" to describe rational creatures. In this way he clearly emphasizes the consubstantiality of the Logos with the Father and humanity's dependence on, and participation in, the Logos. Athanasius adopts as his own the terse phrase of Asterius: "God the word is one (*Logos*), but many are the rational beings (*logika*) (*II Discourse Against the Arians*, 40).

SIN AND THE BLEMISH
OF THE "ACCORDING-TO-THE-IMAGE"

Created in the image of the Logos, humans turned away from the contemplation of this Image and fell into sin.

In this way, then, as has been said, did the Creator fashion the human race, and such did he wish it to remain. But humans, despising better things and holding back from apprehending them, sought, rather, things nearer to them, and what was closer to them was the body and its sensations. So they turned their minds away from intelligible realities and began to focus their attention upon themselves. And in doing so and cleaving to the body and the other senses, and deceived, as it were, in their own interests, they fell into selfish desires and preferred their own good to the contemplation of the divine. Having, then, made themselves

[3]Text: OECT, 6; trans. NPNF 4. 5

at home in these things, and not being willing to leave what was so near to them, they imprisoned in the pleasures of the body their souls which had become disordered and defiled by all kinds of desires, and in the end they forgot the power they had received from God in the beginning.

One could see that all this is true from the first created man, as the Holy Scriptures tell us of him. For, as long as he kept his mind fixed on God and contemplated him, he turned away from the contemplation of the body. But when, at the suggestion of the serpent, he abandoned his contemplation of God and began to consider himself, then they (both Adam and Eve) fell into bodily desires and realized that they were naked and, becoming conscious of it, were ashamed. They realized that they were not so much stripped of clothing as stripped of the contemplation of things divine, and that they had turned their minds in the opposite direction. For, having departed from the consideration of the one and the true, namely God, and from desire of him, they gave themselves up to various and separate desires of the body. Then, as usually happens, clinging to each and every desire, they began to be addicted to these desires, so that they were even afraid to leave them: whence the soul became subject to cowardice and terror, pleasures and thoughts of mortality. For, being unwilling to abandon these desires, it has come to fear death and separation from the body. Furthermore, desiring and not achieving satisfaction, it learned to commit murder and injustice. How it ends up doing such things, we must indicate as best as we can.

Abandoning the contemplation of intelligible realities, and misusing the several faculties of the body, delighting in the contemplation of the body and regarding pleasure as a good thing in itself, the soul was misled to abuse the term 'good' and thought that pleasure was the very essence of the good. It was as if someone, out of his mind, should demand a sword to use against those whom he might meet, thinking this to be a sensible behavior. And, having fallen in love with pleasure, the soul began to enjoy it in various ways. For being easily changeable by nature, even if it had turned away from the good, it did not cease to be in motion. So it moves no longer on the path of virtue, nor with a view to seeing God, but imagining false things, it makes a novel use of its power, abusing it as a means to pursue the pleasures it has devised, since it has been created with free will. For it is able to incline to what is good as well as to reject it; but in rejecting the good it entertains the thought of what is opposite. For it cannot cease from movement altogether, since, as I said before, it is changeable by nature. And knowing its own freedom it sees that it can use its bodily members in both ways—for the pursuit of reality or unreality ... (*Against the Heathen*, 3-4).[4]

In the sequel to his book *Against the Heathen*, the *De Incarnatione*, Athanasius explains the connection between the original fall of humanity and the incarnation of the Logos:

You are wondering, perhaps, why in our proposal to speak about the incarnation of the Word, we are now treating of the beginning of humankind. But this, too, properly belongs to the aim of our treatise. For we must, when speaking of the manifestation of the Savior to us, speak of the beginning of humankind as well, in order that you may know that our own cause was the reason of his coming, and that our own transgression called for the mercy of the Word, so that the Lord came even to us and appeared among humans. For we were the object of his becoming incarnate, and for our salvation he was so compassionate as to being born and appearing in a body. God, then, had so created humans and willed that they shoud remain in incorruption. But when they had despised and rejected the contemplation of God, and devised and contrived evil for themselves ..., then they received the condemnation of death with which they had been threatened, and no longer remained as they had been created, but fell into ruin according to their devices. Consequently, death overcame them and ruled over them....

For God did not only create us from nothing, but he also

[4]Text: OECT, 8-10; trans. NPNF 4. 5-6

granted us by the grace of the Word to live a divine life. But humans, turning away from things eternal and by the suggestion of the devil turning to things corruptible, were themselves the cause of the corruption in death. They are, as I said above, corruptible by nature, but by the grace of participating in the Word, they could have avoided the consequences of their nature had they remained virtuous. For on account of the Word dwelling in them, even natural corruption would not have touched them, as the *Book of Wisdom* says, "God created humanity for incorruption, and made it the image of his own eternity; but by the envy of the devil death entered the world " (*Wisd* 2:23-24). Since this happened, humans died, and corruption henceforth prevailed against them, and was more powerful than the force of nature over the whole race, the more so as it had to its advantage the threat of God concerning the transgression of the Law. For in their trespasses humans had not stopped short of any set limits; but gradually pressing forward they have passed on beyond all measure....

For these reasons death held greater sway, and corruption prevailed upon humanity; the human race was perishing, and humans, who were rational and who had been created in the image, were in the process of dissolution. For death, as I said above, gained from that time forth a legal power over us, and it was impossible to evade the law, since this had been established by God because of the transgression. These consequences were both absurd and unseemly. For it was absurd that, having spoken, God should prove false: when once he had ordained that humans, if they transgressed the commandment, should die the death, and now, after the transgression they did not die—God's word would be made inefficacious. For God would not have been true, if, when he had said we should die, we did not. Furthermore, it would have been unseemly that what had once been created rational and had partaken of his Word, should perish and return again to non-existence through corruption. For it would not have been worthy of the goodness of God that what God had brought into existence should be corrupted on account of the deceit which the devil had played on humanity. And it would have been especially unseemly that

the handiwork of God in humankind should come to
nought, either through its own neglect or through the
deceitfulness of evil spirits.

So, while rational creatures were being corrupted and such
works were perishing, what should God in his goodness do?
Allow corruption to dominate them and death to capture
them? Then to what purpose had they been created in the
beginning? For it was more fitting that they should not be
created than that having come into being, they were left to
neglect and ruin. For neglect would show weakness, and not
goodness, on God's part, that is, if he allows his own work to
be ruined when once he had made it, rather than if he had
not created humanity in the beginning. For if he had not
created humans, there would have been no one to impute
his weakness; but once he had made them and created them
out of nothing, it would be most monstrous for his work to
be ruined, and that before the very eyes of the Maker. It was,
then, out of the question to leave humanity to the current of
corruption; this would be unseemly and unworthy of God's
goodness (*On the Incarnation* 4-6).[5]

THE RESTORATION OF
THE IMAGE AND DIVINIZATION OF HUMANITY

Athanasius consistently uses the verb *theopoiein* and its
cognate noun *theopoiēsis* (meaning to divinize and divinization, respectively), to express the work of sanctification
performed in us by the Logos through his Spirit. Clement of
Alexandria was the first to coin these terms, but it was
Athanasius who canonized them as synonyms for the incarna-
tional activity of the Logos-made-flesh. The divinization is a
gratuitous gift; it consists in our participation in the Word who
alone is the image of the Father. Through this participation
not only are we created in the image, becoming *logikoi*, but
also rendered capable of sharing in the knowledge that the
Logos-Image has of the Father, and thus living the life of God.
The purpose of the Incarnation of the Word is to restore this

5Text: OECT, 142-148; trans. NPNF 4. 38-39

knowledge of God perceivable to humans who had been immersed in the sensible things, and by his death and resurrection he conquered the death that held sway over humanity and gave back to it the gift of immortality and incorruptibility.

For this purpose, then, the incorporeal, and incorruptible, and immaterial Word of God entered our world. In one sense, indeed, he was not far from it before, for no part of creation had ever been without him who, while ever abiding in union with the Father, yet fills all things that are. But now he entered the world in a new way, stooping to our level in his love and revealing himself to us. He saw that the rational race was perishing and that death was reigning over it through corruption; he saw, too, that the threat of transgression was firmly supporting corruption over us, and that it would have been absurd for the Law to be repealed before it was fulfilled. He saw how unseemly it was that the very things of which he himself was the Maker should be disappearing. He saw how the surpassing wickedness of humans was mounting up against them; he saw also their universal liability to death. All this he saw and, pitying our race, moved with compassion for our limitation, unable to suffer that death should have the mastery, rather than that his creatures should perish and the work of his Father for us should come to nought, he took to himself a body, a human body even as ours. Nor did he will merely to become embodied or merely to appear; had that been so, he could have revealed his majesty in some other and better way. No, he took our body.... Thus, taking a body like our own, because all our bodies were liable to the corruption of death, he surrendered his body to death instead of all, and offered it up to the Father. This he did out of sheer love for us, so that in his death all might die, and the law of death thereby be abolished because, having fulfilled in his body that for which it was appointed, it was therefore stripped of its power over humanity. This he did so that he might turn again to incorruption human beings who had turned back to corruption, and give them life for death, in that he had made the body his own, and by the grace of the resurrection had rid them of death as straw is destroyed by fire.

The Word realized that corruption could not be got rid of otherwise than through death; yet he himself, as Word, being immortal and the Father's Son, could not die. For this reason, he assumed a body capable of death in order that this body, by belonging to the Word who is above all, might suffer a death on behalf of all, and because of the Word who was dwelling in it, it might remain incorruptible and put an end to corruption for all others as well, by the grace of the resurrection. Therefore, as an offering and sacrifice free of every stain, he offered to death the body which he had taken to himself, and immediately abolished death from all who were like him by the offering of a like.... *On the Incarnations,* 8-9).[6]

Elsewhere Athanasius describes the work of the Logos more specifically in terms of restoring the image of God that has been marred by sin:

.... Furthermore, even an earthly king, though he is only a man, does not allow lands that he has founded to pass into other hands and become subject to other rulers, but sends letters and friends and, if necessary, even visits them in person to win them over by his presence, rather than allow his work to be destroyed. How much more, then, will God be patient and painstaking with these creatures, that they not be led astray from him to the service of those that are not, especially if such error spells for them utter ruin, and because it is not right that those who had once shared his image should be destroyed. ·

What, then, was God to do? What else could he possibly do, being God, but renew his image in humans, so that through it they might once more come to know him? But how could this have been done, unless the very image of God were to come, our Savior Jesus Christ? Humans could not have done it, for they are only made according to the image; nor could angels have done it, for they are not the images of God. The Word of God came in his own person, because it

[6]Text: OECT, 150-154; trans. NPNF 4. 40-41

was he alone, the Image of the Father, who could recreate humanity made according to the image.

In order to effect this re-creation, however, he had first to do away with death and corruption. He therefore assumed a human body, in order that in it death might once and for all be destroyed, and that humanity might be renewed according to the image. For this none other than the image of the Father himself is capable of achieving.

14. For, as when a figure which has been painted on wood becomes obliterated through external stains, the artist does not throw away the panel, but the subject of the portrait has to come sit for it again, and then the likeness is redrawn on the same material, even so was it with the all-holy Son of God. He, the image of the Father, came and dwelt in our midst, in order that he might renew humankind made after himself, and seek out his lost sheep ... (*On the Incarnation*, 13-14).[7]

By restoring the image of God the Logos also reveals the true knowledge of God which is eternal life:

He deals with them as a good teacher with his pupils, coming down to their level and using simple means of instruction. St.Paul says as much: "Because in the wisdom of God the world did not know God through wisdom, it pleased God to save those who believed through the foolishness of the gospel" (1 Cor 1: 21). Human beings had turned away from the contemplation of God above and were looking for him in the opposite direction, down among created things and things of sense, setting up mortals and demons as gods for themselves. For this reason, the merciful and universal Savior, the Word of God, in his great love took to himself a body and moved as a man among humans, meeting their senses, so to speak, halfway. He became himself an object for the senses, so that those who were seeking God in sensible things might understand the truth from the works

[7]Text: OECT, 164-166; trans. NPNF 4. 43-44

which the Lord did through the actions of his body, and through him might recognize the Father. Because they were human and thought of everything in human terms, wherever they looked in the sensible world, they were taught the truth from all sides. Were they awe-struck by creation? They beheld it confessing Christ as Lord. Were their minds inclined toward humans and supposed them to be gods? The comparison between the works of the Savior with theirs showed that the Savior alone among human beings was the Son of God, since humans had no such works as those done by God the Word. Were they prejudiced for the demons? They saw them driven out by the Lord and learned that the Word of God alone was God and that the demons were not gods at all. Were their minds fixed on the dead, so that they worshipped the heroes and those declared by the poets to be gods? Seeing the resurrection of the Savior, they confessed that the other deities were false, and that only the Word of the Father was the true Lord, he who rules over death. For this reason he was born, and appeared as a man, and died and rose again, eclipsing by his works all other human deeds, in order that from wherever humans were attracted he might lift them up and teach them his true Father, as he himself says, "I have come to save and find that which was lost" (Lk 19: 10) (*On The Incarnation*, 15).[8]

Athanasius himself neatly summarizes the redemptive work of the Logos: "There were thus two things which the Savior did for us by becoming man: he both rid us of death and renewed us; and also, although he is invisible and imperceptible as he is in himself, he became visible through his works and revealed himself as the Word of the Father, the Ruler and King of the whole creation" (*ibid.*, 16).

Sharing the true knowledge of God we humans become partakers in the divine nature (cfr. 2 Pet 1: 4), since fellowship with Christ is fellowship with God; in other words, we became

---

[8]Text: OECT, 168-172; trans. NPNF 4. 44

divinized. Sometimes, as an alternative to the idea of divinization (*theopoiēsis*), Athanasius uses that of adoption as children of God (*huiopoiēsis*). Says he: "By becoming man he made us children of the Father, and he deified humans by himself becoming man" (*I Discourse Against the Arians*, 38) and "Because the Word is in us we are children and gods" (*III Discourse Against the Arians*, 25). This divinization and adoption through the Word does not, however, come naturally to all, but only to those who are in a special relation to him or, to be more precise, who are in intimate union with the Holy Spirit, who unites them to the Son of God, and through him to the Father.

> . . . . The Logos is very God, existing one in essence with the very Father, while other beings, to whom he said, "I said you are gods" (Ps 82: 6), had this grace from the Father, only by participation of the Word, through the Spirit (*I Discourse Against the Arians*, 3, 9).
> . . . . The Savior, on the contrary, being God, and ever ruling in the Father's Kingdom, and being himself the one that gives the Holy Spirit, nevertheless is here said to be anointed, so that, as before, being said as man to be anointed with the Spirit, he might provide for us humans, not only exaltation and resurrection, but the dwelling and intimacy of the Spirit (*ibid.*, 46).[9]

Especially in his four letters to Serapion against the heretical *Pneumatomachoi*, that is, those who denied the divinity of the Holy Spirit, Athanasius argues for the divinity of the Holy Spirit on the basis of his work of divinization. How can he divinize us if he himself is not divine?

> It is, then, in the Spirit that the Logos glorifies creation, and divinizes it, and adopts, and leads it to the Father. But he who unites creation to the Logos would not make part of the created world, just as he who confers filiation upon

[9]Text: PG 26, 28, 108; trans. NPNF 4. 311, 333

creatures would not be a stranger to being a Son. Were this
to be the case, one would have to search for another Spirit
because in the first Spirit humanity is united to the Logos.
This, however, is absurd. The Spirit does not make part of
the created world, but is proper to the divinity of the Father
and it is in him that the Logos deifies the creatures (*1st
Letter to Serapion*, 25).[10]

Indeed, Athanasius declares that the Holy Spirit is the
image of the Son as the Son is the image of the Father: "The
Son is in the Spirit as in his own image, just as the Father is in
the Son" (*ibid.*, 20). Again: "The Spirit is called and is really
the image of the Son. . . . "(*ibid.*, 24); "The Son is the image of
the invisible God, and the Spirit is the image of the Son" (*IV
Letter to Serapion*, 3).

In conclusion, Athanasius' consistent doctrine of the
image—he Logos being the unique *eikōn* of the Father, the
Spirit being the *eikōn* of the Son, and hence the consubstantiality of the three divine persons, and humans as the
kat'eikona of the Father as this image is mediated through the
Son—offers an anthropology which is firmly rooted in
Trinitarian theology. At the same time, this doctrine of the
image functions as the architectonic principle which holds
together in a marvelous synthesis the Christian doctrines of
creation, fall, redemption and grace.

II. Cyril of Alexandria (ca 375/380-444)

Elected patriarch of the Egyptian metropolis after the death
of his uncle Theophilus in 412, Cyril is forever associated with
the second great christological controversy regarding the unity
of the person of Christ, which led to the council of Ephesus
(431) and the condemnation of Nestorius. Most of Cyril's early
writings are devoted to exegesis and polemics against the
Arians, whereas his later works undertook the refutation of the
Nestorian heresy. Though anthropology is not the central

---

[10]Text: PG 26. 589

concern of his theology, it nevertheless occupies an important place insofar as it is the presupposition of his christology.

IMAGE AND LIKENESS

Cyril was very much familiar with the distinction between "image" and "likeness" advocated by his predecessors, Clement and Origen. He refused, however, to accept this distinction. He is convinced that the two terms are indistinguishable in Genesis and proceeds to use them interchangeably. Both realities, image and likeness, were given to humanity in the beginning. To understand Cyril's concept of humanity made according to God's image, it is helpful to follow his distinctions of the various kinds of *eikōn*:

> One—the first—is the image of natural identity by reason of exactly the same properties, as in the case of Abel, born of Adam, Isaac of Abraham. A second is the image according to sheer likeness of distinctive features and the exact modeling of the form in relief, such as a wood carving of the king, or any other artistic medium. Another image has reference to manners, and morals, and way of life by which one strives toward virtue or vice. In this sense we may say that a person who does good is like Paul, whereas one who does evil is like Cain; for it is reasonable to suppose that the same activity, good or bad, effects likeness in each and confers it. Another kind of image is dignity, and honor, and glory, and excellence, as, for instance, one succeeds to another in a position of command and should perform with authority everything that could be fit and proper for his predecessor. An image in another way is that which regards a certain quality or quantity possessed by two persons or things; some shape or proportion of things that are generally by their natures like other things (*Commentary on the Gospel of John*, 2, 8).[11]

---

[11]Text: PG 73. 373; trans. SCA 14. 9, W.J. Burghardt. For what follows, see W.J. Burghardt, *The Image of God in Man According to Cyril of Alexandria* (Woodstock, Maryland: Woodstock College Press, 1957).

Thus Cyril distinguishes five different kinds of image on the basis of generation, artistic representation, moral character, dignity, and the commonality of some aspects. He goes on to describe the radical difference between the image of God that is God, namely the Son, and the image of God that is in humans. Only the Son is the perfect, identical, utterly accurate and exact image of the Father since his likeness is by nature. He is consubstantial with the Father; his image belongs to the first category, which is uniquely his, since he is generated or begotten of the Father.

Humans, on the other hand, are images of God by participation (*methexis*), by imitation (*mimēsis*), by grace (*charis*), and not by nature. In the Son there is identity of nature, in us there is only participation in nature.

Having established the nature of God's image in humans, Cyril goes on to ask whether the distinction between "image" and "likeness" is a valid one.

> Is there a difference between "according to image" and "according to likeness," or are they identical? For they say that we received the former concurrently with creation, but not the latter; this has been reserved for us in the world to come. That is why, so runs the argument, it is written: "When Christ appears, we shall be like to him" (1 Jn 3: 2). And again..."Let us make humanity to our image and likeness" (Gen 1: 26), and after its production.... "And God made humanity; to his own image he made him"(Gen 1: 27), with no mention of "according to likeness," to show...that we had not yet received this, but that it has been reserved for us in that life of blessedness. If they say that "according to image" and "according to likeness" are two different things, let them show the difference! For our judgment is that "according to image" means nothing else than "according to likeness," and conversely "according to likeness" means nothing but "according to image": the likeness to God we obtained in our original constitution, and we are images of God.... Now, if the Holy Scripture said somewhere that God made humans according to his own image, and did not mention "according to his likeness," we should understand that it was sufficient to say "according

to his image," inasmuch as it meant nothing else than "according to his likeness." In fact it is useless to say that the latter has been reserved for us for the life to come; for, since God said: "Let us make humanity according to our image and likeness, " who will dare to say that he made it acccording to his image but not according to his likeness? We shall, it is true, be like to Christ in incorruption...but even now we are not alien to his likeness, if it is really true that he is formed in us through the Holy Spirit..." (*Doctrinal Questions and Answers*, 3) [12]

Since for him "image" and "likeness" are synonymous, Cyril uses the two terms interchangeably.

It is certain and indeed beyond dispute that humans, made according to the image of God (*kat' eikona*), have this likeness (*homoiotēs*) which is not corporeal. God is incorporeal, which fact the Savior himself teaches in saying: "God is Spirit...." That humans are made according to the image of God has another sense and significance. For only a human being, above all other living beings on earth, endowed with reason, is merciful and capable of acquiring every type of virtue. He also possesses the power over all things on earth according to the image of God by which he has been fashioned (*Commentary on the Gospel of Matthew.*)[13]

Where does this image of God reside in humans? When Cyril expressly defines human nature, he terms it "a rational, mortal animal, capable of understanding and knowledge" (*Commentary on the Gospel of John*, 6), or, more simply, "a rational, mortal animal" (*Thesaurus*, 31). This soul had no existence before its union with the body, directly created by God, has no quality, quantity or form, and will never cease to exist. It is precisely in this soul, and not the body, that the image of God resides. It is this image that gives the soul superiority over the rest of animal creation.

[12]Text: Pusey, *In Ioannem* 3, 554; trans. SCA 14, 7, W. J. Burghardt
[13]Text: PG 72. 374

> Humans upon earth, as far as their bodily nature is
> concerned, are dust and ashes; but they have been honored
> by God by having been made in his image and likeness—not
> in their bodily shape, but rather because they are capable of
> being just and good and fitted for all virtues (*Homily 96 on
> Luke*).[14]

Elsewhere, Cyril explicitly affirms that the soul is God's image: "The soul is more noble than the substance of the body, since it is the image and breath of God. The body, however, cooperates with the soul in any good endeavor as its instruments. We must take care of both...and let us refer the soul through its exercise of virtues back to the cause from which it came, namely, God who created it" (*Commentary on the Gospel of Matthew*, 6:23). Fighting against the anthropomorphites who believed that God has a human form because humans are his image, Cyril categorically asserts: "Humans are admittedly made in God's image, but the likeness is not corporeal; for God is incorporeal.... But if they think that God was shaped after the nature of the human body, let them say whether he too has feet to walk, hands to work, eyes to see ...." (*Letter to Calosyrius*). Further, Cyril goes on to argue, if the body shares in the image of God, then the latter can never be lost, which is absurd, since we never lose the essential components of our body.

Being created in God's image humans, in Cyril's view, possess distinctive characteristics. In a concise passage he summarizes them as follows:

> Humanity's formation in God's image has other meanings—
> meanings on the surface and meanings deep within; for the
> human person alone, of all the living creatures on earth, is
> rational (*logikos*), compassionate, with a capacity for all
> manners of virtue, and a divinely alloted dominion over all
> the creatures of earth, after the manner and likeness of God.
> Therefore, it is on account of the fact that he is a rational
> (*logikon*) animal, a lover of virtue, and earth's sovereign

---

[14]Text: *In Lucan* hom. 96 (tr. R. Payne Smith, *A Commentary upon the Gospel according to S. Luke by S. Cyril 2* [Oxford, 1859] 446)

that the human person is said to have been made in God's image (*Letter to Calosyrius*).[15]

The first characteristic, then, is "reason." Human reason, which is God's gift and which, together with the body, constitutes human nature, is, in Cyril's view, a participation in the divine Logos.

> The Word of God "enlightens every human being who comes into the world," not by way of instruction as angels and humans do, but rather as God; in a creative act (*dēmiurgikos*) he stores in each of these who are called into existence a seed of wisdom or of the knowledge of God, and implants the root of intelligence, and thus renders the animal rational (*logikon*), making it partaker of his own nature, and instilling in the mind, as it were, some luminous vapors of the inexpressible splendor, in the manner and proportion known to him (for on subjects like this we should not, I think, say too much). It is, therefore, evident that our forefather Adam did not acquire wisdom in time, as we do, but from the very first moments of his creation, he appears perfect in understanding—as long as he preserved pure and unsullied in himself the enlightenment given to his nature by God, and did not prostitute the dignity of that nature. The Son enlightens, therefore, in creative fashion, inasmuch as he is himself the true Light, while the creature is illumined by participation in the Light, and consequently is called and becomes light, mounting to the supernatural (*ta huper phusin*) through the grace of God who glorifies him and crowns him with various honors (*Commentary on the Psalms*, 18,8).[16]

What Cyril intends to say is that while "reason" is a gift of God to human nature and in this sense is "natural" and cannot be lost, nevertheless it contains the "seed," "root," "vapors" of the Logos and therefore can be fulfilled only in supernatural faith and knowledge of God.

---

[15]Text: Pusey, *In Ioannem* 3, 605; trans. SCA 14.25, W.J. Burghardt

[16]Text: Pusey, 1, 111; trans. SCA 14. 36, W. J. Burghardt

The second component of God's image is freedom:

> For the human person, from the beginning of their creation, had been entrusted with the reins of his own volitions, with unrestricted movement toward his every desire; for the Deity is free, and human beings had been formed after him. It was in this way, I think, and in no other that the human person could win admiration, if it was clear that he practiced virtue of his own accord, and that the purity of his actions was the fruit of judgment, not the result, as it were, of natural necessity which simply would not permit him to be borne beyond the good, even though he might wish to do otherwise. Humans, therefore, had been equipped from the start with unrestricted, unimpeded movement of purpose in all their actions (*Glaphyra on Genesis*, 1).[17]

Freedom, then, is the necessary presupposition for meritorious actions and the practice of virtues. It also accounts for the possibility of the fall of Adam:

> ...the man was made in the beginning with an intelligence that was superior to sin and passions. However, he was not at all incapable of turning aside in any direction he pleased; for the excellent Creator of the universe thought it right to attach to him the reins of his own volitions, and to leave it to self-directed movements to achieve whatever he wanted. The reason is that virtue had to be a matter of deliberate choice, not the fruit of compulsion, nor so firmly fixed by nature's laws that the man could not stumble; for this is proper to the supreme essence and excellence (*On Adoration*, 1).[18]

Human freedom, even though it may turn toward good or evil, is "naturally" inclined toward the good:

[17]Text: PG 69; trans. W.J. Burghardt
[18]Text: PG 68. 145; trans. SCA 14. 46, W. J. Burghardt

The Creator of the universe fashioned the man, that is, his body, from the earth. Animating it with a living and intellectual soul in the manner known to him, he instilled in it a natural appetite for, and knowledge of, everything that is good. This, I think, is the meaning of the blessed evangelist John's words, "He was the true light which enlightened every human being who comes into the world" (Jn 1: 9); for the human animal is born with a natural aptitude for the good. This we learn from the all-wise Paul when he writes: "His workmanship we are, created for good works...." (Eph 2: 10). Humans, you see, govern themselves by their own deliberate choice, and they have been entrusted with the reins of their own purpose, so that they can move quickly in whatever direction they please, to good or to its opposite. Now, their nature has instilled in it the appetite and the desire for every kind of good, and the will to cultivate goodness and justice; for this, we say, is the way humans were made in God's image and likeness, inasmuch as the human animal is naturally good and just. But, since they had to be not merely rational and fit for doing good and justice, but also sharer of the Holy Spirit, in order that they might have the distinctive marks of the divine nature more limpid in them, he breathed into them the breath of life. This is the Spirit given to the rational creature through the Son and transforming it to the Supreme, that is, the Divine form (*Doctrinal Questions and Answers,* 2).[19]

The third characteristic of God's image is dominion over all irrational creatures. In virtue of this dominion, the lord of the earth resembles the heavenly Lord, who rules supreme over the entire universe. Commenting on Ps. 8: 5: "What is a human being that you should be mindful of him?" Cyril writes:

> [What is man? He is] this animal so little, so paltry, earthsprung. God made him somewhat less than the angels; for we are admittedly inferior to the holy angels in nature and glory. And so the God of the universe deigned to

---

[19]Text: Pusey, *In Ioannem* 3, 552, trans. SCA 14. 48, W. J. Burghardt

"crown us with honor and glory" (Ps 8: 6) and made us
illustrious; for he appointed humans to rule over the earth
and "set them over the works of his hands" (Ps 8: 7)
(*Commentary on Hebrews,* 2, 7).[20]

The fourth characteristic of the divine image is sanctification.
Because God is holy, the human person, who images God, is
also holy. Sanctification (*hagiasmos*), which is participation in
God's own Son through his Spirit, is not innate in human
nature but God's gratuitous gift.

We have been formed to God in the primary and most
proper way in which it can be understood: according to
virtue and sanctification (*hagiasmos*); for the Deity is holy
and the fount, beginning, and origin of all virtues. Now, that
we should so understand the creation of humanity in God's
image, the all-wise Paul will tell us in his words to the
Galatians; "Little children, with whom I am in labor again,
until Christ be formed in you" (Gal 4: 19). For he is formed
in us through the sanctification which comes through the
Spirit, through the calling which consists in faith in him.
Now, in those who sin against this faith, the distinctive
features do not shine forth clearly; that is why they need
another spiritual travail and suprasensible regeneration, in
order that they may be formed once more to Christ,
inasmuch as the Holy Spirit makes the divine image gleam
in them through sanctification (*Answers to Tiberius,* 10).[21]

This sanctification, by which the human person participates in
the divine nature or, more specifically, in the Holy Spirit, and
in virtue of which he is selected to do God's will, is, in Cyril's
view, an ontological reality. This created, ontological reality,
however, must be accompanied by the practice of virtue.
Christ, says Cyril, "refashions us once more to his own image,
so that the distinctive marks of his divine nature are conspicuous in us through sanctification and justice and the good
life according to virtue. . . . The beauty of this most excellent

---

[20]Text: Pusey, *In Ioannem,* 3. 382, trans. SCA 14. 56

[21]Text: Pusey, *In Ioannem* 3, 592; trans. SCA 14. 65, W. J. Burghardt

image shines forth in those of us who are in Christ, as long as we have played the part of good people through works themselves" (*Answers to Tiberius,* 8). Because humans are holy they must live a holy life.

As the result of sanctification, humans possess a fifth characteristic: incorruptibility (*aphthasia*). Because the human person has a body, he is essentially mortal and corruptible. But the human soul, because it is spirit, is immortal. Its immortality may be said on the one hand to be "natural" insofar as it belongs to its constitution by God's disposition; on the other hand, it is "supernatural" because it is a free gift of God. Beyond this immortality of the soul, God has given to Adam, and through Christ, to us a richer participation in his life, in his incorruptibility, a sharing in the Spirit of life which constitutes the divinization of human life. This is the true immortality (*athanasia*), the true incorruptibility (*aphthasia*). Thus, for Cyril, corruptibility and incorruptibility do not refer simply to physical death and physical survival; rather a corruptible body is the raw material for sinful concupiscence, and an incorruptible body is one that knows neither physical nor moral imperfection, neither physical weakness nor fleshly concupiscence. The process was initiated when the Son of God quickened corruptible flesh with his Incarnation; it is appropriated by the individual through the reception of the sacraments, in particular the eucharist, and the life of virtue; and finally, it will be consummated in the general resurrection of the dead.

> Since the Word of God is life by nature, he made what was naturally corruptible his own body, in order to transform it to incorruptibility by disabling the power of deadness within it; for, just as iron, when vigorous fire is applied to it, changes its color so as to assume immediately the form of the fire, and gives birth to the power of the prevailing fire, so the nature of the flesh, having welcomed within it the incorruptible and life-giving Word of God, remained no longer in the same condition but became thereafter superior to corruption (*Paschal Homilies,* 17, 4).[22]

[22]Text: PG 77. 785; trans. SCA 14. 92, W. J. Burghardt

The final aspect of the divine image, both as a consequence of sanctification and a basis for incorruptibility, is divine Sonship. Whereas the Logos is Son by nature, our sonship is a participation in his, an adoptive sonship, which is given in the Incarnation.

> [The Word] lowered himself in order to lift to his own height that which was lowly by nature; and he bore the form of the slave, though by nature he was Lord and Son, in order to transport what was slave by nature to the glory of adoptive sonship, after his own likeness, with reference to him. Therefore, just as he became like us, that is, man, in order that we might become like him, I mean gods and sons, he takes to himself what is properly ours and gives us in return what is his. . . . We mount to a dignity which is supernatural through our likeness to him; for we have been called children of God, even though we are not children by nature. . . . By nature and in reality the Father of Christ is the God of the universe; but that does not make him our Father by nature; rather he is God, as Creator and Lord. But the Son, as it were, mingling himself with us, bestows on our nature the dignity that is properly and peculiarly his own, giving the name of common Father to his own Begotten. . . .(*Commentary on the Gospel of John,* 12, 1).[23]

SIN AND REDEMPTION

Human beings, then, according to Cyril, are, before the fall of Adam, the rational, free rulers of the created world, the incorruptible children of God. In paradise, therefore, "human nature lacked nothing for its well-being and its happiness" (*Glaphyra on Genesis,* 2). Gifted with glory and surrounded by delights, Adam and Eve had to realize that God was their King and Lord. And, so that they might remember their utter dependence upon him, God gave them the commandment not to eat the tree of life and threatened with punishment for its transgression. But Satan, envious of their immortal destiny,

[23]Text: Pusey, 3. 122-123, trans. SCA 14. 106-107

tempted the woman—for Cyril, the weaker and the more given to sensual pleasure (cf. *Commentary on Zechariah,* 2)—and she fell; Adam, too, was carried away by guile (cf. *Glaphyra on Genesis,* 1). His transgression was an act of disobedience against God.

What were the effects of Adam's sin on him? As far as rationality and freedom are concerned, Cyril's view is that Adam did not lose these two constitutive components of human nature, that is, he still remained "capable of understanding and knowledge" and of self-determination. Nevertheless, his mind was clouded by sin and concupiscence in its contemplation of God, and his freedom was inhibited by evil in its inclination toward the good.

> Humans were free upon the earth, finely fashioned to the divine image and created, as blessed Paul says, "for good works, which God made ready beforehand that we may walk in them" (Eph 2: 10). But the inventor of iniquity defrauded them beyond all measure. He withdrew them from their love for God and made them worshipers of himself, hanging on them sin's yoke that was hard to escape....(*Commentary on Isaiah* 1, 5).[24]

As for the other four characteristics, dominion over the earth, incorruptibility, holiness, and sonship, Adam lost them all.

> Turn your mind to that ancient Adam, and in the first fruits and root of the race count the whole of humanity as it were in him. Ponder this fact as well, that he had been made to the Creator's image and had been appointed to rule over earthly things, and was, as it were, in God's hand through the life of holiness.... But when, tricked by the serpent's bitterness, he was removed from his original state ... then it was that, torn from his first root and position, he slipped from the hand that held him in holiness and fell down to earth, that is, from the heights of virtue.... In this way he was stripped utterly of the kingship and glory he had in the beginning, and was cast from Paradise and delights. The

[24]Text: PG 70. 249; trans. SCA 14. 145

> Holy Spirit fled from him, because holiness and impurity,
> light and darkness, justice and injustice, are irreconcil-
> able.... (*On Adoration,* 2).[25]

The first sin did not adversely affect Adam only; Cyril
explicitly affirms that the whole human race is affected by it
and its consequences as well: "We have become joint heirs of
the evils that befall the first man" (*Commentary on Isaiah,* 2,
1). Our reason and free will, though not totally destroyed, are
weakened, and we have lost our dominion over the earth, our
incorruptibility, our holiness, and our divine adoptive sonship....

> We must inquire how Adam, our first forefather, transmitted
> to us the penalty imposed upon him for his transgression.
> He had heard "Earth thou art and to the earth shalt thou
> return" (Gen 3: 19), and from being incorruptible he
> became corruptible and was made subject to the chains of
> death. But since he produced children after falling into this
> state we, his descendants, are corruptible, coming from a
> corruptible source. Thus it is that we are heirs of Adam's
> curse; for surely we have not been visited with punishment
> as though we disobeyed with him the divine command
> which he received, but because ... become mortal he
> transmitted the curse to the seed he fathered. We are mortal
> because we come from a mortal source.... (*Doctrinal
> Questions and Answers,* 6).[26]

In his *Commentary on the Romans* (Rom 5:18-19), Cyril is no
less explicit on the existence of "original sin" in us: "Human
nature has, therefore, contracted the malady of sin through the
disobedience of one man, Adam. It is in this way that the many
have been made sinners—not as though they had transgressed
with Adam (for they did not yet exist), but because they are of
his nature, the nature that fell beneath the law of sin...."
    Cyril, of course, was not interested in the fallen state of
human nature as such; like Paul, he spoke of sin only to

[25]Text: PG 68. 244; trans. SCA 14. 146, W. J. Burghardt
[26]Text: Pusey, *In Ioannem,* 3, 560; trans. SCA 14. 151, W. J. Burghardt

celebrate the victory of Christ over it and its consequences. Again and again he proclaims that the Logos, by his Incarnation, has repaired the ravages of sin, given back to humanity its divine image, and by sending his Spirit, restored reason, freedom, dominion, incorruptibility, holiness and adoptive sonship which Adam had lost.

> We say that the very ugly image of the earthly man is visible in certain forms like the filth that is sin, the feebleness that is death and corruption, the impurity involved in fleshly lust and in an earth-bound mind. In like fashion, we think, the image of the heavenly man, Christ, is conspicuous in cleanness and purity, in total incorruption and life and sanctification. But it would have been impossible for us to be restored to our original beauty, once we had fallen from it through the transgression of the first man, had we not achieved that inexpressible communion and union with God. For that is the way in which human nature was adorned in the beginning. Union with God, however, is impossible to achieve for anyone save through participation in the Holy Spirit, instilling in us his own proper sanctification and refashioning to his own life the nature that fell subject to corruption, and thus restoring to God and to God's likeness what had been deprived of this glory. For the perfect image of the Father is the Son, and the natural likeness of the Son is the Holy Spirit. The Spirit, therefore, refashioning as it were to himself the human souls, engraves on them God's likeness, and seals the representation of the supreme essence (*Commentary on the Gospel of John*, 11, 11).[27]

Grace, in Cyril's view, is a created quality, a form (*morphōsis*) whose function is to form Christ in us: "Now, Christ is formed (*morphoutai*) in us "inasmuch as the Holy Spirit implants in us some divine form (*morphōsin*) through sanctification (*hagiasmou*) and justice. It is in this way, you see, that the impress of the substance of God the Father is conspicuous in our souls—since the Holy Spirit reforms us, as I said, to him through sancitification" (*Commentary on Isaiah*, 4, 2).

[27]Text: Pusey, 2. 730-731, trans. SCA 14. 72, W. J. Burghardt

In conclusion, Cyril's magnificent doctrine on sanctification and the presence of the Holy Spirit in the justified souls recapitulates the whole Greek theology of *theopoiēsis,* deification. Unfortunately, this doctrine was elaborated when the West was being engulfed in the Pelagian controversy, and Augustine's doctrine of grace monopolized the attention of the West. As a consequence, Cyril's anthropology was ignored. But since the seventeenth century, when Petau's patristic studies retrieved Cyrillian doctrine of grace, this has been of great profit both for theology and spiritual life.

6

The Cappadocian Fathers

The three bishops, St. Basil of Caesarea, St. Gregory of Nazianzus and St. Gregory of Nyssa, often referred to as the Cappadocian Fathers on account of their common place of origin, are linked together in more ways than one. They were intimately united with each other either by family ties (the first and the third were brothers) or by friendship, as existed among all three, or by literary activities (Basil and Gregory of Nazianzus, schoolmates at Athens and, composing together the *Philocalia,* a selection from the writings of Origen). Though quite different in temperaments and talents, Basil the pragmatic ecclesiastic and founder of Cenobitic Monasticism, his brother the speculative thinker, and Gregory the poetic theologian, they were all ardent defenders of the Nicene faith regarding the divinity of the Son (the two brothers wrote against Eunomius, the Arian bishop of Cyzicus) and of the divinity of the Holy Spirit, defined as an article of faith at the council of Constantinople in 381. Thanks to their ecclesiastical and theological activities, the Cappadocians have exercised a lasting influence on the life of the Church and on later theological thought.

I. Basil of Caesarea (ca 330-379)

One of the ten children of rich and deeply Christian parents (besides Gregory of Nyssa, one of his brothers, Peter, was also a bishop, and one of his sisters, St. Macrina, whose life is celebrated by her brother Gregory, was quite influential thanks to her establishment of a religious community on the family estate in Pontus), Basil acquired the title 'the Great' on account of his outstanding talent for organization (his construction of the church and episcopal residence, hospitals and hostels for the poor), his struggle against Arianism (his three *Books Against Eunomius*), his defense of the divinity of the Spirit (*On the Holy Spirit*), and his establishment of Cenobitic Monasticism (*The Moralia,* the *Longer Rules* and the *Shorter Rules*).

For our purpose, Basil's most important work is his nine homilies on the opening chapters of Genesis, entitled the *Hexaemeron.* They were Lenten sermons, delivered *extempore* at both the morning and evening services, and were later constantly drawn upon as a source for theological cosmology by Ambrose, Augustine, and even medieval authors. In these sermons Basil avoids the allegorical exegesis of Origen and offers a literal interpretation of the story of the origin of the world.

GOD, THE FREE AND PERSONAL CREATOR

In his critique of Greek cosmology Basil particularly disputed the assumption of eternal matter as well as the Aristotelian doctrine of eternal creation. He expressly repudiates Platonic and Gnostic dualism as well as Stoic immanentism. He holds fast to the Christian idea of a free, personal, divine Creator and of the Trinity's involvement in the work of creation.

> "In the beginning God created the heaven and the earth." I am struck with admiration at this thought. What shall I say first? Where shall I begin my narration? Shall I expose the vanity of the heathens? Or shall I proclaim our truth? The philosophers of Greece wrote many books to explain nature, and yet not one of their systems has remained firm and unshaken, each being overturned by its successor. As a consequence it is not necessary to refute them; they are sufficient in themselves to destroy one another. Those, in fact, who were too ignorant to rise to the knowledge of God,

did not concede that an intelligent cause was the author of the creation of the universe; they drew their successive conclusions in keeping with this primary error. Some had recourse to material principles and attributed the origin of the universe to the elements of the world. Others imagined that the nature of visible things is formed by the union of atoms, and invisible bodies, molecules and interstices. Atoms, in their opinion, now united with each other, now separated, produce births and deaths, and the most durable bodies derive their consistency from the strengths of their mutual adhesion.

Truly, it is a spider's web that these writers weave who assign such weak and unsubstantial beginnings to the heavens, and earth, and sea. It is because they did not know how to say, "In the beginning God created." What a glorious order! He first establishes 'the beginning,' so that it might not be supposed that the world never had a beginning. Then he adds 'created' to show that what was made required a very small part of the power of the Creator. In fact, just as the potter, though he has formed innumerable vessels with equal effort, has exhausted neither his art nor his talent, so also the Creator of the universe, possessing creative power not commensurate with one world, but infinitely greater, by the weight of his will alone brought the immensities of the visible world into being. If, then, the world has a beginning and was created, inquire: Who is he that gave it the beginning, and who is the Creator? Rather, lest human reasonings may make you wander from the truth, Moses has taught us beforehand, imprinting upon our hearts as a seal and a security, the highly honored name of God, saying: "In the beginning God created." It is the beneficient Nature, Goodness without measure, the Beloved of all beings endowed with reasons, the much desired Beauty, the Origin of things created, the Fount of life, the spiritual Light, the inaccessible Wisdom, he is the one who "in the beginning created the heavens and the earth" (*The Hexaemeron,* 1, 2).[1]

[1]Text: SC 26^2.92; trans. FOTC 46.5-6

HUMANITY CREATED IN GOD'S IMAGE

The last homily of the *Hexaemeron* deals with the production of land animals. In this context Basil briefly mentions the creation of humans in God's image and the role of the Logos in it:

> ...And God said: "Let us make humankind." Does not the light of theology shine in these words, as through windows, and does not the second person show himself in a mystical way, without yet manifesting himself until the great day? Where are the Jews who resisted the truth and pretended that God was speaking to himself? It is he who spoke, it is said, and it is he who made. "Let there be light and there was light." But then their words are obviously absurd. What coppersmith or carpenter or shoemaker, sitting down alone among the tools of his craft, would say to himself: "Let us make a sword," or "Let us make a plow," or "Let us make a shoe?" Does he not accomplish the work undertaken in silence? Truly, is it not utter nonsense to say that any one has seated himself to command himself, to watch over himself, to hurry himself, with the tone of a master? But the unhappy creatures are not afraid to calumniate the Lord himself: What will they not say with a tongue so well practiced in lying? Here, however, the words block their mouth. "And God said, 'Let us make humankind.'" Tell me: is there then only one person? It is not written: "Let humankind be made," but: "Let us make humankind." As long as the one to be instructed had not yet appeared, the preaching of theology was still deeply hidden, but now that the creation of humankind was expected, faith was revealed, and the doctrine of truth was more clearly disclosed. "Let us make humankind." You, O enemy of Christ, hear God speaking to his cooperator, to him by whom also he made the worlds, who upholds all things by the word of his power.....To whom does he say "in our image," to whom if not to him who is "the brightness of his glory and the express image of his person" (Heb 1: 3), "the image of the invisible God" (Col 1: 15)? It is then to his living image, to him who has said: "I and my Father are one" (Jn 10: 30),

"he that has seen me has seen the Father" (Jn 14: 9), that God says: "Let us make humankind in our image." Where is the unlikeness in these Beings who have only one image? "So God created humankind." It is not "They created." Here Scripture avoids the plurality of the persons. After having enlightened the Jews, it dissipates the error of the Gentiles by returning to the singular, to make you understand that the Son is with the Father and to guard you from polytheism. "In the image of God he created him." Again, the co-worker is introduced, because it is not said, "In his own image," but "In the image of God" (*The Hexaemeron,* 9, 6).[2]

Basil cut short his homily for want of time and promised that "if God permits, we will say later in what way humans were created in the image of God and how they share this resemblance (*ibid*). In a homily on Ps 48, Basil returned to the text of Genesis and the theme of the image-likeness of God. For him the distinctive dignity granted both to angels and humans made according to the image of the Creator consists in "the power of understanding and recognizing their own Creator and Maker":

> "Humans are great, and even a pitiful human being is honorable" (Prov 20: 6) because his honor is based upon his nature. For what other beings on earth have been made according to the image of the Creator? To which of the animals that live on the land, or in the water, or in the air, has the rule and power over all things been given? Humans have fallen a little below the dignity of the angels because of their union with the earthly body. In fact God made them from the earth, as it is said: "And his ministers a flame of fire" (Heb 1: 7). But still, the power of understanding and recognizing their own Creator and Maker also belongs to them. "And he breathed into his nostrils" (Gen 2: 7), that is to say, he placed in humans some share of his own grace, in order that they might recognize likeness through likeness.

[2]Text: SC 26².514; trans. FOTC 46.147-149

Nevertheless, being in such great honor because they were created in the image of the Creator, they are honored above the heavens, above the sun, above the choirs of stars. For, which of the heavenly bodies was said to be an image of the most high God? What sort of an image of its Creator does the sun preserve? The moon? The stars? They possess only inanimate and material bodies that are clearly discernible, but in which nowhere there is a mind, no voluntary movements, no free will; on the contrary, they are servile through the necessity imposed upon them, through which they always behave precisely the same in the same circumstance . . . (*Homily on Ps 48,*, 8).[3]

This "according to the image of God," Basil suggests, resides in the mind: "The mind is a wonderful thing and therein we possess that which is according to the image of the Creator" (*Letter 233,* 1). Humans are called to perfect this "according to the image" and to grow in the likeness to God: "It is proposed to us to resemble God as far as it is possible to human nature" (*On the Holy Spirit,* 1, 2). This is done through contemplation and knowledge of the good and through good actions:

. . . The operation of the mind is a thing of beauty; and, since the mind is ever active, it frequently forms images of nonexistent things as though they did exist; and it frequently is carried straight to the truth. But there are in it two faculties, according to the view of us who believe in God, the one wicked, which is of the demons, drawing us along to their apostasy; the other divine and good, which brings us to the likeness of God. Whenever, therefore, the mind remains alone and unaided, it contemplates small things, commensurate with itself. When it yields to those who deceive it, it nullifies its own judgment and is concerned with monstrous fancies. Then it considers wood to be no longer wood, but a god; then it looks on gold no longer as money, but as an object of worship. If, on the other hand, it assents to its more divine part and accepts the grace of the Spirit, then it is able to discern the more divine things as far as its

[3]Text: PG 29.449; trans. FOTC 46.324-325

nature allows.... The mind that is permeated with the divinity of the Spirit is capable of viewing great objects; it beholds the divine beauty, though only so far as grace imparts and its natures receives.... The judgment of our mind has been given us for the comprehension of the truth. So, the principal duty of our mind is to know our God, but to know him in such a way as the infinitely Great One can be known by the very small.... If the mind is misled by the demon, it will practice idolatry or will turn aside to some other form of impiety. If, however, it has yielded to the aid of the Spirit, it will have understanding of the truth and will know God (*Letter 233,* 1-2).[4]

FALLEN HUMANITY

In his letters and homilies Basil mentions, in passing, not only the account of creation, as we have seen above, but also the fall of humanity. As the result of their fall, humans threw aside "the image of the heavenly" and took on "the image of the earthly":

> Humans, then, having been advanced above these things in honor, failed to understand, neglecting to follow God and to become like their Creator. Becoming slaves of the passions of the flesh, they are compared to senseless beasts and become like them; they are now like an amorous horse which neighs after his neighbor's wife (cf. Jer 5: 8); now like a ravenous wolf lying in wait for strangers (cf. Ex 22: 27); at another time, because of their deceit toward their brethren, they make themselves like the villainous fox (cf. Ez 13: 4). Truly, is it not exessive folly and beastlike lack of reason that they, made according to the image of the Creator, neither perceive their own nature from the beginning, nor even wish to understand such great plans as were made for their sake and to learn, at least, their own dignity from them? Furthermore they become unmindful of the fact that

having thrown aside the image of the heavenly, they have taken up the image of the earthly (*Homily on Ps. 48,* 8).[5]

In his treatise against the Manichaeans, designed to show that God is not the author of evil, Basil traces the origin of moral evil to created freedom. This statement leads him to speak of Adam's sin and so back to the sin of the angels. The devil is not created a devil: he is a fallen angel. Jealous of humans' happiness, he brought about their fall. In terms reminiscent of neo-Platonism and Origen, Basil describes this fall:

> This misfortune happens when through satiety the soul loses its taste for the blessed delectation. Then through a lack of vigilance it grows heavy and falls from the superior regions. It mixes then with the flesh, goaded on by the desire of shameful joys of earthly pleasures. . . . There was a time when Adam lived on high, not with regard to place, but by his will. This was when, having just been animated by the breath of life, he had his gaze turned towards heaven. He loved the Creator who had placed him in paradise. He lived in the company of the angels. Protected by God he enjoyed all his goods. But, as if he had had enough of this happiness, he preferred to spiritual beauty that which allured his eyes of flesh; to spiritual joys, the taste of an earthly sustenance. Driven out of paradise, he was suddenly deprived of this blessed life and became wicked; withdrawing from life he drew near to death; for God is life and death is the privation of life (*God Is Not the Author of Evil,* 6).[6]

The result of this sin, which for Basil was one of pride (*Homily* 20, 1, *On Humility*) or greed (*Homily* 8, 7), is vividly described as the marring of the beauty of the image of God:

> Humanity was made according to the image and likeness of God; but sin marred the beauty of the image by dragging the soul down to passionate desires. Now, God, who created

[5]Text: PG 29.449; trans. FOTC 46.325
[6]Text: PG 31.344

humanity, is the true life. Therefore, when humans lost their likeness to God, they lost their participation in the true life; separated and estranged from God as they are, it is impossible for them to enjoy the blessedness of the divine life. Let us return, then, to the grace which was ours in the beginning and from which we have alienated ourselves by sin, and let us adorn ourselves again with the beauty of God's image, being made like to our Creator through the quieting of our passions. He who, to the best of his ability, copies within himself the tranquility of the divine nature attains to a likeness with the very soul of God; and, being made like to God in the manner described above, he also achieves in full a resemblance to the divine life and abides continually in unending blessedness. If, then, by mastering our passions we regain the image of God and if the likeness of God bestows upon us everlasting life, let us devote ourselves to this pursuit in preference to all others, so that our soul never again be enslaved by vice, but that our understanding may remain firm and unconquerable under the assaults of temptation; in this way we may become sharers in the divine beatitude (*An Ascetical Discourse,* 1).[7]

At other times Basil's language may be interpreted as affirming the existence of original sin in us, even though it must be admitted that his expressions are vague and ambiguous, passing without warning from Adam to the children of Adam, from personal sin to collective sin. So, in his homily on Psalm 114, speaking of God's mercy and justice, he says:

> ...Everywhere Scripture joins justice with the mercy of God, teaching us that neither the mercy of God is without judgment, nor his judgment without mercy....Mercy presupposes compassion, as when one sees a wealthy person dispossessed, or a man in good health suddenly stricken by illness. So it is with regard to us. Formerly in paradise, we were glorious, but now we are fallen, degraded (*Homily on Psalm 114:* 3).[8]

[7]Text: PG 31.869
[8]Text: PG 29.489; trans. FOTC 46.355

LIFE IN THE HOLY SPIRIT

Basil strongly emphasizes that human beings, captives of the devil and slaves of sin, cannot save themselves. Only the God-Man, Jesus Christ, could and did save us through his death.

> ...In fact, what can humans find great enough that they may give it for the ransom of their souls? But, one thing was found worth as much as all humans brought together. This was given for the price of ransom of our souls, the holy and highly honored blood of our Lord Jesus Christ, which he poured out for all of us; therefore, we were bought at a great price. If then, a brother does not redeem, will a man redeem us? But if a man cannot redeem us, he who redeems us is not a man. Now, do not assume, because Christ sojourned among us 'in the likeness of sinful flesh' (Rom 8: 3), that our Lord is only man, failing to discern the power of divinity, who had no need to give God a ransom for himself nor to redeem his own soul because "he committed no sin, neither was deceit found in his mouth" (1 Pet 2: 22). No one is sufficient to redeem himself, unless he comes who turns away the captivity of the people, not with ransoms nor with gifts, as it is written in Isaiah (cf. 52: 3), but in his own blood (*Homily on Ps. 48*).[9]

Like Athanasius, Basil associates the Holy Spirit with Christ in the task of restoring humanity to its former dignity of "according to the image." Even though he never calls the Holy Spirit explicitly 'God' in his treatise *On the Holy Spirit,* and though he never uses the expression 'consubstantial with the Father' (*homoousios tō patri*) of the third person in the Trinity (for which he was accused by his contemporaries as a crypto semi-Arian), there is no doubt that for Basil the Holy Spirit is divine. He speaks unequivocally of his divinity in his *Against Eunomius* 3, 4 and 3, 5 and proves it all through his treatise *On the Holy Spirit,* 41-47, 58-64, 71-75. The Holy Spirit is divine precisely because his task is to sanctify, that is, divinize us. He

---

[9]Text: PG 29.440; trans. FOTC 46.318

restores the image of God in us. Explaining the expression "*in* the Holy Spirit," Basil writes:

> Now, short and simple as this utterance is, it appears to me, as I consider it, that its meanings are many and various. For the senses in which "*in*" is used, we find that all help our conceptions of the Spirit. *Form* is said to be *in matter; power* to be *in* what is capable of it; *habit* to be *in* him who is affected by it, and so on. Therefore, inasmuch as the Holy Spirit perfects rational beings, completing their excellence, he is analogous to form. For the one who no longer "lives after the flesh" (Rom 8: 12), but being "led by the Spirit of God" (Rom 8: 14), is called the Son of God, being "conformed to the image of the Son of God" (Rom 8: 29), and is described as spiritual. And as the power of seeing is in the healthy eye, so is the operation of the Spirit in the purified soul. Wherefore also Paul prays for the Ephesians that they may have their "eyes enlightened" by "the Spirit of wisdom" (Eph 1: 17-18). And as the art is in him who has acquired it, so is the grace of the Spirit ever present in the recipient, though not continuously in operation. For as the art is potentially in the artist, but only in operation when he is working in accordance with it, so also the Spirit is ever present with those that are worthy, but works, as need requires, in prophecies, or in healings, or in some other actual realization of his potential action. Furthermore, as in our bodies is health, or heat, or, generally, their variable conditions, so, very frequently is the Spirit in our soul; since he does not abide with those who, on account of the instability of their will, easily reject the grace they have received...(*On the Holy Spirit,* 26, 61).[10]

In a striking passage, Basil details not only the permanent presence of the Spirit in the just, but also the various activities he performs:

> The creature is a slave, the Spirit sets free; the creature is in need of life, the Spirit gives life; the creature needs

[10]Text: SC 17².466; trans. NPNF Second Series, 8.38

instruction, the Spirit instructs; the creature is sanctified, the Spirit sanctifies. Even if you would speak of angels, or archangels, or all the heavenly powers, it is through the Spirit that they receive their holiness. For the Spirit of himself has a natural holiness not received through grace but joined essentially to him, whence he has gained in a special manner the name of 'Holy.' Accordingly, him who is holy by nature, as the Father is holy by nature, and the Son holy by nature, we ourselves do not dare to separate and sever from the divine and blessed Trinity, and we do not approve those who carelessly reckon him among creatures (*Letter 159*).[11]

Thus for Basil it is the Holy Spirit that restores the image of God in us, communicating to our intellect a special light by which we can contemplate the Son, the image of the Father, and in this way effects our sanctification and deification.

II. Gregory of Nazianzus (ca 330-389)

Called the 'Christian Demosthenes' for his oratorical skills, Gregory of Nazianzus (or Gregory 'the Theologian') found monastic life very congenial to his contemplation and retiring spirit. Under the pressure of circumstances, however, he let himself be ordained a priest and then consecrated by Basil to the see of Sasima, a miserable little village which he never visited. In 379 he was summoned out of his solitude in Seleucia to Constantinople, where his eloquent preaching was greatly responsible for the restoration of the Nicene faith and its final establishment at the Council of Constantinople in 381. Elected bishop of Constantinople, he resigned the see before the end of the year, retiring first to Nazianzus and later to his own estate, where he died.

Gregory's literary legacy consists solely of orations, poems and letters. Of the forty-five extant orations, the five *Theological Orations* (27-31), delivered at Constantinople in the

---

[11]Text: PG 32.621; trans. NPNF 8.212

summer or fall of 380, are the most famous. They contain the most mature expression of Trinitarian theology of the fourth century. With the Trinity as the radiant point Gregory works out God's plan of salvation for humanity, beginning with creation and culminating in the Incarnation.

IN THE BEGINNING: A THREEFOLD CREATION

Echoing a Johannine metaphor, Gregory affirms that God is Light. Though self-existent and self-contemplating, God, because he is Light, pours himself out on that which is external to him. This shedding forth of God's illuminating self is, for Gregory, the symbol of creation, with God's goodness as the sole motive. Gregory interprets God's gracious creative act as a three-stage process. God first created the spiritual world, then the material, and finally the human, which is the formation out of the first two.

> But since this movement of self-contemplation alone could not satisfy the Good, the Good must be poured out and go forth beyond itself to multiply the objects of its beneficence. This is essential to the highest Good. That is why God first conceived the heavenly and angelic powers. And this conception was a work fulfilled by his Word and perfected by his Spirit. And so the secondary lights came into being as the servants of the First Light, whether we are to conceive of them as intelligent spirits, or as fire of an immaterial and incorruptible kind, or as some other nature approaching this as near as may be. I should like to say that they were incapable of moving toward evil, and capable only of moving toward good, as being about God and illumined with the first rays from God—for earthly beings have but the second illumination; but I am obliged to stop short of saying that, and to conceive and speak of them as having difficulty in moving in either direction on account of him who for his splendor was called Lucifer, but became and is called darkness through his pride, and the apostate hosts who are subject to him, creatures of evil by their revolt against good and our temptors.

Thus, then, and for these reasons, God gave being to the world of thought, as far as I can reason upon these matters and explain great things in my own poor language. Then when his first creation was in good order, God conceives a second world, material and visible, composed of earth and heaven and all that is in the midst of them—an admirable creation indeed, when we look at the beauty of every part, but yet more worthy of admiration when we consider the harmony and the unison of the whole, and how each part fits in with every other, in fair order, and all with the whole, tending to the perfect completion of the world as a unit. . . . Mind and sense, thus distinguished from each other, had remained within their boundaries, and bore in themselves the magnificence of the Creator-Word, silent praisers and thrilling heralds of his mighty work. There was not yet any mingling of both nor any mixtures of these opposites, tokens of a greater wisdom and generosity in the creation of natures; not as yet were the whole riches of Goodness made known. Now the Creator-Word, determining to exhibit this and to produce a single living being out of both, I mean, the visible and invisible creations, fashioned the man. He took a body from already existing matter and placed in it a breath taken from himself which he knew to be an intelligent soul and the image of God, as a sort of second world. He placed the man, great in littleness, on the earth, a new angel, a composite worshipper, fully inserted into the visible creation but only partially into the intellectual, king upon the earth but subject to the King above, earthly yet heavenly, temporal yet immortal, visible yet intellectual, half-way between greatness and lowliness. In him spirit and flesh are combined into one; spirit, because of the favor bestowed upon him; flesh, because of the height to which he had been raised; spirit, so that he might continue to live and praise his Benefactor; flesh, so that he might suffer, and by suffering he might remember who he is, and corrected if he became proud of his greatness. A living creature trained here, he will be moved elsewhere, and to complete the mystery, deified by his inclination to God. For to this, I think, tends that Light of Truth which we here possess but in measure, that we should both see and experience the Light of God, which is worthy of him who made us and will remake us again in a loftier fashion (*Oration* 38, 9-11).[12]

In the above quotation Gregory explicitly affirms the role of the Logos in the creative act. He is here called the *technitēs logos* (Creator-Word) and elsewhere the *dēmiurgos logos* (*Oration* 32, 10). Further, Gregory affirms that creation is made *ex nihilo* (cf. *Oration* 40, 7). Of special interest, too, is his doctrine of the image of God. Gregory insists, as Athanasius did, that humans are not immediately, but only mediately, the image of God. The original model is the Father, the perfectly similar derived image is the Son, and humans are in their turn the derived image of the Son.

> He (i.e. the Son) is also called the Image, as of one substance with him (i.e. the Father), and because he is of the Father, and not the Father of him. For this is of the nature of an image, to be the reproduction of its archetype, and of that whose name it bears; only that there is more here. For in ordinary parlance an image is a motionless representation of that which has motion; but in this case it is the living reproduction of the living one, and is more exactly like than was Seth to Adam, or any son to his father. For such is the nature of simple existences that it is not correct to say of them that they are like in one aspect and unlike in another; but they are a complete resemblance, and should rather be called identical than like (*Oration* 30, 20).[13]

Gregory applies the technical expression *to kat' eikona* to humans. Preaching on Easter, he says:

> Yesterday I was crucified with him, today I am glorified with him; yesterday I died with him, today I am quickened with him; yesterday I was buried with him, today I rise with him. But let us offer to him who suffered and rose again for us—you will think perhaps that I am going to say gold, or

[12]Text: PG 36.320; trans. NPNF 7.347
[13]Text: SC 250.268; trans. NPNF 7.317

> silver, or woven work, or transparent and costly stones, the
> mere passing material of earth, that remains here below,
> and is for the most part always possessed by bad people,
> slaves of the world and of the Prince of the world. Let us
> offer rather ourselves, the possession most precious to God,
> and most fitting; let us give back to the image *what is made*
> *after the image.* Let us recognize our dignity; let us honor
> our archetype; let us know the power of the mystery, and for
> what Christ died (*Oration* 1, 4).[14]

Again, speaking of the priestly office, and comparing its
healing ministry with that of the physician, Gregory writes:

> But the scope of our art is to provide the soul with wings, to
> rescue it from the world and to give it to God, and to watch
> over *that which is in his image,* if it abides; to take it by the
> hand, if it is in danger; or to restore it, if ruined; to make
> Christ dwell in the heart by the Spirit, in short, to deify and
> bestow heavenly bliss upon the one who belongs to the
> heavenly host (*Oration* 2, 22).[15]

Our kinship to God, then, consists in our being made
according to God's image which Gregory, following the
Alexandrian tradition, locates in our intellectual soul (see the
text from *Oration* 38, 11, given above). This preeminence
given to the soul sometimes led Gregory to speak in disparaging
terms of the body, especially in its fallen condition ("the body
of our humiliation" [*Oration* 2, 91]). Nevertheless, it must be
remembered, for him human dignity stems not from the soul
alone, but from the body as well, or, more precisely, from our
composite nature of body and soul. Our future hope is not to
rid ourselves of the body, but to look for the salvation of "body
and soul" (*Oration* 14, 8). In one passage, Gregory suggests
that the body exercises a pedagogical role in its relation to the
soul, testing it and forcing it to obtain its goal through its own
efforts; and that the soul, on the other hand, has the specific
role of raising the body to a higher level:

[14]Text: SC 247.76; trans. LNPF 7.203
[15]Text: SC 247.118; trans. LNPF 7.209

The other (i.e. the priestly office) is concerned with the soul, which comes from God and is divine, and partakes of the heavenly nobility, and presses on to it, even if it is bound to an inferior nature. Perhaps, indeed, there are other reasons also for this, which only God, who bound them together, and those who are instructed by God in such mysteries, can know; but as far as I, and people like myself can perceive, there are two: one, that it may inherit the heavenly glory by means of a struggle and wrestling with earthly things, being tried as gold in the fire by things below, and gain the objects of our hope as a prize of virtue, and not merely as the gift of God. This, indeed, was the will of Supreme Goodness, to make the good even our own, not only because sown in our nature, but also because cultivated by our own choice, and by the motions of our will, free to act in either direction. The second reason is that it may draw to itself to raise to heaven the lower nature, by gradually freeing it from its grossness, in order that the soul may be to the body what God is to the soul, itself leading on the matter which ministers to it, and uniting it, as its fellow-servant, to God (*Oration* 2, 17).[16]

FREEDOM AND THE FALL

Intimately connected with the concept of dynamic growth of the human person toward God is that of freedom, which Gregory calls, like Origen before him, *autexousia*. This gift was bestowed upon us so that we might perfect our likeness to God through our free choice. Together with this gift God also gave the gift of the Law, so that, as the soul has to work on the body, our free will might have some material upon which to work.

These beings (i.e. the man and the woman) God placed in Paradise, whatever the Paradise may have been, having honored them with the gift of free will in order that God might belong to them as the result of their choice, no less than they to him who has planted the seeds of it. In Paradise

[16]Text: SC 247.112; trans. LNPF 7.208

then were they placed to till the immortal plants, by which is perhaps meant the divine conceptions, both the simpler and the more perfect. Naked they were in their simplicity and inartificial life, and without any covering or screen, for it was fitting that they who were from the beginning should be such. God also gave them a Law, as a material for their free will to act upon. This Law was a commandment as to what plants they might partake of, and which one they might not touch. This latter was the Tree of Knowledge; not, however, because it is evil from the beginning when planted; nor was it forbidden because God grudged it to us.... Let not the enemies of God wag their tongues in that direction, or imitate the Serpent.... But it would have been good if partaken at the proper time, for the tree was, according to my theory, contemplation, upon which it is only safe for those who have reached maturity of habit to enter; but which is not good for those who are still somewhat simple and greedy in their habits; just as solid food is not good for those who are yet tender and have need of milk. But when through the Devil's malice and the woman's caprice, to which she succumbed as the more tender, and which she brought to bear upon the man, as she was the more apt to persuade, alas for my weakness (for that of my first father was mine), he forgot the commandment which had been given to him. He yielded to the baleful fruit; and for his sin he was banished, at once from the Tree of Life, and from Paradise, and from God; and to put on the coats of skins...that is, perhaps, the coarser flesh, both mortal and contradictory. This was the first thing he learnt—his own shame, and he hid himself from God. Yet here too he makes a gain, namely death, and the cutting off of sin, in order that evil may not be immortal. Thus his punishment is changed into a mercy; for it is in mercy, I am convinced, that God inflicts punishments (*Oration* 38, 12).[17]

For Gregory, then, the possibility of humanity's fall lies in the dynamics of human freedom. It was occasioned by the envy of

---

[17]Text: PG 36.324; trans. LNPF 7.348

Satan who had fallen because of his pride: "We were deceived because we were the objects of the Evil One's envy" (*Oration* 45, 28). The substance of Satan's trickery was to make the first parents impatient of waiting to be mature enough of the blessings of knowledge and immortality. It is, as it were, a sin of "prematurity," an idea we have already found in Clement. The result of this fall is threefold: death, interior conflict between the "higher" and "lower" natures in us, and the infection of Adam's descendants with the consequences of the first sin.

The first two results have already been alluded to. As to the third (the *peccatum originale originatum*), though Gregory, out of pastoral concern, avoids assigning the "guilt" of Adam's sin to his children, nevertheless, he clearly affirms the fact that all of us, himself included, participate fully in Adam's sin. He does not explicate, however, the mode of transmission; he simply asserts that humankind as a whole is fallen (cf. *Oration,* 16, 12; 19, 14; 22, 13; 33, 9; 38, 12).

DEIFICATION

Gregory was not interested in describing the fall as such; rather, his concern was to show that God has created us for the purpose of deifying us, the "new creation" or "re-creation" (*anaplasis*) being "more godlike and exalted" than the first (cf. *Oration* 40, 7). No Christian theologian prior to Gregory had used the term *theōsis* and the idea therein expressed with as much consistency and frequency as he did. He urged that the term and concept of *theōsis* are indeed Christian and have nothing to do with pagan parallels of idolatry, cultic imperial apotheosis, polytheism and pantheism. He understood *theōsis* as a process having its first roots in God's creative act, realized by Christ in his incarnation, passion, death and resurrection of Jesus, perfected in the economy of the Holy Spirit, appropriated individually in baptism as well as in ascetic and philanthropic acts and finally consummated in the future life.

Sometimes Gregory describes *theōsis* as an ascent to God. Speaking of solitude he says that it is "the collaborator and mother of the divine ascent and as deifying man" (*Oration* 3, 1).

Whoever has been permitted to escape by reason and contemplation from matter and this fleshly cloud or veil (whichever it should be called) and to hold communion with God, and be associated, as far as human nature is capable, with the purest light, blessed is he, both from his ascent from here and for his deification there, which is conferred by true love of wisdom, and by rising superior to the dualism of matter, through the unity which is perceived in the Trinity (*Oration* 21, 2).[18]

Again, after having described the various titles of Jesus, Gregory urged us to "walk through them":

Walk through them, those that are lofty in a godlike manner; those that belong to the body in a manner suitable to them; or rather, altogether in a godlike manner, that you may become a god, ascending from below, for the sake of him who came down from a high for ours (*Oration* 30, 21).[19]

At other times Gregory conceives *theōsis* as a reflection of God's light and brightness:

God is Light: the highest, the unapproachable, the ineffable, that which can neither be conceived in mind nor uttered with the lips, that which gives life to every reasoning creature. He is in the world of thought what the sun is in the world of sense, presenting himself to our minds in proportion as we are cleansed, and loved in proportion as he is presented to our minds, and again, conceived in proportion as we love him, himself contemplating and comprehending himself, and pouring himself out upon what is external to him.... A second light is the angel, a kind of outflow and communication of that first Light.... A third light is human, a light which is visible to external objects. For they call humans light because of the faculty of speech in us. And the name is applied again to those of us who are more like

[18]Text: SC 270.112; trans. LNPF 7.270
[19]Text: SC 250.274; trans. LNPF 7.317

God and who approach God closer than other (*Oration,* 40, 5).[20]

As reflection of God's light in us, *theōsis* gives us a deeper knowledge of him:

> What God is in nature and essence, no human ever yet has discovered or can discover. Whether it will even be discovered is a question which he who will may examine and decide. In my opinion it will be discovered when that within us which is godlike and divine, I mean our mind and reason, shall have mingled with its like, and the image shall have ascended to the archetype, of which it has now desire...(*Oration,* 28, 17).[21]

Theōsis as proximity to, illumination by, and knowledge of God demands on our part an imitation (*mimēsis*) of Christ and acts of love for the neighbor (*philanthrōpia*). Gregory urges the Christian to imitate Christ:

> Let us accept anything for the sake of the Word. By our sufferings, let us imitate his suffering; by our blood, let us dignify his blood. The nails are sweet, even though painful. For to suffer for and with Christ is more to be desired than a life of ease with others (*Oration* 45, 23).[22]

This attempt to imitate the asceticism of Christ is accompanied by acts of love for the neighbor. Indeed, asceticism is seen by Gregory as a necessary prerequirement for pastoral oversight and not as an end in itself:

> Before one has, as far as possible, risen superior to the passions, has sufficiently purified one's mind, and has surpassed others in nearness to God, I do not see how one could expect to undertake the rule over souls or the role of

[20]Text: PG 36.364; trans. LNPF 7.361
[21]Text: SC 250.134; trans. LNPF 7.294
[22]Text: PG 36.656; trans. LNPF 7.431

mediator between humanity and God; for this, I believe, is what a priest is (*Oration,* 2, 91).[23]

Furthermore, a purification of mind, soul, and body that is not also embodied in philanthropic works is, Gregory suggests, not a "purification" but a "defilement" (*Oration,* 14, 37). Preaching on baptism, he says:

> If, then, you will listen to me, you will bid a long farewell to all such arguments, and you will jump at this blessing and begin to struggle in twofold conflict: first, to prepare yourself for baptism by purifying yourself; and next, to preserve the baptismal gift. Indeed, it is equally difficult to obtain a blessing which we have not, and to keep it when we have gained it. For often what zeal has acquired sloth destroys, and what hesitation has lost diligence regains. Things that will greatly help you attain what you desire are vigils, fasts, sleeping on the ground, prayers, tears, pity and almsgiving to those who are in need. And let these be your thanksgiving for what you have received and at the same time your safeguard of them. You have the benefit to remind you of many commandments; so do not transgress them. Does a poor man approach you? Remember how poor you once were, and how rich you were made. Does one in want of bread or of drink, perhaps another Lazarus, come to your door? Respect the sacramental table to which you have approached, the bread of which you have partaken, the cup in which you have communicated, being consecrated by the sufferings of Christ. If a stranger falls at your feet, homeless and a foreigner, welcome in that person him who for your sake was a stranger.... Does a sick or a wounded man lie before you? Respect your own health and the wounds from which Christ delivered you. Do you see someone naked? Clothe him in honor of your own garment of incorruption, which is Christ, for as many as were baptized into Christ have put on Christ...(*Oration* 40, 31).[24]

[23]Text: SC 247.208; trans. LNPF 7.223
[24]Text: PG 36.401; trans. LNPF 7.371

Though Gregory strongly emphasizes the necessity of ascesis and philanthropy for *theōsis,* which he says is "a prize for virtue" (*Oration,* 2, 17), he is no less aware that it is a gift of God. He insists that ascetic and philanthropic effort is impossible apart from the initial and sustaining grace of God. For him salvation by "works" and salvation by "grace" are not opposites but the obverse sides of a single reality. It is not the question of grace *or* free will, but of grace *and* free will. Gregory himself states that he is attempting to achieve a balance between what is natural to him and what he freely chooses, i.e., between what is given him and what he himself achieves (cf. *Oration* 37, 13 and 20). Elsewhere, after urging the necessity of good works, he warns against the temptation of thinking that these are performed by one's strength:

> If you receive all the Word, you will bring therewith upon your own soul all the healing powers of Christ, with which separately these individuals were healed. Only be not ignorant of the measure of grace; only let not the enemy, while you sleep, maliciously sow tares. Only take care that as by your cleansing you have become an object of enmity to the evil one, you do not again make yourself an object of pity by sin. Only be careful lest, while rejoicing and lifted up above measure by the blessing, you fall again through pride. Only be diligent as to your cleansing, "setting ascensions in your heart" (Ps 84: 6), and keep with all diligence the remission which you have received as a gift, in order that, while the remission comes from God, the preservation of it may come from yourself also (*Oration,* 40, 34).[25]

This *theōsis,* which is both God's gift and a reward for human effort, Gregory attributes specifically to the Holy Spirit. It is well known that Gregory did not hesitate, as Basil did, to give a clear and formal expression of the divinity of the Spirit: "Is the Spirit God? Most certainly. Well, then, is he consubstantial (*homoousios*)? Yes, if he is God" (*Oration,* 31, 30). The divinity of the Holy Spirit is, however, linked with his work of deification:

[25]Text: PG 36.408; trans. LNPF 7.372

If the Spirit is of the same order or creation as myself, how
can he deify me or join me to the Godhead? (*Oration* 34, 4).
If the Holy Spirit is not God, let him first be deified, and
then let him deify me his equal! (*Oration* 34, 12).[26]

III. Gregory of Nyssa (c. 330-c. 395)

Of the three Cappadocians, Gregory of Nyssa is certainly
the most gifted speculative theologian and mystic and the most
versatile and successful writer. Made bishop of Nyssa by his
brother Basil, he was deposed from his see by a synod of Arian
bishops in 376 but returned to it in 378 after the death of the
Arian emperor, Valens, In 381 he took a prominent part in the
council of Constantinople side by side with Gregory of
Nazianzus.

Gregory's thought has been described as prismatic rather
than systematic. That is to say, though he possesses a relatively
coherent understanding of the Christian revelation, he tends in
his writings to treat a single theme in all its manifold aspects on
the basis of his profound knowledge of Scripture and of
neo-Platonic and Stoic philosophies in such a way that it is
intimately linked with and reflects the other central themes of
his thought. Gregory's anthropology involves and presupposes,
therefore, his theology of the Trinity, his christology, his
pneumatology, his conception of the triple character of
Christian life as moral, intellectual, and spiritual, his mystical
doctrine of contemplation and "epectasy," and his vision of the
transfigured physical universe.

Among Gregory's numerous writings, two are of topical
interest here. First, his *Great Catechetical Discourse,* composed
about 385, is a compendium of Christian doctrine on the scale
of Origen's *De Principiis.* On the basis of Scripture as well as of
metaphysics, Gregory expounds in chapters 1-4 the doctrine of
the one God in three persons, the consubstantiality of the Son
and the divinity of the Holy Spirit. The second part of this
book, chapters 5-7, discusses the creation of humanity, the

[26]Text: PG 36.252; trans. NPNF, Second Series 2,7. 337

nature of evil and the fall. In the third part, chapters 8-32, Gregory treats of the restoration of humankind, the Incarnation and atonement. In the last part, chapters 33-40, he deals with baptism, eucharist, faith, and repentance.

The other work is *On the Making of Humankind,* written about 379, intended to complete the unfinished homilies of Basil on the *Hexaemeron.* Here Gregory deals extensively with humanity's original state and with the doctrine of the resurrection. In our exposition of Gregory's anthropology we shall give preeminence to his doctrine of the image of God in us. It is the foundation of his teaching not only on the intuition of God but also on the mystical ascent of humanity.

THE CREATION OF HUMANITY IN GOD'S IMAGE

Gregory of Nyssa's approach to the doctrine of creation is closely akin to that of the Alexandrians and to the Platonic and Philonic idea of creation. He accepts, for instance, the teaching that the participation in the Logos is the motive of creation (cf. *Great Catechetical Discourse,* 5), the doctrine of the double creation (cf. *ibid.,* 6) and that of the generic sexlessness of primordial human beings (*On the Making of Humankind,* 16, 7-8). The first creation consisted in the production of the ideal or archetypal humanity, in the platonic sense, perfect and without sexual differentiation, comprising in itself all possible men and women. It was because God foresaw that, being creaturely and therefore mutable, humanity would sin, that he divided it, by a second creative act, into male and female, thus inaugurating the present human race.

Central, however, to Gregory's anthropology is his insistence on the biblical teaching that humans are created in God's image and likeness. Contrary to most of his predecessors Gregory does not sharply distinguish between "image" (*eikōn*) and "likeness" (*homoiōsis*). These are seen rather as two aspects of the one human being: the likeness is the result of an effort to imitate the original according to the exigencies of the image that God has placed in us as a rough draft to be perfected. The image becomes "beastly" or "demonic" if we turn away from God, or it becomes "divine" if we submit ourselves to him. The image and likeness are only temporarily distinct; in the perfect in this world and in heaven in the resurrection they coincide with one another. They should not be interpreted as indicating two different orders of reality, *eikōn* the natural likeness to God by reason, and *homoiōsis* the supernatural likeness to God by grace. In Gregory, *eikōn* is already the divine perfection which God shares with humanity and which *homoiōsis* attempts to achieve.

The image indicates both similitude and dissimilitude. Insofar as the image "participates" in the original, it is similar to it. While all beings, even infrahuman beings, "participate" in God, only humans are made "according to the image of God." On the other hand, there is also dissimilarity between the original and the image. For Gregory, this dissimilarity consists, not in the attributes of Being and beings—these are the same— but in their modes of existing: uncreated in God and created in humans. God is Being, Goodness, and Life by nature, whereas humans, being made in his image, are existent, good, and alive, not by nature, but by participation in God. There is, however, one unique exception in which the image and the archetype coincide so that all essential differences between them are excluded and that they are distinguished from one another only as the opposed terms of a subsistent relation. Gregory refers, of course, to the Son as image of the Father.

Because humans participate in God as the image in the archetype, there exist certain links between them. Participation produces kinship (*suggeneia*), kinship is the ground for knowledge, knowledge leads to desire, and desire is consummated in love.

The following quotations contain some of the elements of Gregory's anthropology as expounded above.

> If anyone wants to call him Word, or Wisdom, or Power, or God, or any other sublime or dignified title, we will not quarrel with him. For whatever word or name is invented to describe this subject, one thing is intended by the expressions, namely the eternal power of God, which creates things that are, discovers the things that are not, sustains things that are brought into being, and foresees things that are yet to be. This, then, is the gist of our argument: that he

who is God the Word, and Wisdom, and Power created human nature. He was not, indeed, driven by any necessity to create humankind; but out of his abundant love he fashioned and created such a creature. For it was not right that his light should remain unseen, or his glory unwitnessed, or his goodness unenjoyed, or any other attribute observed in the divine nature should lie idle with no one to share or enjoy it.

If, then, humans come into being for these reasons, that is, to participate in the divine goodness, they had to be fashioned in such a way as to be adapted to share in this goodness. For just as the eye shares in the light by virtue of the brightness inherent in it, and by this innate power attracts what is akin to itself, so something akin to the divine had to be mingled with human nature. In this way the eye desires for something corresponding to what is native in it. Even the natures of irrational creatures, whose lot is to live in water or air, are fashioned to correspond with their mode of life. Each of them has an organization adapted to its kind of life, so that by a peculiar formation of their bodies, one would find the air, the other water, appropriate and congenial to them. In the same way, human beings, who were created to enjoy God's goodness, had to have some element in their nature akin to what they were to share. Hence they were endowed with life, reason, wisdom, and all the good things of God, so that by each of these they might have their desire set upon that which is not unnatural to them. And since immortality is one of the good attributes of the divine nature, it was essential that the constitution of our nature should not be deprived of it. It had to be immortal so that, by its inherent faculty, it might both recognize what is transcendent to it and desire God's divine and eternal life.

The account of creation sums all this up in a single expression when it says that humans were created "in the image of God." For in this likeness, implied in the word "image," there is a summary of all things that characterize divinity; and whatever Moses relates by way of a narrative, presenting doctrines in a form of a story, expresses the same teaching. For the Paradise he mentions, with its peculiar fruits, the eating of which does not satisfy the appetites but grants to those who taste of them knowledge and eternal life—all this corresponds to what we have been saying about humans, how our nature in its origin was good and set in the midst of goodness...(*Great Catechetical Discourse,* 5).[27]

In what then does the greatness of humans consist, according to the teaching of the Church? Not in their likeness to the created world, but in their being in the image of the nature of the Creator.

How, then, you will perhaps ask, is "image" defined? How is the incorporeal likened to the corporeal? How is the temporal likened to the eternal? The mutable to the immutable? The passible and corruptible to the impassible and incorruptible? That which constantly dwells with evil and grows up with it to that which is absolutely free of evil? There is a great difference between that which is conceived in the archetype, and a thing which has been made in its image. The image is properly so called if it keeps its resemblance to the prototype. If, however, the imitation is perverted from its original, the thing is something else and no longer an image of the original.

How then can human beings, who are mortal, passible and shortlived, be the image of that nature which is immortal, pure and eternal? The true answer to this question, indeed, perhaps only the very Truth knows; but this is what we understand concerning the matter in our effort to discover the truth as far as possible by conjectures and inferences. Neither does the word of God lie when it says that humans were made in the image of God, nor is the pitiable suffering of human nature like to the blessedness of the impassible life. Were anyone to compare our nature with God, one of the following two things must be acknowledged if the definition of the likeness is to be apprehended in both cases in the same terms: either the Deity is passible, or humanity is impassible. But if neither the Deity is passible nor our nature free from passion, what other account remains whereby we may say that the word of God speaks truly, which says that humans were made in the image of God?

[27]Text: PG 45.21; trans. LNPF, Second Series, 5.478-1479

We must, then, take up once more the Holy Scripture itself, if we wish to find some guidance in the question by means of what is written. After saying, "Let us make humankind in our image," and explaining the purpose for which it was said, "Let us make him," Scripture adds: "and God created humankind; in the image of God he created it; male and female he created them." We have already said above that this saying was uttered to destroy heretical impiety, so that with the knowledge that the Only-begotten God made man in the image of God, we should never distinguish the Godhead of the Father and the Son, since Holy Scripture gives to each equally the name of God, to him who made man and to him in whose image he was made.

However, let us leave aside our discussion of this topic and turn attention to the issue before us: How it is that while the Deity is in bliss and humanity is in misery, the latter is yet in Scripture called "like" the former?

We must examine the words carefully. If we do so, we will find that which was made "in the image" is one thing, and that which is now manifested in wretchedness is another. "God created humankind," it says; "in the image of God he created it." There ends the creation of that which was made "in the image." Then Scripture resumes the account of creation and says, "male and female he created them." I presume that everyone knows that this is a departure from the prototype. For, "in Christ Jesus," as the Apostle says, "there is neither male nor female." The quotation then declares that humankind is divided.

Thus the creation of our nature is in a sense double: one made like to God, the other divided according to this distinction. This is something obscurely conveyed by the passage with its arrangement where it first says, "God created humankind, in the image of God he created it," and then, adding to what has been said, "male and female he created them,"—a thing which is alien from our conception of God. I think that by these words Holy Scripture conveys to us a great and lofty doctrine; and the doctrine is this. While two natures—the divine and incorporeal nature and the irrational life of brutes—are separated from each other as extremes, human nature is the mean between them. In the composite nature of human beings we may behold a part of each of the natures I have mentioned: First, the divine, rational and intelligent element, which does not admit the distinction of male and female; secondly, the irrational, which constitutes our bodily form and structure and is divided into male and female. Such a division is in fact found in all that partakes of human life...(*On the Making of Humankind,* 16, 2-9).[28]

Gregory goes on to affirm that God brought humans into being "from nothing" and that God's purpose in creating is no other than to share with them all his attributes: "The language of Scripture therefore expresses it concisely by a comprehensive phrase which says that humans were made "in the image of God": for this is the same as to say that he made human nature participant in all his goodness; for if the Deity is the fullness of God, and this is his image, then the image finds its resemblance to the Archetype in being filled with all good" (*ibid.,* 16, 10). This participation in all the attributes of God, Gregory is careful to point out, does not imply any pantheism, since there remains an ontological difference between God and humans, between the uncreated and the created:

Thus there is in us the principle of all excellence, all virtue and wisdom and every higher thing that we conceive. However, preeminent among all is the fact that we are free from necessity and not in bondage to any natural power, but have decision in our own power as we please. Virtue, in fact, is a voluntary thing, subject to no dominion; that which is the result of compulsion and force cannot be virtue. Now the image bears in all points the semblance of the excellence of the archetype. But if it does not differ from the archetype in some respects and in no way diverges from it, it will no longer be a likeness but will obviously be absolutely identical with the archetype. What difference then is there between the divine and that which has been made divine later? It consists in the fact that the former is uncreated,

28Text: PG 44; trans. LNPF Second Series, 5.404-405

while the latter derives its being from creation. This distinction of property brings with it a train of other properties; for it is very certainly acknowledged that the uncreated nature is also immutable and always remains the same, while the created nature cannot exist without change. The latter's very passage from non-existence to existence is a certain motion and change of the non-existent transmuted by the divine purpose into being.

As the Gospel calls the stamp upon the coin "the image of Caesar" (Mt 22: 20), whereby we learn that in that which was fashioned to resemble Caesar there was resemblance as to external appearance but difference as to material, so also in the present saying, when we consider the attributes contemplated both in the divine and human natures, we find that the likeness consists in the attributes participated and the difference in their modes of being which are uncreated, on the one hand, and created, on the other (*ibid.,* 16, 11-13).[29]

As a result of this ontological distinction, Gregory emphasizes that whereas God is by essential identity his own perfections, and hence is simple, infinite, immutable, and eternal, humans possess their perfections by participation and hence are composite, finite, mutable and temporal.

In summary, Gregory of Nyssa's entire anthropology is recapitulated in the famous biblical expression: "Humans are made in God's image." For Gregory this means not only that humans possess a complex of attributes that make them similiar to God, but also that all the divine attributes are found in them, of course, in the created mode. This divine image does not, however, reside in their body. Indeed, Gregory explicitly affirms in his first homily, "On these words: Let us make man in our image. . . . "; "It is not in the form of the body that the likeness resides" (*hōti ouk ekhomēn to kat' eikona ēn morphē sōmatos,* PG, 44, 261 C). Strictly speaking, only the soul is in the image of God, but its nobility overflows onto the body insofar as it is the instrument of the soul. In virtue of this

[29]Text: PG 44; trans. LNPF Second Series, 5.405-406

image, humans share in the divine intelligence and Word (*nous kai logos*), they become *logikoi,* which means not "reasonable" but "participating in the Word." Thus, human beings are both and at the same time "natural" and "supernatural"—the latter by participation and not by nature, human nature being, says Gregory "both divine and intellectual" (*theia te kai noera ousia: On Infants' Early Death,* PG, 46, 172 D, 173 B). Finally, by virtue of this participation, humans are given to rule over the rest of creation, are endowed with freedom, tend toward God in love, and are made immortal.

THE FALL AND THE GARMENTS OF SKIN

This description of humanity as made in God's image sounds highly optimistic and seems not to correspond to the real condition of humanity as we know it. Hence, one may ask: "Where is the soul's likeness to God? Where is the body's freedom from suffering? Where is eternal life? Human life is fleeting, subject to passion, mortal, liable in soul and body to every type of suffering" (*The Great Catechetical Discourse,* 5). In reply Gregory affirms that the present condition was not intended by God in the beginning but is the result of human fall. The ultimate ground of this fall is human freedom. Since all created things are by nature changeable, it follows that created freedom could separate itself from God.

> The fact that human life is at present in an unnatural condition is no proof that humanity was never created in a state of goodness. For since humans are a work of God, who out of his goodness brought them into being, one cannot rightly suppose that he was made by their Creator in the state of evil. For their nature was created in goodness. Therefore the cause of our present condition and of our being deprived of our original surroundings is to be sought elsewhere. Here again the premise of our argument is not something with which our opponents will disagree. He who made humans to share in his own goodness and incorporated in them the instincts for everything that was excellent, in order that their desires, in each case, correspond to that to

which they were directed, would not have deprived them of the most excellent and precious of blessings, namely the gift of liberty and free will. For were human life governed by necessity, the "image" would be falsified in that respect and so differ from the archetype. For how can a nature which is under a yoke and bondage to any kind of necessity be called an image of a Supreme Being? What, therefore, is in every respect made similar to the divine, must certainly possess free will and liberty by nature, so that participation in the good may be the reward for virtue.

But, you will ask, whence comes it that he who had been distinguished throughout with the most excellent endowments exchange these good things for the worse? The answer to this, too, is clear. Evil does not originate in the divine will. For no blame, indeed, would be attached to vice if evil could claim God as its creator and father. But evil is, in some way or other, engendered from within, springing up in the will at that moment when the soul withdraws from the good. For as sight is an activity of nature, and blindness a deprivation of that natural operation, such is the kind of opposition between virtue and vice. It is, in fact, impossible to conceive of the origin of vice than as the absence of virtue. Just as in the removal of light darkness follows and never appears as long as light remains, so as long as goodness is present in a nature, evil does not exist. But when there is a withdrawal from the good, its opposite supervenes. Since, then, it is the mark of free will to choose as it likes the thing that pleases it, God is not the author of your present evils, for he made your nature independent and free. The cause is rather your thoughtlessness in choosing the worse instead of the better (*The Great Catechetical Discourse,* 5).[30]

The remote cause of the fall is, therefore, human freedom in its changeable nature. Its proximate cause, Gregory suggests, is the jealousy of the angel to whom the universe had been entrusted, and who resented that God had produced in his realm human beings, "a blending of the intelligible and the

---

[30]Text: PG 45.24; trans. LNPF Second Series, 5.479-480

sensible . . . the earthly being raised to union with the divine, and a single grace equally extending through all creation. . . ." (*ibid.*, 6).

When the intelligible creation was already in existence, and the authority which governs all things had assigned a certain activity in connection with the framing of the universe to each of the angelic powers, one of them was appointed to maintain and take charge of the region of the earth. He was equipped for this very purpose by the power that rules the universe. Then there was created that being formed of earth, which was an image of the power above; and this creature was the human being. In him was the divine excellence of the intelligible nature, an excellence blended with a certain ineffable power. In consequence, that angelic power, to whom the governance of the earth had been assigned, took it amiss as something insufferable that, out of the nature subject to him, there should be produced a being bearing likeness to the transcendent dignity. . . .

Uncreated nature is incapable of the movement implied in mutability, change, and variation, while everything that exists through creation has an innate tendency to change. For the very existence of creation had its origin in change, non-being becoming being by divine power. Now that angelic power we have already mentioned was created, and by the movement of his own free will chose whatever he liked. But when he closed his eyes to the good and the generous, that power, by his unwillingness to acknowledge the good, contrived its opposite, just as one only sees darkness when one closes the eyelids in sunlight. That is how envy arose. . . .

When he saw that humans, empowered by God's blessing, have been elevated to a lofty position—for they were appointed to rule over the earth and all the creatures on it; their form was beautiful, being created as the image of the archetypal beauty; by nature they were free from passion, being a copy of him who is without passion; they were full of candor, revelling in the direct vision of God—all this was to the adversary the fuel to his passion of envy. But he could not fulfill his purpose by force or violence, for the power of

God's blessing was superior to his own force. For this reason his plan was to withdraw humans from this enabling force and so render them an easy prey to his treachery. As in a lamp, when the flame has caught the wick too much and one is unable to blow it out, one mixes water with oil and by this means dims the flame, so, in the same way, the enemy, by craftily mixing up evil with the human will, in some measure quenched and obscured God's blessing. When this failed, the opposite necessarily enters. Now the opposite of life is death; of power, weakness; of blessing, curse; of candor, shame; and of every good thing, its contrary. That is why humanity is in its present plight; for that beginning provided the occasion for such a conclusion (*ibid.,* 6).[31]

But, one may object, why did God create humanity when he foresaw the disaster that would result from this thoughtlessness? Gregory answers that as humans turned away from God, they were deprived of immortality and were clad in the garment of skin. This garment, though in itself a punishment, was intended by God as a remedy. In his work *On the Dead,* Gregory explains that the garment of skin allows humans to turn back again freely to God. This garment would cause them to experience a disgust with the things of the world and thus "would willingly desire to return to their former blessedness" (PG, 46, 524 B). In the *Great Catechetical Discourse* Gregory proposes another reason for the garment of skins. Symbolizing our present state of mortality, it permits the human body to be destroyed, and since evil is so closely bound with the body, evil too is destroyed, and thus humanity is restored to its original innocence.

It was by a movement of free will that we became associated with evil. Owing to some sensual gratification we mingled evil with our nature, like some deadly drug sweetened with honey. So, falling away from that blessedness we think of as freedom from passion, we have been transformed into evil. For this reason humans, like a clay pot, are again resolved into the dust of the ground in order that, when once they

---

[31]Text: PG 45.25; trans. LNPF Second Series, 5.480-481

have been separated from the filth now attaching to them, they may be refashioned after the original pattern through the resurrection, at least if in the present life they have preserved what belongs to that image.

A doctrine such as this is expounded by Moses by way of a story and in a veiled manner. But what the veiled allegories teach is quite plain. For after, as he tells us, the first human beings were implicated in things forbidden and were stripped naked of blessedness, the Lord clothed his first creatures with coats of skins. In my opinion we are not bound to take the expression "coats of skins" literally. For to what sort of animals, when slain and flayed, did this covering fabricated for them belong? But since every skin taken from an animal is a dead thing, I am sure the skins mean the attribute of death, which is the special characteristic of the brute creation. In his care for humans, he who heals our wickedness subsequently provided them with the capacity to die, but not to die permanently. For a coat is an external covering for us. The body is given the opportunity to use it for a while, but it is not an essential part of its nature.

Mortality, then, taken from the brute creation, provisionally clothed the nature created for immortality. It enveloped his outward, but not his inward, nature. It affected the sentient part of human nature, but not the divine image. The sentient part, to be sure, is dissolved, but is not destroyed. For destruction means passing into non-being, while dissolution means separation once more into those elements of the world from which something was constituted. When this happens, it does not perish, even if we cannot grasp this with our senses. . . . We can illustrate the point as follows. Suppose that some vessel has been composed of clay, and then, for some mischief or other, filled with molten lead, which has hardened and cannot be poured out. Suppose, too, the owner recovers the vessel and, being skilled in ceramics, he pounds to pieces the clay surrounding the lead. He then remolds the vessel, now rid of the intruding matter, into its former shape and for his own use. In the same way, the Creator of our vessel, I mean our sentient and bodily nature, when it became mingled with evil, dissolved the material which contained the evil. And then, once it has been freed from its opposite, he will remold it by the resurrection, and will reconstitute the vessel into its original beauty. . . . To thoughtless people this (mortality) is a threat and a harsh means of correction, so that by fear of a painful retribution we may be brought to our senses and flee evil. The more thoughtful, however, believe it to be a healing remedy provided by God, who thus restores his own creation to its original grace. . .(*The Great Catechetical Discourse,* 8).[32]

THE UNIVERSAL RESTORATION

Subjection to change, Gregory of Nyssa has suggested, especially in freedom, is the remote cause of the human fall. This change or motion is characteristic of the biological world; it is cyclic, repetitious, insubstantial and illusory. It is movement without progress, motion which is in reality immobility.

But there is another kind of movement which is a perpetual growth in good, a state of perfection. Perfection is constituted by progress itself.

For humans do not merely have an inclination to evil; were this so, it would be impossible for them to grow in good, if their nature possessed only an inclination toward the contrary. But in truth the finest aspect of our mutability is the possibility of growth in good; and this capacity for improvement transforms the soul, as it changes, more and more into the divine. And so. . . what appears so terrifying, I mean the mutability of our nature, can really be a wing in our flight toward higher things, and indeed it would be a hardship if we were not susceptible of the sort of change which is toward the better. One ought not, then, to be distressed when one considers this tendency in our nature; rather let us change in such a way that we may constantly evolve toward what is better, being transformed from glory to glory, and thus always improving and ever becoming more perfect by daily growth, and never arriving at any limit of perfection. For that perfection consists in our never stopping in our growth in good, never circumscribing our perfection by any limitation (*On Perfection*).[33]

We arrive here at a striking paradox: permanence in good is the very principle of authentic change. This kind of permanence constitutes unceasing movement. This doctrine of perpetual ascent (*"epectasis,"* tension, expansion) is one of the foundational ideas of Gregory's anthropology and spirituality. "The perfection of human nature," says he, "consists perhaps in its very growth in goodness" (*The Life of Moses,* I, 10). He later dedicates a long section of the book (II, 219-248) to develop this doctrine of perpetual progress.

> ...Bodies, once they have received the initial thrust downward, are carried downward by themselves with greater speed without any additional contact, provided that the surface on which they move is graded and sloping, and that they meet no obstacle to interrupt their motion. So too, the soul moves in the opposite direction. Once it is released from its sensuous and earthly attachments, it moves swiftly upward, soaring from the world below up toward the heavens. And if nothing comes from above to intercept its flight, for the nature of the good attracts to itself those who look to it, the soul keeps rising even higher and higher, stretching with its desire for heavenly things, straining ahead for what is still to come (cf. Phil 3: 13), as the Apostle tells us, and thus it will always continue to soar even higher. Made to desire and not to abandon the heights that lie beyond it, the soul moves ceaselessly upward, always reviving its tension for its onward flight by means of the progress it has already realized. Indeed, activity directed toward virtue causes its capacity to grow through exertion; it does not slacken its tension by action but rather increases it. This is the reason why we say that the great Moses, moving ever forward, did not stop his ascent nor did he set a

---

[33]Text: PG 66.285 B.C.; trans of H. Musurillo, *From Glory to Glory, Gregory of Nyssa's Mystical Writings,* 83-84

limit in his upward course. But once he had put his foot upon the ladder on which the Lord had leaned, as Jacob tells us, he continually climbed to the step above and never ceased to rise higher, because he always found a step higher than the one he had reached (*The Life of Moses,* II, 224-227).[34]

Commenting on the famous text Phil 3: 13, in which the word *epecteinomenos* occurs, Gregory says that what Paul intends to teach is that "the graces we receive at every point are indeed great, but the path that lies beyond our immediate grasp is infinite" and that those who share in the divine goodness "will always enjoy a greater and greater participation in grace throughout eternity" (PG, 44, 940 C - 941 C).

Thus Gregory comes to speak of a paradox: the identity between motion and stability:

> Here we have a very great paradox: motion and stability are identical. For usually speaking, one who is rising is not standing still, and the one who is standing still is not rising. But here the ascent takes place by means of the standing still. By this I mean that the firmer and more immovable one remains in the Good, the more one progresses in the course of virtue. . . . It is like people who try to climb uphill in sand. Even though they take long strides, their footing in the sand always slips downhill, so that, although there is much motion, no progress results from it. But if, in the words of the psalmist, a person drags his feet from the mire of the pit and sets them firmly upon the rock, . . . the more steadfast and unshakeable he becomes in good, so much the more quickly he will finish his course. His very stability becomes a wing in his flight toward heaven; his heart becomes winged because of his stability in good (*The Life of Moses,* II, 243-244).[35]

---

[34]Text: SCI ter, 260; trans. *Gregory of Nyssa, From Glory to Glory*, H. Musurillo, 57-58

[35]Text: SCI ter, 272; trans. cf. Malherbe/ Ferguson, 117-118

The "wing" refers to the transformation into Spirit, into the Dove; it becomes a new principle of activity, a new step in the soul's never-ceasing movement upward from glory to glory.

> Participation in the divine good is such that, where it occurs, it makes the participant even greater and more spacious than before, bringing to it an increase in size and strength, in such wise that the participant, nourished in this way, never stops growing and keeps becoming larger and larger. Indeed, as the source of good keeps flowing and welling up without end, so too the participant, as it becomes larger, grows more and more in desire, by the fact that nothing that it receives is lost or left unused, and everything that flows in produces an increase in capacity (*On the Soul and Resurrection*).[36]

This movement and growth does not however occur in the individual soul only; for Gregory, it will happen to humanity as a whole, humanity in its fullness (*plērōma*). The divinization of humanity has already occurred in time with the Incarnation of the Logos, but it will be fulfilled in the general resurrection. For Gregory of Nyssa, there can be no eternal hell. The victory of good would not be complete, the image would not be restored, the body of Christ would not be whole, Christ's face would not be radiant, God would not be all in all, if human beings persist, eternally, in their sin. Gregory sees in the *apocatastasis* the magnificent ending of the entire history of salvation, when every creature will give thanks to the Savior and when the "author of evil" will be healed.

> When after long periods of time, the evil of our nature, which is now mixed up with it and has grown with its growth, has been expelled, and when there has been a restoration of those who are now lying in sin to the original state, a hymn of thanksgiving will arise from all creation, from those who in the process of purification have suffered chastisement as well as from those who needed no

---

[36]Text: PG 46.105; trans. FOTC 58.244

purification at all. This is the sort of teaching we derive from the mighty revelation of God's Incarnation. By his intimate union with humanity, he shared all the marks of our nature. He was born, reared, grew up, and went so far as even to taste death. Thus he brought about all we have mentioned. He freed humanity from evil, and healed the very author of evil himself (*The Great Catechetical Discourse,* 26).[37]

[37]Text: PG 45.69; trans. NPNF Second Series, 5.496

7

Antiochene Anthropology:
John Chrysostom

In the third, fifth and sixth chapters we have expounded what may be loosely called Alexandrian anthropology. Though these Fathers—Clement, Origen, Athanasius, the Cappadocians and Cyril—did not form a theological school in the strict sense of the term, there is no doubt that, despite their differences, they all shared the same philosophical and cultural background, largely Platonic and Neo-Platonic, the same allegorical method of biblical interpretation, and at times consciously adopted certain concepts and themes of their predecessors' anthropologies.

In this chapter we will turn our attention to the writers of the other equally famous, if less influential, theological school, that of Antioch in Syria. The Church of Antioch, where the disciples of Christ were first called 'Christians' (Acts 11: 26), could boast of such great martyrs as Ignatius and, from the fourth century, ranked after Rome and Alexandria as the third patriarchal see of Christendom. Lucian, who was martyred in 312, founded a theological school there which in time rivalled that of Alexandria. In contrast to the latter, the school of Antioch favored a literal interpretation of the Scripture and an historical and grammatical study of its sense.

The Antiochene tradition is seen in heretics and orthodox alike. Among the former are found Arius and Eusebius of Nicodemia, who both inherited subordinationist ideas from their teacher Lucian, as well as Apollinaris of Laodicea and Nestorius. Among the orthodox, we find Diodore of Tarsus, his disciples Theodore of Mopsuestia and John Chrysostom, and Theodoret of Cyrus, though Diodore, Theodore and Theodoret were later condemned as heretics, the first in 499, the second and the third in 553. Of all Antiochene theologians there is no doubt that John Chrysostom was the greatest, or at least the most prolific, author.

After having discharged for twelve years (386-398) his preaching duty in the principal church of Antioch with such zeal and success that he earned the title of the "Golden Mouth," John was chosen to succeed Nectarius as patriarch of Constantinople. The appointment to the see of the imperial capital proved to be his greatest misfortune. His lack of political astuteness, his forthright character, and his over-zealous plan of reform for the clergy and laity, coupled with the jealousy of his episcopal colleagues, in particular Theophilus of Alexandria, and the hatred of the empress Eudoxia, brought him exiled first to Bithynia (from which he was recalled on the following day) and then to Pityus, a wild spot on the eastern end of the Black Sea. Forced to travel on foot in severe weather, Chrysostom died at Comana in Pontus before reaching his destination.

Among the Greek Fathers none has left so extensive a literary legacy as Chrysostom, which, fortunately, is well preserved. Though he wrote some treatises on practical matters (the most famous of which is the treatise *On the Priesthood*) and a great number of letters (236 letters are extant), most of his works are in sermon form. For our theme, two exegetical homilies are of interest, namely *Homilies on Genesis* and *Homilies on Romans*. In addition, of special importance are the *Eight Baptismal Catecheses* discovered in 1955 by A. Wenger and published as Volume 50 in the *Sources chrétiennes* series.

I. Creation and the Fall

The first series of homilies on Genesis (*Nine Homilies on Genesis* [PG 54, 581-630]) were delivered at Antioch during Lent 386. Except the last, all of the homilies deal with the first three chapters of Genesis. Chrysostom takes notice of the plural form of the verb "let us create" in Gen 1: 26 and understands it to refer to a dialogue between the Father and his Word. The man is created in the image of God and the woman is in the image of the man; both are in God's image by reason of their soul. In virtue of their being in God's image, humans are the masters of the animal kingdom and of the whole earth. Chrysostom did not interpret the two accounts of creation in the manner of Philo and other Alexandrians as a double creation; for him the second account simply repeats the first account and makes it more precise.

> So who is this to whom he says, "Let us make a human being?" Who else is it than the Angel of Great Counsel, Wonderful Counsellor, Figure of Authority, Prince of Peace, Father of the age to come, Only-begotten Son of God, like the Father in being, through whom all things were created? To him is said, "Let us make humankind in our image and likeness." This text also deals a mortal blow to those entertaining the position of Arius. I mean, he did not say by way of command, "Make such a creature," as though to a subordinate or to one inferior in being, but, "Let us make," with great deference to an equal. And what follows shows us further the equality in being; it says, you see, "Let us make humankind in our image and likeness." Here again, however, other heretics arise assailing the dogmas of the Church; they say, Look: he said, "In our image"—and from these words they want to speak of the divine in human terms, which is the ultimate example of error, namely, to cast in human form him who is without shape, without appearance, without change and to attribute limbs and forms to the one who has no body. What could match this madness, people not simply refusing to derive any profit from the teaching of the inspired Scriptures, but even incurring severe harm from them? I mean, they are in a similar predicament as people who are ill and suffering impairment of their bodily vision: just as the latter have a revulsion for the sunlight on account of their weakness of vision and invalids turn away from the healthier foods, so too those ailing in spirit and handicapped in their mind's vision have lost the power to look directly at the light of truth.

So let us do for them what lies in our power and offer them a helping hand, conversing with them in a spirit of great kindness. Blessed Paul, after all, encouraged us to do this when he said, "Instruct your adversaries with gentleness, in the hope that God will grant them a change of heart leading to knowledge of truth, and they may return to a sober mind and escape from the snare of the devil, by whom they were held as captives at his pleasure." Do you see how he declared in the words he chose that they were overcome, as it were, by some drunken stupor? To say, "Return to a sober mind," after all, suggested they were in a state of intoxication. Likewise he says, "held captive by the devil," as though to say they are ensnared in traps. What is required of us is much kindness and tolerance so as to be able to rescue them and lead them out of the devil's snares. So let us say to them, "Make your escape slowly but surely, look towards the light of righteousness, study the precision of the words." You see, in saying, "Let us make humankind in our image and likeness," he did not stop there, but through the following verse made clear to us what was the reason for choosing the word "image." What in fact does the text go on to say? "Let them have control of the fish of the sea, the birds of heaven, and all the reptiles creeping on the earth." So "image" refers to the matter of control, not anything else; in other words, God created the human being as having control of everything on earth, and nothing on earth is greater than the human being, under whose authority everything falls (*Nine Homilies on Genesis*, 8: 8-9).[1]

Chrysostom goes on to describe the fall, first of Eve and then of Adam:

But acting impetuously—how, I know not— she got involved in conversation with the serpent and through him as through an instrument she took in the devil's deadly words; so it ensued that she learned from the devil's speech the very opposite to the words' real sense, and that whereas

---

[1] Text: PG 54; trans. FOTC 74.109-110, R.C. Hill

the Creator gave one set of directions, the devil said the opposite. . . . In fact, through her grave negligence she not only failed to turn away but revealed the whole secret of the Lord's direction, thus casting pearls before swine and fulfilling what was said by Christ: "Don't cast your pearls before swine, lest they trample them underfoot, turn on you and tear you to pieces," as in fact happened in this case. I mean, she exposed herself to swine, to that evil beast, that is, to the demon acting through it, the divine pearls; he not only trampled on them and opposed them with his words, but turned and led into the rupture of disobedience not only her but also the first-formed man with her. Such is the evil of idly and casually exposing to all and sundry the divine mysteries. Let those give heed who idly and indiscriminately open their mouths to everyone. . . .

Let us, however, listen to what she says to him in reply. That is, when he said, "Why is it that God said, Do not eat of any tree of the garden?" the woman replied to the serpent, "We do eat of every tree of the garden; but of the fruit of the tree in the middle of the garden God said, Do not eat or even touch it in case you die." Do you see his malice? He said what was not the case so as to entice her into conversation with him and thus learn what was the case. The woman, you see, is evidently encouraged as though he were kindly disposed to her, and she reveals the whole of the instruction, tells him all in detail, and by her reply deprives herself of any excuse. I mean, what could you say in your defense, woman? "God said, Do not eat of any tree in the garden." You ought to have turned away from the speaker and said to him, "Be off, you are a cheat, you do not know the force of the direction given us, nor the extent of the enjoyment we have, nor the abundance of good things given us. For your part you said God has told us to taste nothing of any tree, whereas out of his great goodness the Lord and Creator has permitted us enjoyment and control of them all, bidding us keep away only from one, and this likewise out of great care for us lest we taste it and die." You should, had you been in your right mind, have addressed these words to him, turned away from him utterly, and have had nothing to do with him and not listened to anything said by him. . . .

Well and good, then: so you cast yourself into such an abyss and robbed yourself of your pre-eminent dignity. Why did you make your husband a partner in this grievous disaster, why prove to be the temptress of the person whose helpmate you were intended to be, and why for a tiny morsel alienate him along with yourself from the favor of God? What excess of folly led you to such heights of presumption? Wasn't it sufficient for you to pass your life without care or concern, clad in a body yet free of any bodily needs? To enjoy everything in the garden except for one tree? To have all visible things under your own authority and to exercise control over them all? Did you instead, deceived as you were by vain hopes, set your heart on reaching the very pinnacle of power? On that account you will discover through experience itself that not only will you fail to achieve that goal but you will rob yourself and your husband of everything already given you, you will fall into such depths of remorse that you will regret your failed intentions while that wicked demon, responsible for concocting that deadly plan, will mock and insult you for falling victim to him and incurring the same fate as he. I mean, just as he had ideas above his station, was carried away to a degree beyond what was granted him, and so fell from heaven to earth, in just the same way did you have in mind to proceed, and by your transgression of the command were brought to the punishment of death, giving free rein to your own envy, as some sage has said: "By the devil's envy death entered the world." (*Nine Homilies in Genesis, 16, 6-12*).[2]

All in all, Chrysostom gives a fairly literal interpretation to the Genesis text: paradise was a real place. His interest, however, was not on Adam and Eve and their fall; rather, he focuses on redemption and the tree of the cross:

The first tree introduced death into the world, the second gave us immortality. The one banished us from Paradise, the other takes us back to heaven. The one, for a single transgression, condemns the wretched Adam to the most

[2]Text: PG 54; trans. FOTC 74.210-215, R.C. Hill

fearful chastisement; the other frees us from the burden of a
great number of sins and gives us back confidence in God
(*Nine Homilies on Genesis*, 16, 20).[3]

Later, in his *Eight Baptismal Catecheses*, Chrysostom comes
back to the same themes:

> From the very beginning God has always filled the human
> race with goods. As soon as he had created the first human
> being, he gave him Paradise as his dwelling place and graced
> him with a blessed life, allowing him to enjoy all goods of
> Paradise except the one tree. But the man, giving in to his
> intemperance by the trickery of the woman, transgressed
> the commandment which he had received and offended the
> honor which had been given him.
> But see how far, even then, divine goodness went. It would
> have been just for God to consider Adam unworthy of
> forgiveness, ungrateful as he had comported himself to the
> kindnesses of his benefactor, and to exclude him from the
> plan of his Providence. Not only did God not do so, but, as a
> tender father, when his son rebels against him, lets himself
> be touched by the voice of nature and does not measure the
> punishment to the sin, without however renouncing all
> sanction but moderating the penalty that he inflicts so that
> the son may not fall deeper into evil, so does God treat
> Adam in his goodness. Because the man has committed a
> serious act of disobedience, God, on the one hand, excluded
> him from his blessed state, and, on the other hand, holding
> in check his pride for fear he would rebel further, he
> condemned him to work and pain. It is as if God had
> said: "This complete unrestraint, this full freedom has led
> you to a grave disobedience and made you forget my
> commandments. You had nothing to do, and that led you to
> lift your thoughts above your own nature, since 'idleness is
> the mother of all vices.' That is why I condemn you to work
> and pain so that in cultivating the earth you may remember
> without ceasing both your disobedience and the weakness

[3]Text: PG 54; trans. FOTC 74.210-216, 220, R.C. Hill

of your nature. You have dreamed of great things and did not want to stay within your limits; that is why, to the dust from which you have been taken I want you to return, because 'dust you are, and to dust you shall return'. . . ."

And, so that you may know both the snare of the wicked devil and the wise arrangements of our Master, understand what the devil wanted to do to humans by means of trickery and what loving kindness our Master has shown to them. The wicked devil envied them their sojourn in Paradise. He made them hope for a future increase of their privileges and deprived them of the privileges they were possessing. Making them to imagine that they were equal to God, he drew upon them the chastisement of death.

Such are, in fact, his baits: not only did he make us lose the goods we have, but also he seeks to throw us into a deeper precipice. On the contrary, the good God, even in this circumstance, did not abandon the human race. To show to the devil how foolish his attempts were, and to humans how he cared for them, God granted them, through death, immortality. See then how the evil has thrown the human race out of paradise and how the Master has led it to heaven. The profit is greater than the punishment (*Baptismal Catecheses*, II, 3-7).[4]

Does Chrysostom think that the guilt of the original sin is transmitted to Adam's descendants? In other words, is there in Chrysostom a doctrine of original sin? A passage in the third catechesis seems to indicate a negative answer and it was used by the Pelagian, Julian of Eclanum, to argue that Chrysostom had denied original sin. Discussing the benefits of baptism, he says: ". . . Have you seen the number of benefits of baptism? While many believe that its only benefit is the remission of sins, we have counted at least ten honors conferred by it. It is for this reason that we baptize even little children, *even though they have no sins*, so that they may receive justice, sonship, inheritance, the grace of being brother and members of Christ, and of becoming the temple of the Holy Spirit" (III, 6).

---

[4]Text: SC 50.134-137; cf. 4 ACW 31.44-46, trans. P.W. Harkins

Augustine replied that the plural "sins" referred to personal sins (*propria peccata*) and therefore Chrysostom cannot be made to deny original sin. Augustine's retort is ingenious enough, but, I believe, is off the mark. In the previous paragraph, Chrysostom has enumerated the ten benefits of baptism: "Those who were captives yesterday are today free people and citizens of the Church. Those who were in the shame of sin before are now in assurance and justice. They are not only free but also holy, not only holy but also just, not only just but also brothers of Christ, not only brothers of Christ but also his coheirs, not only his coheirs but also his members, not only his members but also temples, not only temples but also instruments of the Spirit" (III, 5). In speaking of the benefits of baptism for little children, however, Chrysostom deliberately omitted the first benefit, namely the deliverance from sins (*eleutheroi*), precisely because they are free from all sins.

Elsewhere, speaking of the dwelling place of little children killed by sorcerers (according to popular belief their souls became the dwelling place of demons), Chrysostom says that such belief is wrong because the souls of the just are in the hand of God, and if this is true of the souls of the just, "then those children's souls also, for neither are they wicked" (*Homily 28 on the Gospel of Matthew*, 3).

Though Chrysostom does not explicitly affirm the existence of original sin, nevertheless he repeatedly points out that the consequences or penalties of Adam's sin affect not only our first parents but also their descendants:

> Be careful not to fall victims again to the old contract. Christ has come once; he has found the ancestral obligation of Adam. For it was Adam who began contracting the debt; and we, on our part, have increased the charges with our subsequent sins. And the debt brought forth malediction, sin, death, and condemnation by the law (*Baptismal Catecheses* III, 21).

Again, commenting on Rom 5: 19, he says:

> What is the question? It is the saying that through the offence of one many were made sinners. For the fact that

when he had sinned and become mortal, those who were of him should be so also, is nothing unlikely. But how would it follow that from his disobedience another would become sinner? For at this rate a person of this sort will not even deserve punishment, if, that is, it was not from his own self that he became a sinner. What then does the word 'sinners' mean here? To me it seems to mean liable to punishment and condemned to death (*Homily 10 on Romans*, 2, 3, 4).[5]

In brief, then, though falling short of Augustinianism, there was here an outline of a doctrine of original sin which would be elaborated in greater detail by Augustine, especially in his struggle against Pelagius and his disciples.

II. The Life of Grace

We have already seen above how Chrysostom explicates the effects of baptismal grace. Faithful to the Word-man christology of the Antiochene school, he emphasizes the reality of Christ's complete humanity, composed of body and soul and the details of the earthly life of Jesus. As regards Christ's saving work, he tends to adopt the "realist" view rather than the "mystical" or "physical" view of the Alexandrians, which stresses the Incarnation as the means of redemption, and the "Ransom" theory according to which Jesus' death is the price paid to the devil. The "Realist" view focuses instead on the suffering and death of Christ. To return to the grace of God, sinful humanity must expiate its sins and satisfy divine justice. Christ took our place, and taking upon himself the punishment that our sins deserved, he offered himself as a sacrifice to the Father on the cross, satisfied divine justice and reconciled humanity to God.

Chrysostom teaches that humankind was condemned to death by God and was indeed virtually dead; but Christ has delivered us by his sacrificial death on the cross, substituting himself in our place (cf. *Homilies on Hebrews* 15, 2). Furthermore, Christ died for all, a sacrifice of surpassing

[5]Text: PG 60.477; trans. LNPF XI.403

efficacy, sufficient to save the entire human race: "He died for all, to save all, so far as he was concerned; for that death was a fair equivalent in exchange for the destruction of all" (*ibid.*, 17, 2). In a compact paragraph, Chrysostom describes the work of Christ:

> In all this the Son of God, because of his goodness and solicitude, suffered death for you, in order to suppress the tyranny of sin, to destroy the citadel of the devil, to break the bonds of death, to open for us the gates of heaven, to remove the curse, to wipe away the first sin, to teach you patience, to train you for resistance, so that nothing of the present life may afflict you, neither death, nor insults, nor injuries, nor mockeries, nor attacks, nor denunciations, nor evil suspicions, nor anything of the kind (*On Providence*, 8, 7).[6]

In another place, he describes the benefits of the Cross for our life:

> It is the cross of Christ that has lifted up the world, dissipated error, transformed earth into heaven, broken the forces of death, conquered hell, destroyed the citadel of the devil, shut the mouths of the demons; it is the Cross that has transformed humans into angels, destroyed the altars, demolished the temples, implanted a new religion, and produced a thousand good benefits (*ibid.*, 15, 1).[7]

Given this grace, humans must, Chrysostom points out, cooperate with it. Of course he does emphasize that without God's grace we are unable to perform good works; nevertheless, even if grace takes the lead, it cooperates (*symprattei*) with free will (cf. *Nine Homilies on Genesis*, 25: 7; 58: 5). Commenting on Rom 6: 17, he writes:

> After shaming them by the slavery, after alarming them by the rewards, and so exhorting them, Paul again corrects

---

[6]Text: SC 79.136
[7]Text: SC 79.214; trans. LNPF XI. 412

them by calling the benefits to mind. For by these he shows that they were great evils from which they were freed, and that not by any labors of their own, and that things henceforth would be more manageable. Just as anyone who has rescued a prisoner from a cruel tyrant, and advises him not to run back to him, reminding him of his terrible slavery, so does Paul set the former evils most emphatically before us, by giving thanks to God. For it was no human power that could set us free from all those evils, but "thanks be to God," who was willing and able to do such great things. And Paul says well, "You have obeyed from the heart." You were neither forced nor pressed; rather you came over of your own accord, with a willing mind. Now this is like one that praises and rebukes at once. For after having willingly come, and not under any duress or necessity, what allowance can you claim, or what excuse can you make, if you run away back to your former condition? Next, that you may learn that it came not of your own will only, but the whole of it of God's grace also, after saying "You have obeyed from the heart," Paul adds, "that form of doctrine which was delivered you." In the obedience from the heart shows the free will. But the deliverance indicates the grace of God (*Homilies on Romans*, 11, 17).[8]

Again, commenting on Ephesians 1:4-5 Chrysostom emphasizes the gratuity of grace and the necessity of cooperating with it:

> ...After speaking of the good works of men, Paul goes back to the grace of God. For all this does not come about by toil and good works, but by love: yet not by love alone, nor by our virtue alone. For if it were by love alone, then everyone would be saved; and if it were by our virtue alone, then the Incarnation and all that is accomplished would be superfluous. So it is not by love alone, nor by our virtue alone, but comes from both. "He chose us," says the text; and the chooser knows what he is choosing. "He predestined

---

[8] Text: PG 60.489; trans. LNPF XI.412

us in love." For virtue without love would never have saved
anybody. Where would Paul have got to, how would he
have achieved what he did, if God had not first of all called
him and in his love drawn him to himself? In any case the
fact that he bestows such great benefits on us is the outcome
of his love and not of our virtue. Our becoming virtuous,
our believing and our coming to him—these are all the work
of him who called us, though admittedly they are our works
also. But to bestow such great honors on those who come to
him, translating them immediately from enmity to adopted
sonship, is most emphatically the outcome of a love that
knows no bounds (*Homilies on Ephesians*, 1, 1).[9]

Speaking to the neophytes, Chrysostom explains how they
have been made a "new creation," basing on Paul's saying, "If
anyone is in Christ, he is a new creation" (2 Cor 5: 17).

How are these things not new and unheard of when the
person who only yesterday and the day before yesterday
lived in softness and excess suddenly embraces temperance
and frugality? How are these things not new and unheard of
when the person who until now was a libertine and who
wasted his life in the pleasures of the present life suddenly
masters his passions and dedicates himself to temperance
and purity as if he were no longer enclosed in a body?
Have you seen how what has happened is really a new
creation? God's grace has entered; it has remodelled and
refashioned the souls, making them other than what they
were, not by transforming their nature but changing their
will. It no longer allows the tribunal of the eyes of the mind
to form judgments contrary to the facts: as though it had
removed the speck, it enables the eyes to see with precision
the ugliness and deformity of vices and the beauty and
brightness of virtues (*Baptismal Catechesis*, IV, 13-14).[10]

Here Chrysostom enunciates one of the basic principles of his
anthropology. Grace does not do any violence to human

[9]Text: PG 62.12-13; trans. LNPF XIII.51
[10]Text: SC 50.190; trans. ACW 31.71

nature. It does not change nature, which is immutable. But it enlightens the free will and enables the eyes of the soul to get rid of the false notions which it has formed of things.

Finally, for Chrysostom, Christian life is the life in the Spirit who confers on the baptized the gift of immortality and eternal glory.

> As soon as we are baptized, our soul, purified by the Spirit, becomes more luminous than the sun. Not only do we behold the divine glory but also we participate in its light. Like a piece of polished silver which reflects the rays it receives, less by the strength of its nature than by the force of the light which is reflected, so our soul, purified and becomes more luminous than purest silver, receives and reflects the glory of the Spirit. Wherefore it is said: "Reflecting as a mirror we are transformed into the same image" (2 Cor 3: 18). The glory of the Spirit becomes our own glory, since it is communicated to us as if it came from the Lord the Spirit himself (*Homilies on 2 Corinthians*, 7, 5).[11]

The Christians, washed of their sins, become totally spiritual, "pneumatic," and participate, by the power of the Spirit who dwells in them, in the glory of God and Trinitarian life, and in this way, are made again in the image of God.

---

[11] Text: PG 61.448; trans. LNPF XII.314

8

Ambrose of Milan (c. 333-397)

Born at Trier into a distinguished Roman family (his father was the Pretorian Prefect of Gaul) and moved to Rome after his father's death with his mother, his older sister Marcellina and older brother Uranius Satyrus, Ambrose undertook studies to prepare himself for a public career. After completing their education, Ambrose and Satyrus left Rome in 365 for Sirmium as advocates to the Court of the Italian Prefecture. Probably in 370, Satyrus was made a provincial governor and Ambrose 'Consular' or Governor of the province of Aemelia Liguria.

In 373, Auxentius, the intended Arian bishop of Milan, died, and by this time, the exiled Catholic Bishop Dionysius was also dead. It was necessary to elect a new bishop, and the Catholics and Arians campaigned violently for their candidates. Suddenly, with surprising unanimity, both parties agreed on Ambrose, who was still a catechumen, as bishop. Protesting in vain, Ambrose was baptized on November 24 and consecrated bishop on December 1.

Ambrose's responsibilities as the bishop of a large city and as the sole metropolitan of northern Italy were numerous and heavy. He dedicated himself with zeal to the administration of baptism and penance, the supervision of the charities of the Church to which he donated his acquired property, the defense of the oppressed, the hearing and determining of civil cases, and the discipline of his clergy. In addition, in his struggle against Arianism and paganism, he had to deal with various imperial authorities from Gratian, to whom he acted as confidant; to Justina, to whom he refused to hand over first the Portian Basilica and later the New Basilica for Arian worship; to Valentinian II whom he defended against the usurper Maximus, and whom he urged to reject paganism (the Altar of Victory affair); to Theodosius, whom he excommunicated for his excessively severe punishment of the people of Thessalonica. In his dealings with the Roman emperors Ambrose succeeded in establishing the *modus operandi* of the Church and the state as two independent authorities, each autonomous within its own sphere, but each rendering general assistance and support to the other.

Despite his heavy pastoral and political responsibilities Ambrose found time to devote himself to the study of the sacred sciences with which he had not been familiar as a catechumen. In exegesis he followed Philo and Origen, while in theology he was heavily indebted to Athanasius, Didymus, Basil, Gregory of Nazianzen and Cyril of Jerusalem. As we shall see, many of his important writings are Latin adaptations of Greek works, such as the *Hexaemeron* (Basil), *On the Holy Spirit* (Didymus), *On the Mysteries* (Cyril of Jerusalem), whereas in his famous *On the Duties of the Clergy*, the influence of Cicero and Stoicism is apparent.

I. Creation as the Common Work of the Trinity

Ambrose's commentary on the six days of creation is, as has been alluded to above, an adaptation of Basil's celebrated homilies which had been delivered some seventeen years previously. Despite its many quotations from Virgil and Cicero, the *Hexaemeron* does not intend to reconcile the Christian doctrine of creation with Greco-Roman thought. Rather its purpose is to expound the religious and moral relevance of the doctrine of creation. Against pagan philosophers Ambrose emphasizes that the world had a beginning, that is, it is not eternal but created, (cf. I, 1-3) and that "in the beginning" means "in Christ."

> A beginning in a mystical sense is denoted by the statement: "I am the first and last, the beginning and the end" (Apoc

1: 8). The words of the Gospel are significant in this connection, especially wherein the Lord, when asked who he was, replied: "I am the beginning, I who speak with you" (Jn 8: 25). In truth, he who is the beginning of all things by virtue of his divinity is also the end, because there is no one after him.... Therefore, in this beginning, that is, in Christ, God created heaven and earth, because "all things were made through him and without him was made nothing that was made" (Jn 1: 3). Again: "In him all things hold together and he is the first-born of every creature" (Col 1: 15)....

We can also understand that the statement, "In the beginning God created heaven and earth," refers to a period. The beginning of a journey is not yet a completion, nor is the beginning of a building yet the finished house.

Finally, others have interpreted the Greek phrase *en kephalaio* to mean *in capite*, by which is meant that in a brief moment the sum of the operation was completed. Then there are also others who interpret the beginning not in a temporal sense, but as something before time. Hence they use the Greek word *kephalaion* in the sense of its Latin equivalent, *caput*, indicating by this the sum of the work. Heaven and earth, in fact, are the sum of the invisible things which appear not only as the adornment of this world, but also as a testimony of invisible things.... We can find it easy to understand, then, that the Creator of Angels, Dominations, and Powers is he who in a moment of his power made this great beauty of the world out of nothing, which did not itself have existence, and gave substance to things or causes that did not themselves exist (*Hexaemeron*, I, 4, 15-16).[1]

At other times Ambrose explicitly says that creation is the work of the Trinity, and especially of the Holy Spirit.

... "And the Spirit of God moved over the waters" (Gen 1: 2). Although some consider this Spirit to be air, others think of it as the vital breath of the air which we take in and

---

[1] Text: CSEL 32,1.13; trans. FOTC 42.14-16, tr J.J. Savage

emit. However, in agreement with the saints and the faithful we consider this to be the Holy Spirit, so that the operation of the Holy Trinity clearly shines forth in the making of the world. Preceded by the statement that "In the beginning God created heaven and earth," that is, God created it in Christ, or the Son of God, as God, created it, or God created it through the Son, since "all things were made through him and without him was made nothing that was made" (Jn 1: 3). There was still to come the fullness of the operation in the Spirit, as it is written: "By the word of the Lord the heavens were established and all the power of them by the Spirit of his mouth" (Ps 32: 6). As we are instructed in the psalm concerning the operation of the Word, which is the work of God, and on the power which the Holy Spirit bestowed, so is echoed here the prophetic oracle, namely, that "God said" and "God created" and "the Spirit of God moved over the waters." While adorning the firmament of the heavens, the Spirit fittingly moved over the earth, destined to bear fruit, because by the aid of the Spirit, it held the seeds of new birth which were to germinate according to the words of the Prophet: "Send forth your Spirit and they shall be created and you shall renew the face of the earth" (Ps 103: 30).

Finally, the Syriac text, which is close to the Hebrew and agrees with it in word for the most part, expresses it in this way: "And the Spirit of God brooded over the waters," that is, gave life, in order to help the birth of new creatures and by cherishing them give them the breath of life. For the Holy Spirit, too, is called Creator, as we read in Job: "The divine Spirit made me" (Job 33: 4) . . . (*ibid.*, I, 8, 29).[2]

Because of his polemics against Arianism, Ambrose tends to emphasize with vigor the active role of Christ in the creative act. Everything has been created by the Word; the Son is a mediator and not simply an instrument of creation. He is at the side of God the Father, he is God himself. Further, in his stress on the consubstantiality of the Son with the Father, Ambrose also tends to view creation as a common activity of the Trinity

[2]Text: CSEL 32, 1.28; trans. FOTC 42.33

(he often speaks of creation as "*inseparabilis, communis, una operatio Trinitatis*"), with the result that each divine person is wisdom, power, goodness, and creative cause in the same way.

II. Humanity in God's Image and Its Original Condition

In his discussion of the primitive condition of Adam, Ambrose takes into consideration both Adam's external environment and interior, spiritual condition, though his ascetical-mystical bent, coupled with his preference for allegory, leads him to focus more extensively on the second element. In his vision, humanity's external environment is constituted by three successive levels: earth, 'Paradise', and heaven. Commenting on Gen 1: 26 and 2: 7, Ambrose suggests that humans were first formed in a lower place, then placed in 'Paradise', complete in their essential being, and destined for heaven.

> "And God took the man whom he has created and placed him in the garden of Eden to till it and keep it" (Gen 2: 15). Note, now, the person who was taken and the land where he was formed. The power of God, therefore, took the man and breathed into him, so that the man's strength will advance and increase. God set him apart in Paradise that you may know that humanity was taken up, that is to say, was breathed upon by the power of God. Note the fact that the man was created outside Paradise, whereas the woman was made within it. This teaches us that each person acquires grace by reason of virtue, not because of place of birth or of race. Hence, although created outside Paradise, that is, in an inferior place, the man is found to be superior, whereas the woman, created in a better place, is found to be inferior. She was the first to be deceived and was responsible for deceiving the man....
> 25. Therefore the man was placed in Paradise, while the woman was created in Paradise. The woman, even before she was deceived by the serpent, shared grace with the man, since she was taken from the man. Yet, "this is a great mystery" (Eph 5: 32), as the Apostle said. Wherefore he

traced the source of life from it. And so Scripture refers only to the man in the words: "He placed him in the garden of Eden to till it and keep it" (Gen 2: 15). The act of tilling and the act of keeping are one and the same thing. In tilling there is a certain exercise of the man's virtue, while in keeping it is understood that the work is accomplished, for protection implies something completed. These two acts are required of the man ... (*Paradise*, 4, 24-25).[3]

It is not clear whether Ambrose intends to propose a double creation taking place in two different places and moments or whether he merely distinguished two kinds of creation to illustrate the different origin of the constitutive elements of the human person, namely, the soul, which comes from God and tends toward him, and the body, which comes from the earth and tends toward it. At any rate, the paradise, "God's great gift to humanity" (*Paradise* 11, 51), in which the woman was created and to which the man was moved, was both a place and a spiritual condition. Placed in this garden of delights, Adam led a blessed and happy life similar to that of the angels (cfr. *ibid.*, 9, 42-44). However, Paradise is not a definitive dwelling place for the first humans, but only a place and a condition of waiting in which they "expect the revelation of the sons of God, just as the sun, which God placed in heaven, awaits lordship over the heavens" (*ibid.*, 1, 5). It is merely a preparatory phase for their entrance into the kingdom of heaven. Ambrose consistently distinguished between Paradise and the kingdom of heaven, the former being the way to the latter (cfr. *Letter*, 19, 71, 8). The definitive dwelling-place for our first parents was heaven, the abode of God, where they would find eternal life.

> ...and so, because God is a refuge, and because he is, moreover, in heaven and above the heavens, surely we must flee from here to there, where there is peace and rest from labors and where we can feast upon the great sabbath, even as Moses said: "And the sabbaths of the land shall be food for you" (Lev 25: 6). For it is a banquet, and one filled with

[3]Text: CSEL 32,1.280; trans. FOTC 42.301,302

enjoyment and serenity, to rest in God and to look upon his delight...(*Flight from the World*, 8, 45).[4]

Following the teaching of Genesis, Ambrose affirms that humans are made in God's image. Like most Latin Fathers, he does not differentiate between "image" and "likeness." God's image, however, does not reside in the body but in the soul, which is rational, immortal, incorporeal, and spiritual.

> ...Attend, rather, to your soul and mind, in which all our deliberations take place and to which the profit of your works is accrued. Here only is found the fullness of wisdom, the plentitude of piety and justice of which God speaks—for all virtue comes from God: "Behold, Jerusalem, I have painted your walls "(Is 49: 16). That soul of yours is painted by God, who holds in himself the radiant beauty of virtue and the splendor of piety. That soul is well painted in which shines the imprint of divine operation. That soul is well painted in which resides the splendor of grace and the reflection of its paternal nature. Precious is that picture which in its brilliance is in accord with that divine reflection. Adam before he sinned conformed to this image. But after his fall he lost that celestial image and took on one that is terrestrial. Let us flee from the image which cannot enter the city of God, for it is written: "In your city, O Lord, you will bring their image to nothing" (Apoc 21: 27)....
>
> Our soul, therefore, is made to the image of God. In this is the human person's entire essence, because without it, he is nothing but earth and into earth he shall return. Hence, in order to convince you that without the soul the flesh is nothing, Scripture says: "Do not be afraid of those who kill the body but cannot kill the soul" (Mt 10: 28).
>
> Why, then, do you presume in the flesh, you who lose nothing when you lose the flesh? Rather, be fearful lest you be deprived of the aid of your soul. "What will a person give in exchange for his soul?" (Mt 16: 26). In this is no small part of himself, rather, it is the substantial part of the entire human race. This is the means by which humans rule over

[4]Text: CSEL 32,2.199; trans. FOTC 65.315, M.P. McHugh

living things, wild beasts, and birds. Your soul is made in the image of God, whereas your body is related to the beasts. In one there is the holy seal of imitation of the divine. In the other there is found base association with beasts and wild animals.

But let us define more accurately the meaning of the phrase "in the image of God." Is it true that the flesh is made "in the image of God"? In that case, is there earth in God, since flesh is of earth? Is God corporeal, that is to say, weak and subject like the flesh to the passions...?

The flesh, therefore, cannot be made in the image of God. This is true, however, of our souls, which are free to wander far and wide in acts of reflection and counsel. Our souls are able to envisage and reflect on all things....

That, therefore, is made in the image of God which is perceived, not by the power of the body, but by that of the mind. It is that power which beholds the absent and embraces in its vision countries beyond the horizon. Its vision crosses boundaries and gazes intently on what is hidden....

The soul, then, is made in the image of God, in form like the Lord Jesus. Those people are saints who are conformed to the Son of God...(*Hexaemeron*, VI, 7, 42-3, 44-46).[5]

In their original state humans could be considered as heavenly and angelic beings living on earth. Their nakedness indicates innocence, the absence of sin, and the presence of virtues:

> "And their eyes were opened," we are told, "and they realized that they were naked"(Gen 3: 7). They were naked, it is true, before this time, but they were not devoid of the garments of virtue. They were naked because of the purity of their character and because nature knows nothing of the cincture of deceit. Now, on the contrary, the human mind is veiled in many folds of deception (*Paradise* 13, 63).[6]

[5]Text: CSEL 32,1.233; trans. FOTC 42.255-259
[6]Text: CSEL 32,1.322; trans. FOTC 42.343

Despite their innocence and happiness, however, the first parents were not yet perfected. Their perfection was not yet definitive, their happiness not yet complete, and their grace not yet confirmed. Between the initial condition and the definitive state there was an interval in which they would have to develop their spiritual life in accordance with divine grace. Ambrose uses his favorite contrast between shadow (*umbra*), image (*imago*), and reality (*veritas*) to explain the three phases through which the first parents had to pass before they could reach the kingdom of heaven.

> We should be aware of the fact, therefore, that where God has planted a tree of life he has also planted the tree of the knowledge of good and evil in the midst of Paradise. It is understood that he planted it in the middle. Therefore, in the middle of Paradise there were both a tree of life and a cause for death. Note that humans did not create life, but that by carrying out and observing the precepts of God they could find life. This was the life mentioned by the Apostle: "Your life is hidden with Christ in God" (Col 3: 3). Humans, therefore, were, figuratively speaking, either in the shadow of life—because our life on earth is but a shadow—or they had life, as it were, in pledge, for they had been breathed on by God. They had, therefore, a pledge of immortality, but while in the shadow of life they were unable, by the usual channels of senses, to see and attain the hidden life of Christ with God. Although not yet a sinner, they did not possess an incorruptible and inviolable nature. Of course later on they fell into sin, but as yet they were not sinners. Hence they were in the shadow of life, whereas sinners are in the shadows of death... (*Paradise*, 5, 29).[7]

III. Original Sin

In Paradise, then, the first human beings received the promise of eternal glory, the blessing of the kingdom of heaven, where they would obtain "true perfection" (*vera*

[7]Text: CSEL 32,1.285; trans. FOTC 42.306

perfectio) and "the inheritance of God" (*hereditas dei*) [cfr. *Explanations on the Psalms*, 118, 8, 10] Unfortunately, they fell into sin and their situation was drastically disturbed. As the result of this very grievous sin (*maximum peccatum*), which consists in pride (cfr. *ibid.,* 118, 8, 8-10), they were wounded, lost the divine grace, and suffered a general degradation (cfr. *Exposition on the Gospel of Luke*, 7, 73). Ambrose insists on the first parents' loss of their "unspoilt and incorrupt nature" (*integrae incorruptaeque naturae*); he points out how, because of their sin, they were stripped of all the extraordinary gifts they had received when they were placed in Paradise. They became naked of their virtues.

> When, therefore, they saw that they had been despoiled of the purity and simplicity of their untainted nature, they began to look for objects made by human hands with which to cover the nakedness of their minds and hearts.... "So they sewed fig leaves together and made themselves coverings" (Gen 3: 7). We are taught by the content of Holy Scripture how we should interpret the meaning of the word "fig" in this passage. Scripture relates that the saints are those who find rest beneath the vine and the fig (cfr. Mich 4: 4). Solomon has said: "Who plants the fig tree and does not eat the fruit thereof?" (Prov 27: 18). Yet the owner may come to the fig tree and may be offended at finding there only leaves and no fruit. I gather from Adam himself the meaning of the leaves. He proceeded to make a covering for himself out of the leaves of the fig tree after he had sinned, whereas he should have had its fruit instead. The just person chooses the fruit; the sinner, the leaves. What is the fruit? We read: "The fruit of the Spirit is charity, joy, peace, patience, kindness, modesty, continence, love" (Gal 5: 22). He who possessed no fruit possess no joy. The one who violated the command of God had no faith, and the one who ate of the forbidden tree had no virtue of continence. Whoever, therefore, violates the command of God has become naked and stripped, a reproach to himself ... (*Paradise*, 13, 63-65).[8]

---

[8]Text: CSEL 32,1.323; trans. FOTC 42.343-344

Ambrose examines the objection that Adam should not have been punished because, not yet knowing the difference between good and evil, he was like a child and therefore was not responsible for his sin. Ambrose flatly rejects such explanation: "It is certainly false to hold that the person who does not know good and evil is similar to a child. If he was not a child, then surely he is liable to sin, inasmuch as he is not a child. If he is subject to sin, then punishment follows the sin, because the person who can avoid sin is reckoned to be liable to punishment" (*ibid.*, 6, 31).

Banished from Paradise and deprived of all divine aids, the first parents lost their special likeness to God (cfr. *Explanations on the Psalms*, 118, 11, 14), fell to a lower condition, and became "earthly." They experienced the revolt of their body against their soul, the former becoming an instrument of sin and the prison of the latter. Having followed the suggestion of the devil, they became his slaves. And lastly, they brought death upon themselves: ". . .since disobedience was the cause of death, for that very reason, not God, but humans themselves were the agent of their own death" (*Paradise*, 7, 35).

The sin of Adam and Eve did not harm themselves only but, Ambrose insists, also their descendants. Adam's sin was a sin of pride; this sin was our sin, for Adam is in each one of us: "Pride is the most serious sin in humans; it is the source of our sin. It was with this weapon that the devil first struck and wounded us" (*Explanations on the Psalms*, 118, 7, 8). Again: "Adam is in each one of us. It was in him that the human race fell, because it was through one man that sin passed to all" (*Apology of Prophet David*, II, 71).

Ambrose is a clear witness to the existence of original sin in us. He developed this doctrine at length in his commentary on the parable of the Good Samaritan (cfr. Lk 10: 30-37). The traveler from Jericho to Jerusalem, assaulted by robbers and left for dead, represents Adam and sinful humanity.

> Jericho is in fact the symbol of this world where Adam, expelled from Paradise, that is, the heavenly Jerusalem, descended as the result of his fall, passing from life to hell. It is a change not only of place but also of way of life, which is now in exile. How different was he from the former Adam

who was enjoying a secure happiness, when he lowered himself to the sinful world and therein met the robbers; he would not have met them had he not deviated from the heavenly command. Who are these robbers if not the angels of the night and darkness, who sometimes disguise themselves in angels of light but cannot keep up for long? They first strip us of our garments of spiritual grace which we have received and in this way are able to inflict wounds upon us. For if we keep our garments which we have put on intact, we would not feel the strikes of the robbers. Let us take care not to be stripped, as Adam was stripped naked, bereft of the protection of the heavenly command and of the garment of faith. It was in this way that he received the fatal wound, which the whole human race would have incurred, had not the Samaritan come to heal his mortal wounds (*Exposition on the Gospel of Luke*, 7, 73).[9]

Later, Ambrose, commenting on the parable of the Prodigal Son (cfr. Lk 15: 11-32), made a famous statement, which Augustine quoted seven or eight times in his controversy with Julian, in which the link between the sin of Adam and our fallen condition is made explicit: "Adam existed, and in him we all existed; Adam perished, and in him all perished" (*Fuit Adam et in illo fuimus omnes: periit Adam et in illo omnes perierunt*) (*ibid.*, 7, 234).

Finally, as regards the existence of original sin, the Church of Ambrose practiced the washing of feet, a rite peculiar to the Church at Milan, and Ambrose dwelled especially on the hereditary sins, *peccata hereditaria*, which are remitted by baptism together wih personal sins.

Peter was clean, but he should have washed his feet, for he had the sin of the first man by succession, when the serpent overthrew him and persuaded him to sin. So his feet are washed, that hereditary sins may be taken away; for our sins are remitted by baptism (*On the Mysteries*, 32).[10]

[9]Text: SC 52.33
[10]Text: SC 25².172; trans. FOTC 44.16

In *The Sacraments*, the authenticity of which has been convincingly shown by O. Fallen and others, Ambrose defended the rite of washing the feet against the absence of it in the Church of Rome on the ground that it washes away "the poisons of the serpent":

> The Lord answered him, because he had said "hands and head": "He that is washed, needs not to wash again, but to wash his feet alone" (Jn 13: 10). Why this? Because in baptism all guilt is washed away. So guilt is done away with. But since Adam was overthrown by the Devil, and venom was poured out upon his feet, accordingly you wash the feet, that in this part, in which the serpent lay in wait, greater aid of sanctification may be added, so that afterwards he cannot overthrow you. Therefore, you wash the feet, that you may wash away the poisons of the serpent...(*The Sacraments*, 3, 7).[11]

In another text, Ambrose writes forcibly: "In Adam I fell, in Adam I was cast out of Paradise, in Adam I died. How should God restore me, unless he finds in me Adam, justified in Christ, exactly as in that first Adam I was subject to guilt (*culpae obnoxium*) and destined to death?" *(On the Death of Brother Satyrus*, 2, 6). This solidarity with Adam suggests, at least in the last quotation, that the human race is affected with Adam's actual guilt. In general, however, it must be said that for Ambrose the inherited "sin" consists rather in a congenial propensity to sin (the "*lubricum delinquendi*," as Ambrose calls it) than in positive guilt. The moment of transmission Ambrose identifies with the act of physical generation.

IV. Salvation as the Return to Paradise and as a New Humanity

Ambrose was deeply convinced that God in his goodness and mercy would never abandon fallen humanity. The

---

[11] Text: SC 25².94; trans. FOTC 44.292

parables of the lost sheep, the lost coin and the prodigal son (cf. Lk. 15: 1-32) form the background for his theology of redemption (cf. *Exposition on the Gospel of Luke*, 7, 201-243). Redemption, for Ambrose, is a gratuitous initiative of God, "not as a reward for works nor a justification of virtues, but the gift of the generosity of the giver and the decision of the redeemer" (*Explanations on the Psalms*, 43, 48). God accomplished his salvation through Christ, in him he reconciled the world to himself, and sent him as the Savior of all humankind.

The salvation which Christ offered is, according to Ambrose, universal, complete, and definitive. Universal, insofar as it is given to all human beings; complete, insofar as it affects the whole person, his physical as well as spiritual dimensions; and definitive, insofar as it needs no further complement (cfr. *The Prayer of Job and David*, 4, 4; *Joseph*, 34; *Explanations on the Psalms*, 118, 2, 15; *Exposition on the Gospel of Luke*, 5: 39; 83-86; 10: 44). And though the whole life of Christ was efficacious as far as salvation is concerned, nevertheless a special significance is attributed to the death of Jesus, which Ambrose calls "*causa salutis publicae*" and to the cross, which he calls "*sacramentum salutis*":

> . . . . By the death of one the world was redeemed. For Christ, had he willed, need not have died, but he neither thought that death should be shunned as though there were any cowardice in it, nor could he have saved us better than by dying. And so his death brought life to all, we are signed with the sign of his death, we show forth his death when we pray; when we offer the sacrifice we declare his death, for his death is victory, his death is our mystery, his death is the yearly recurring solemnity of the world. What now should we say concerning his death, since we prove by this divine example that death alone found immortality, and that death itself redeemed death. Death, then, is not to be mourned over, for it is the cause of salvation for all; death is not to be shunned, for the Son of God did not think it unworthy of him, and did not shun it . . .(*On the Death of Brother Satyrus*, 2, 46).[12]

[12]Text: CSEL 73.273; trans. FOTC 22.215

Ambrose describes Christ's gift of grace and salvation as enabling us to return to the Paradise from which Adam and his descendants have been banished.

> The cross of Christ gave back Paradise to us; this is the tree which the Lord showed to Adam when he pointed to the tree of life, which was in the middle of the garden, saying that it should be eaten, whereas the tree of the knowledge of good and evil should not be eaten. Adam erred, he did not keep the command, he tasted the forbidden fruit; we began to hunger for the tree which the flesh received as its food. That is why God united in Christ the flesh to the tree, so that the ancient hunger might cease, and that the life of grace might be restored. Blessed is the tree of the Lord, which crucified the sins of all; blessed is the flesh of the Lord, which nourished all (*Explanations on the Psalms*, 35, 3).[13]

The return to Paradise implies first of all a return to a place, inasmuch as Christ, the second Adam, reopened the gate of Paradise to all and allowed them to go back to where they could not stay, bringing them back from their exile in the world to live a life of rest and peace in expectation of the definitive coming of the kingdom of heaven. Commenting on Jesus being stripped of his clothes before the crucifixion, Ambrose writes:

> It is important to note in which condition Christ went up. I see him stripped naked. It is in this way that he should go up, he who was about to conquer the world, without the help of the world. Adam was vanquished, he who looked for a garment (Gen 3: 7); the Conqueror, on the contrary, abandoned his garment. Then he came up as nature has formed us under the guidance of God. It was in this condition that the second man entered Paradise. And in order to be conqueror not only for himself alone but also for all, he extended his hands to draw everything to himself (Jn 12: 32), to break the bonds of death, to submit all to the

---

[13]Text: CSEL 64,6.51

yoke of faith, and to unite to heaven what before was of the earth (*Exposition on the Gospel of Luke*, 10, 110).[14]

In fact, because Christ did not stop at Paradise but ascended "above all the heavens to the seat of God" to prepare a "place" for those who believe in him, the redeemed souls will also ascend to the heavens, and participate in the unity, glory and blessedness of God.

To the return to Paradise as a place there corresponds, according to Ambrose, an interior restoration of the human person, understood as a recovery of the original condition of Adam by means of a spiritual ascesis which is begun here on earth, continues in paradise, and is perfected in heaven: "Humanity is therefore reformed in the very man who died, and that which was made in the likeness and image of God is restored by the patience and magnanimity of God" (*Exposition on the Gospel of Luke*, 7, 234). In this way, humans are delivered from sin, death, the devil, and ignorance, and acquire a higher freedom, a "glorious slavery" (*gloriosa servitus* [*Explanations on the Psalms*, 118, 3, 6]) by which they are subjected to the divine wisdom given by Christ.

It must be pointed out, however, that for Ambrose Christ did not simply restore us to the original condition of Adam but also, and more importantly, created a new humanity which enjoys a condition superior to that of Adam. For one thing, Christ gave us a greater measure of grace and more numerous means to attain it. But, more significantly, he enables us to be children of God, making us the perfect image of God according to God's perfect image that he is.

> Therefore, as the Father is holy and perfect, so also holy and perfect is the Son, as it were, the image of God. Moreover, he is the image of God, because all things which belong to God, that is, eternal divinity, omnipotence, and majesty, are seen in the Son. Thus, such is God who is seen in his image. Therefore, you ought to believe that his image is such as is God. For, if you detract from the image, this surely will also

[14]Text: SC 52.192

seem to have been detracted from him of whom he is the image. If you believe the image lesser, God will appear lesser in the image. For such as you consider the image, such will be seen to you, of whom, the invisible, the image is. The image said: "He that sees me sees the Father also" (Jn 14: 9). And such as you consider him, whose image you believe the Son to be, such necessarily must the Son be considered by you. Thus, since the Father is uncreated, the Son also is uncreated; since the Father is not lesser, the Son is not lesser; since the Father is omnipotent, the Son is omnipotent (*The Sacrament*, 112).[15]

Human beings, made "in the image and likeness of God," are made in the perfect image of God which is the unbegotten Son; thus they share, in a finite way, in his nature and perfection. Ambrose continually urges us to remember that we are made in God's image and to behave accordingly.

Be fully aware, O beautiful soul, of the fact that you are the image of God. And, man, be aware that you are the glory of God. . . . Know then, man , your greatness and see to it that you never on any occasion become entrapped in the snares of the devil, so as not to fall, perchance, into the jaws of that dread beast "who as a roaring lion goes about seeking someone to devour" (I Pet 5: 8). . . .
God has made you a hunter, not a harrier, for he says: "Behold I will send you many hunters (Jer 16: 16) — hunters, not of crime, but of absolution therefrom; hunters, certainly not of sin, but of grace. You are a fisher of Christ, for whom it is said: "Henceforth you shall make men live" (Lk 5: 10). Spread your nets, direct your eyes, and control your tongue in such a way as to destroy no one, but bring rescue to those who struggle in the water . . . (*Hexaemeron*, 6, 50).[16]

---

[15]Text: CSEL 79.278; trans. FOTC 44.260
[16]Text: CSEL 32,1.241; trans. FOTC 42.263

Finally, Ambrose counterbalances his emphasis on the gratuitous nature of God's grace with a warning on the need for us to collaborate with it: "In everything the Lord's power cooperates with the human person's efforts" (*Exposition on the Gospel of Luke*, 2, 84). And again: "Our free will gives us either a propensity to virtue or an inclination to sin" (*Jacob*, 1, 1). Even though grace is not bestowed as a reward for merit, but "simply according to the will of the Giver" (*Exhortation to Virginity*, 43), and though a person's decision to become a Christian, Ambrose insists, has really been prepared in advance by God (cfr. *Exposition on the Gospel of Luke*, 1, 10), and indeed every holy thought we have is God's gift (cfr. *On Cain and Abel*, 1, 45), nevertheless Ambrose repeatedly asserts that the grace of salvation will come only to those who make the effort to bestir themselves (cfr. *Explanations on the Psalms*, 43, 7; 118, 12, 13).

9

Pelagius, Augustine's
Anti-Pelagian Writings,
and The Council of Carthage of 418

For good or ill, Western theology of the human condition
and divine grace is linked forever with the names of two
protagonists, Pelagius and Augustine, and their respective
followers. In this chapter we will first of all give a summary of
the Pelagian controversy, including Augustine's struggle with
Julian of Eclanum; then follows an exposition of Pelagius'
anthropology. Next, a selection of Augustine's writings against
Pelagius and Julian will be given, though a full exposition of
his anthropology will be postponed to the next chapter.
Finally, we will conclude with a presentation of the teaching of
the Sixteenth Council of Carthage on the problems of sin and
grace.

I. A Brief Overview of the Pelagian Controversy

So far we have seen two major religious philosophies that
formed the intellectual climate in which the Fathers of the
Church elaborated their anthropologies. The first of these was
the Gnostic doctrine, against which Irenaeus, Tertullian and
Hippolytus fought a vigorous battle; the second was Platonism
and its later development by Plotinus, which was adopted and
transformed by such Fathers as Clement, Origen, Athanasius,
the Cappadocians, and Cyril of Alexandria in the East, as well

as Ambrose and, as we will see, Augustine in the West.

A third influence on patristic anthropologies was the ascetical and monastic movement. It had its origin in the practice of fasting, almsgiving, prayer, continence, and even virginity in the primitive Christian communities. As a stable form of life, it flourished first in Egypt towards the end of the third century, either in the anchoretic form (St. Antony) or in the coenobitic one (St. Pachomius). It was then introduced into the West in the second half of the fourth century (St. Martin of Tours and John Cassian). The first Western monks followed Eastern models, especially the rule of Pachomius and Basil, which were often marked by extreme austerity.

The ascetical and monastic movement, in whatever form it took, rested on an optimistic estimate of human nature which was deemed to be capable of obeying God's commandments and achieving perfection. It believed that humans are endowed with the light of reason to recognize the good and the freedom to choose it. Of course, because of Adam's fall, his descendants have to serve God in a hostile environment. Nevertheless they can avail themselves of external aids, such as the good examples of Christ and the saints, the teaching of the Law, the prophets and Christ, the encouragement of the community, to determine themselves freely for good and avoid evil. This free self-determination for good may be enhanced or hampered by the environment, but the latter's influence depends on the individual's own prior consent. It is therefore of paramount importance for the ascetical and monastic movement to emphasize the existence in the human person of this power of self-determination for good or evil and to strengthen it by means of traditional pious practices.

It was in this spiritual tradition that Pelagius first came to the notice of the West. A lay monk from the British Isles, Pelagius came to Rome in the time of Pope Anastasius (399-401), where he gained fame for learning and devotion and engaged in various literary works, including a commentary on St. Paul's letters. Shocked by the moral laxity of the time, he began urging his contemporaries to adopt a stricter asceticism and a deeper loyalty to the Gospel. It was during this period, too, that he became a close friend of Caelestius, a fellow Briton, who was practicing as an advocate and whom he induced to turn from secular pursuits to dedicate himself to moral reform.

The first certain event of Pelagius' life took place in 405, and is recorded by Augustine himself (cfr. *Against Two Letters of the Pelagians*, 4, 8, 21). A bishop read with approval to Pelagius the famous prayer from Augustine's *Confessions*, X, 40: "Give what you command and command what you will" (*Da quod jubes et jube quod vis*). Pelagius was deeply scandalized by it since it appeared to him to imperil the whole moral enterprise. If a person were not responsible for his good or evil deeds, there would be nothing to restrain him from indulgence in sin.

We hear no more of Pelagius for four years, but in 409, with Alaric at the gates of Rome, Pelagius and Caelestius departed, first for Sicily, and then for North Africa. Augustine was then deeply involved in the Donatist controversy, and was absent from Hippo. Pelagius spent a short while there, before moving on to Carthage (June, 411), so that the bishop and the monk never had the opportunity to meet each other formally to discuss their views. Before long, Pelagius made his way alone to Palestine. Left behind, Caelestius, full of zeal to propagate his ideas, talked and wrote with vigor with the result that he won to his views quite an alarming number of people of the Christian community.

Meanwhile, in 412, a deacon from Milan, Paulinus, who had come to Carthage to collect material for his biography of Ambrose, accused Caelestius of heresy before Bishop Aurelius of Carthage. A short charge ("*libellus minor*") was drawn up on seven counts, reported by Augustine in his *On the Proceedings of Pelagius*, 23 and *On Original Sin*, 2-3. He was accused of teaching:

1. That Adam was created mortal and would have died even if he had not sinned.

2. That the sin of Adam injured himself alone and not the human race.

3. That infants at the moment of birth are in the same condition as Adam was before the Fall.

4. That infants, even though they are not baptized, have eternal life.

5. That the human race as a whole does not die by the death

or fall of Adam, nor does the human race as a whole rise again by the resurrection of Christ.

6. That the Law has the same effect as the Gospel in introducing humans into the kingdom of heaven.

7. That even before the coming of Christ there were humans without sin.

Caelestius faced the charges with legal acumen, but when asked whether he believed in an inherited taint, he tergiversated and was condemned. For a moment he thought of appealing to Rome, but when he finally departed it was for Ephesus and the East.

By now Augustine had more leisure to study the new doctrine carefully. He discovered that a distinction was made between salvation and the higher sanctification, or between "eternal life" and "the kingdom of heaven." He discovered, too, that, in the Pelagius' view, original sin is not transmitted from Adam to his descendants by generation but by imitation. Gradually he realized that Pelagianism was a most pernicious attack on the Christian faith, and from 412 he began a relentless campaign to eradicate it through his personal influence at various councils, in his letters, sermons and books. Of these and of his subsequent struggle against Julian of Eclanum we will deal at greater length in the later parts of this chapter.

Meanwhile Pelagius had been living in Palestine since his departure from Carthage. There he found in Jerome a formidable enemy whose work against Jovinian (*Contra Jovinianum*, 393) he had criticized in 394 while still in Rome. Pelagius attempted a reconciliation with Jerome, through his friend Ctesiphon, but only succeeded in provoking him into the offensive. The latter wrote in reply to Ctesiphon a lengthy letter (letter 133) in which he attacked Pelagius' presumed teaching on apathy and impeccability. He carried on the attack in 415 in a long treatise in three books, in dialogue form (*Dialogues Against the Pelagians*).

In the same year a young Spanish priest, Paulus Orosius, came to Augustine to consult him about the spread of Priscillianism and Origenism in Spain. Augustine recommended him to read his books against the Manichaeans and to visit Jerome for further advice, at the same time asking him to bear two letters (letters 131 and 132) to Jerome, dealing with the origin of the soul and the exegesis of James 2: 10. On July 28, there was a diocesan synod at Jerusalem, and Orosius was summoned by Bishop John to attend. Orosius informed the synod that Caelestius had been condemned by the council of Carthage and that Pelagius had said to him personally: "My teaching is that a person can, if he will, live without sin, and easily keep God's commandments." Pelagius acknowledged the statement and replied: "I did not mean that human nature has a natural endowment of sinlessness; I meant that the person who is prepared to toil and strive to avoid sin and to walk in the commandments of God on behalf of his own salvation, is granted by God the possibility of so doing." On further questioning, he roundly anathematized anyone who would say that apart from the help of God a person could advance in virtue. Pelagius' position was judged orthodox and the charge of heresy was dropped.

His troubles did not end there, however, for, towards the end of the same year, two deposed bishops from Gaul, Heros and Lazarus, who had made their home in Palestine, drew up a formal indictment on the basis of Pelagius' "Testimonia," some of his letters, an anonymous work of Caelestius, and the records of events at Carthage and in Sicily. They presented this "libellus" to Eulogius, metropolitan of Caesarea, who called a synod at Diospolis. The first part of the "libellus" accused Pelagius of teaching the following errors:

1. That no one can be without sin except those who have knowledge of the Law (*On the Proceedings of Pelagius* 1, 2).

2. That all human beings are governed by their own free will (*ibid.*, 3, 5).

3. That in the day of judgment there will be no mercy for sinners and wrongdoers, but they must be consumed in eternal fire (*ibid., 4, 12*).

4. That evil does not even enter the thought (*ibid.*, 4, 12).

5. That the kingdom of heaven is promised in the Old Testament as well (*ibid.*, 5, 13).

6. That human beings can, if they will, be without sin (*ibid.*, 6, 16).

7. That the Church is here without blemish or wrinkle (*ibid.*, 12, 27).

Pelagius met all the accusations to the satisfaction of the bishops. He still clung to the central proposition about the possibility of sinlessness (the sixth accusation), but qualified it in two ways. First, sinlessness was only possible by a combination of personal effort and the grace of God ("*proprio labore et Dei gratia*"). And, second, he did not mean to assert that there was *de facto* a sinless person but only that sinlessness was not a theoretical impossibility. In addition, Pelagius was able to produce letters from Augustine and other Church leaders written in terms of affection and friendship, and uttered a general anathema upon all doctrines alien to that of the Church. He was acquitted of all the charges of heresy and declared to be within the communion of the Catholic Church (*ibid.*, 20, 44).

The Church of Africa was not satisfied with the results of the two Palestinian councils. In June or July 416, a synod was held in Carthage, and the bishops, after Orosius had given his testimony and produced a letter of Heros and Lazarus, resolved to condemn Pelagius and Caelestius, a judgment of particular importance because it associated officially, for the first time, the two leaders of the error. A letter was drawn up to Innocent, the bishop of Rome, asking him to add the anathema of the apostolic see upon this heresy. It was signed by Aurelius, the bishop of Carthage, and sixty-seven other bishops. The bishops of the neighboring churches of Numidia in their turn met at Mileve in the same year and drew up a document in similar terms, which was forwarded to Innocent. In addition, five of the most influential bishops, Aurelius, Augustine, Alipius, Evodius and Possidius, wrote a personal letter to the Pope, explaining the various errors of Pelagius. Enclosed with the letter was a copy of Pelagius' *De Natura* as exemplifying the views they wished to be condemned.

Innocent first called a local synod to assist his deliberations, and finally replied in three letters dated January 27, 417. He found Pelagius' *De Natura* blasphemous in its denial of the necessity of grace and excommunicated Pelagius, Caelestius and their supporters until they should return to orthodoxy. Forty-four days after this solemn sentence he died.

Meanwhile in answer to Jerome, Pelagius wrote a work in four books entitled *On Free Will*. The work is now unfortunately lost, except for a few fragments cited and examined by Augustine in his *On the Grace of Christ* and *On Original Sin.* We shall come back to it in our exposition of Pelagius' teaching. In the meantime Augustine wrote a full and critical account, addressed to Aurelius, of the proceedings of the synod of Diospolis called *De Gestis Pelagii.* When news of the papal condemnation came, Augustine was elated. In a sermon (sermon 131) he proclaimed: "The cause is ended: would that the error might some day end!"

Under Innocent's successor, Zosimus (417-19) Pelagius' case was taken up again in Rome. In his defense, Pelagius had sent to Innocent a *"Libellus fidei"* in which he summarized his beliefs (see Augustine's *On the Grace of Christ*, 31, 33 ff.) Now Caelestius came to Rome to defend his cause in person before Zosimus. The pope, impressed by Caelestius' apparent humility and willingness to anathematize whatever doctrines were condemned by the pontifical see, and perhaps also because he was a Greek and therefore little inclined to make much of this Western controversy, wrote a sharp letter to Africa, proclaiming Caelestius "catholic," and requiring the Africans to appear within two months at Rome to prosecute their charges, or else to abandon them. A little later, he followed with another letter in which he declared both Pelagius and Caelestius to be orthodox, and severely rebuked the Africans for their hasty judgment.

In 418, more than two hundred African bishops met at Carthage and replied to Zosimus that their sentence against Pelagius and Caelestius would remain in force until they recognize that "we are aided by the grace of God, through Christ, not only to know, but to do what is right, in each single act, so that without grace we are unable to have, think, speak, or do anything pertaining to piety." Zosimus, challenged by such firmness, wavered and wrote in reply that he would reconsider the case. His letter arrived in Africa on April 29, and on the next day an imperial decree was issued from Ravenna ordering Pelagius, Caelestius and their followers to be banished from Rome. On May 1, a plenary council of two hundred fourteen bishops met at Carthage, and in nine canons condemned all the essential features of Pelagianism. Zosimus then published his *Epistola tractoria* in which he gave a brief history of Pelagianism, pointed out its errors, ratified the acts of the council of Carthage, and renewed his predecessors's excommunication of Pelagius and Caelestius.

Zosimus further required subscription to his letter from all bishops as a test of orthodoxy. Eighteen Italian bishops refused, among whom was Julian of Eclanum, who henceforth became the champion of the Pelagian party. A formidable dialectitian, he conducted a violent polemic against Augustine whom he accused of innovating on the question of original sin and of falling back into Manichaeism. Augustine had written in 419-420 a book *On Marriage and Concupiscence*, addressed to Valerius, which Julian attacked. In response Augustine was forced to clarify his view, defending the goodness of marriage, in another book, now known as the second book of *On Marriage and Concupiscence*. Julian's works include two letters to Zosimus, a *Confession of Faith*, the two letters answered by Augustine in his *Against Two Letters of the Pelagians* of 420 (though Julian repudiated the former of these), and two large books against Augustine, the first of which was a four-book volume against Augustine's first book of *On Marriage and Concupiscence*. In response, Augustine undertook in 421 a detailed refutation of Julian's four books in his first *Against Julian*, consisting of six books. The first two books establish Catholic teaching on the authority of the Greek and Latin Fathers. The last four books follow closely Julian's works, on the subjects of original sin and marriage (book II), on concupiscence (books IV and V), on infant baptism (book VI).

Julian, from Cilicia, where he had fled, sent a violent pamphlet in eight books against Augustine, who received it only in 428. In spite of his seventy-four years, the Bishop of Hippo again took up the pen and replied point by point to all of Julian's assertions. He was writing the sixth book of his voluminous and incomplete second treatise, *Contra Julianum opus imperfectum,* when death interrupted his work (430).

Before his death, however, Augustine had to be drawn into another controversy regarding the relationship between God's grace and human freedom. Of this we will treat in the next chapter. Meanwhile, Nestorius was deeply shaken by Zosimus' condemnation. He longed for reconciliation with Augustine, but it was useless. A synod, called under the chairmanship of Theodotus of Antioch, excluded him from the holy places of Jerusalem. It is likely that he left Palestine for Egypt. In any case he faded out of history, surrounded by abuse and contempt.

Caelestius made a final but unsuccessful attempt to vindicate himself before Pope Celestine. Banished once more from Italy, he went to Constantinople, whither Julian and three other bishops arrived in 428 or 429 and were befriended by Nestorius. In spite of Nestorius's protection, Pelagianism was condemned by the ecumenical council of Ephesus in 431 along with Nestorianism. This council dealt a death blow to Pelagianism, which, opposed by both East and West, henceforth ceased to exist as an organized movement.

II. Pelagius: Stoicism and Christian Asceticism

As we have seen, Pelagius was primarily a spiritual director engaged in helping others achieve Christian perfection. While Jerome was busy advising the aristocratic Aemilii family (including Paula and her two daughters Eustochium and Blesilla), Pelagius was guiding the members of the Anician clan, Pinianus and his wife Melania, the virgin Demetrias and her mother Juliana and grandmother Proba, and the deacon Syxtus (later Pope Syxtus III). Of course such spiritual direction could not be done without some theological understanding of God and the human condition. In his *De fide trinitatis*, which survive only in fragments, Pelagius strongly defends the doctrine of the Trinity, and we possess fragments which appear to have been a treatise on christology in which Pelagius opposed Apollinarianism. Furthermore, in his commentary on the letters of Paul, Pelagius often engages in polemics against Arians, Macedonians, Photinians, Apollinarians, Novatians, Marcionites and Jovinianists.

But more importantly, and more *a propos* to our theme, Pelagius develops an anthropology in which human freedom and human capacity to do good apart from God's grace are vigorously affirmed against the fatalistic tendency of Manichaeism. For Pelagius what distinguishes humans from non-human creatures is that the former are endowed with free will, whereas the latter act by natural necessity. Further, human freedom means for him "the capacity for either direction," that is, for good or evil; and this in turn implies that humans are able to be without sin. He recognizes that God has endowed human beings with the capacity (*possibilitas*) or ability (*posse*) for doing good, and in this sense this capacity or ability is a grace, but he asserts that the desire for (*velle*) and realization of (*esse*) the good lies within human power apart from divine grace.

From this fundamental principle Pelagius draws three corollaries. First, it is possible for humans to be without sin, even though admittedly the majority of people are held by the power of sin produced by the habit of successive acts of sinning; thus the doctrine of universal sinfulness is denied. Secondly, each person comes into the world in a kind of morally neutral condition; there is therefore no such thing as original sin. Understood as a constitutive element of the human condition, Adam's sin harmed the whole human race, and not merely himself, only in the sense that he gave a bad example. Thirdly, because of the integrity of their freedom, humans do not need supernatural grace, especially prevenient grace, to choose the good. Pelagius, of course, spoke often of grace; but for him grace means (1) the original endowment of free will by which humans have the capacity to be without sin; (2) the law of Moses; (3) the forgiveness of sin in virtue of the redemptive death of Christ; (4) the example of Christ; and (5) the teaching of Christ. In other words, for Pelagius grace still remains an external aid; he has no knowledge of grace as both *healing* sinful human nature and *elevating* it to share in the divine life.

Pelagius expounds his anthropology in various works, some of which survive only in quotations in the works of Augustine. We will give extracts from his letter to Demetrias, and from his treatises *On Nature* and *On Free Choice*.

THE LETTER TO DEMETRIAS

Demetrias, daughter of Julian, resolved to take the vow of virginity. Her Christian education had been under the guidance of Augustine and Alypius (Augustine's letter 150). Jerome, too, wrote to her (letter 130), directing her to a life of study and fasting, labor and good works through her wealth, and warning her not to worry about difficult theological problems. Pelagius, in his turn, sent her a letter in which, besides imparting to her advice on religious life, he asserted that God has given us a capacity for right or wrong action and that the possibility of wrong choice is given us so that our fulfillment of his will may be the result of our will, not his. There is thus a kind of natural holiness which, Pelagius points out, exists in many of the pagan philosophers and the patriarchs of the Old Testament. Of course we are weighed down by our evil habits, but what evil habits have done, good habits can undo. Our salvation is in our hands. Augustine will react to this letter in his own to Juliana (letter 188) in which he protests that Demetrias' virtues did not come from her own strength but are God's gifts.

> (2) In my discussion of the norms of right conduct and a holy life, I often begin by showing the strength and characteristics of human nature. By explaining what it is capable of doing, I encourage my hearers to practice different virtues. To ask a person to do something he considers impossible does him no good. We must have hope as our guide and companion when we set out to practice virtue; otherwise, despair of success will jeopardize every enterprise to acquire the impossible. The method I have adopted in other exhortations should, I believe, be especially observed in this one. Where a more perfect form of life is to be established, the explanation of nature's goodness should be correspondingly fuller. If the soul has a lower estimation of its capacity, it will be less diligent and insistent in pursuing virtue. Not realizing its inner power, it will assume that it lacks the capacity. We must therefore reflect fully on the power that is to be exercised, and explain clearly the good of which nature is capable. Once something has been shown possible, it ought to be accomplished. The first foundation for a pure and spiritual life, therefore, is that the virgin recognize her strengths. She will be able to exercise them well once she realized she possesses them. . . .

The first way to form a judgment of the goodness of human nature is to look upon it as created by God. He made the whole world and all the good things in it. How much more excellent, then, did he fashion human beings, for whose sake he made everything else. The goodness of humanity was indicated even before it was created when God prepared to form it in his image and likeness....

Though he was made without external armament, the human person was given the better interior weapons of reason and judgment. Thus, through the exercise of his intellect and mind, by which he was superior to other animals, he alone could acknowledge the creator of all. He was to use the same faculty to dominate the beasts and to serve God. The Lord wanted him to accomplish justice voluntarily rather than by coercion. He gave him the power of his own counsel and placed before him life and death, good and evil....

(3) We must take care that you are not disturbed by what tends to upset the ignorant people. You must not think that human nature was not created truly good because it is capable of evil and because it is not, on account of its impetuosity, bound by necessity to immutable good. If you reflect more carefully and bring your mind to a deeper understanding of the matter, you will realize that what seems to be inimical to it actually makes the human condition better and superior. The glory of the reasonable soul consists precisely in its having to face a parting of the ways, in its freedom to choose either direction. In this, I submit, lies the dignity of our nature; this is the source of honor, reward, and praise merited by the best people. If a person could not choose evil, he would not practice virtue in persevering in the good. It pleased God to endow rational creatures with the gift of good will and the power of free choice. By making a person naturally capable of good and evil, so that he could do both and would direct his will to either, God arranged that what an individual actually chose would be properly his own. The good could be done voluntarily only by a creature which was also capable of evil. Therefore the most excellent Creator decided to make us capable of both.

It was, of course, God's intention and command that we should do what is good. His only purpose in giving the capacity for evil was that we accomplish his will by our own will. Our ability to do evil is, therefore, itself a good. The reason for this is that it makes its opposite, the capacity for doing good, better. It removes the bonds of necessity, enables the person to decide freely, and makes the will voluntary in its own right. Thus we have the freedom to choose or oppose, to accept or reject. All other creatures have only the goodness which comes from their nature and condition; the rational beings excel them all in having the goodness coming from their own will. . . .

(4) . . . Our souls possess, as it were, a natural integrity which resides in their depths and passes judgments of good and evil. It approves upright and correct actions as well as condemns the evil ones. According to the testimony of the conscience, by a kind of interior law, it distinguishes the quality of each deed. It does not deceive us by contrived or clever arguments; rather, it uses the most faithful and incorruptible testimony of our own feelings to accuse or defend us. . . . Once you realize how nature itself taught justice in place of the law, you will easily understand how good it is. . . .

(8) In defending the goodness of nature we do not affirm that it can do no wrong. Certainly we do recognize that it is capable of both good and evil. We do, however, reject the notion that nature's inadequacy inevitably leads us to do evil. We do either good or evil only by our own will; since we always remain capable of both, we are always free to do either . . .[1]

HUMAN NATURE AND HUMAN FREEDOM

In his *Retractations* written in 426-427 in which he reviewed his works, Augustine noted that he wrote his *On Nature and Grace* (415) in response to "a certain book of Pelagius, in which he defends, with all the argumentative skill he could muster, the human nature in opposition to the grace of God

[1]Text: PL 30.15-46; trans. J. Patout Burns, *Theological Anthropology,* 39-55.

whereby the unrighteous is justified and we become Christians" (c. 68). The book Augustine referred to is Pelagius' *De Natura (On Nature)* which Timasius and James had sent to him with the request that he reply point by point to it. This book is unfortunately now lost, but from Augustine's quotations and summaries, it is possible to gather the main outline of Pelagius' teaching on grace. Pelagius begins by distinguishing between the possible and the actual. He is not maintaining that any sinless person actually existed, but that it is possible for one to be so. Further, he argues that humans have this possibility by their natural endowment, and hence do not need the aid of special grace. God does not command impossibilities; if our nature made it impossible for us to be free from sin, our wills would not be truly free; in the endowment of our human nature, God has granted us the power of not sinning, and this power, coming from God, may rightly be called ours by God's grace, or we would be introducing an illegitimate division in God. In what follows, we will give Augustine's quotation of Pelagius' words:

> For he (Pelagius) first of all makes a distinction: "It is one thing," says he, "to inquire whether a thing can be, which has respect to its possibility only; and another thing, whether or not it is...." Observe, however, what he means by this distinction, true and manifest enough in itself, and what he attempts to make out of it. "We are treating," says he, " of possibility only; and to pass from this to something else, except in the case of some certain fact, we deem to be a very serious and extraordinary process...." And among the many passages in which he treats of this subject, occurs the following: "I once more repeat my position: I say that it is possible for a human person to be without sin. What do you say? That it is impossible for a person to be without sin? But I do not say," he adds, "that there actually is a person without sin; nor do I say that there is not a person without sin. Our contention is about what is possible and not possible; not about what is, and is not ... (*On Nature and Grace*, 7, 8).[2]

[2]Text: CSEL 60.237; trans. LNPF 5.123, ed. Philip Schaff

He then starts an objection to his own position, as if, indeed, another person had raised it, and says, "A person," you will say, "may possibly be without sin; but it is by the grace of God." He then at once adds the following, as if in answer to his own objection: "I thank you for your kindness, because you are not merely content to withdraw your opposition to my statement, which you just now opposed, or barely to acknowledge it; but you actually go so far as to approve it. For to say, 'A person may possibly, but by this or by that,' is in fact nothing else than not only to assent to its possibility, but also to show the mode and condition of its possibility. Nobody, therefore, gives a stronger assent to the possibility of anything than the person who allows the condition thereof; because, without the thing itself, it is not possible for a condition to be." After this he raises another objection against himself: "But," you will say, "you seem here to reject the grace of God, inasmuch as you do not even mention it?" He then answers the objection: "Now, is it I that reject grace, who, by acknowledging the thing, must also confess the means by which it may be effected, or you, who, by denying the thing, must also deny whatever may be the means by which the thing is accomplished...?" (*ibid.*, 10,11).[3]

At reading this statement of Pelagius, Augustine rejoiced because it seems not to deny the necessity of grace for justification. On further perusal of his book, however, Augustine grew alarmed at the comparisons Pelagius employs which, in fact, deny the necessity of such supernatural grace:

> ...For he says, "If I were to say, a human being is able to dispute, a bird is able to fly, a hare is able to run, without mentioning at the same time the instrument by which these acts can be accomplished—that is, the tongue, the wings, and the legs—should I then have denied the conditions of the various offices, when I acknowledged the very offices themselves?" It is at once apparent that he had here

instanced such things as are by nature efficient, for the members of the bodily structure which are here mentioned are created with natures of such a kind—the tongue, the wings, the legs. He has not here pointed any such thing as we wish to have understood by *grace*, without which no human person can be justified; for this is a topic which is concerned about the cure, not the constitution, of natural functions...(*ibid.*, 11, 12).[4]

In the survey of the history of the Pelagian controversy given above we have already given a summary of Pelagius' doctrine as reported in Augustine's *On the Proceedings of Pelagius*; it remains to give another extract of Pelagius' work *On Free Will* which he wrote in answer to Jerome. This work is now lost and fragments of it are found in Augustine's *On the Grace of Christ and On Original Sin*. In his work Pelagius makes four important points.

First, according to Pelagius we are born in a kind of morally neutral condition with the capacity for good and evil alike. This is a flat denial of original sin. Pelagius, however, did not think that his doctrine would entail the denial of the necessity of baptism for infants; this baptism, according to him, is still needed for them to be able to enter the kingdom of heaven, which is different from salvation.

> ...Pelagius says: "Everything good and everything evil, on account of which we are either praiseworthy or blameworthy, is not born with us but with the capacity for either conduct; and so we are procreated without virtue as well as without vice, and previous to the action of our own proper will, that alone is in humans which God has formed..." (*On the Grace of Christ and on Original Sin*, Book II, 13, 14).[5]

Secondly, Pelagius distinguishes three elements in any course of action: *posse*, *velle*, and *esse*—the power, desire, and realization. The power is in our nature and is God's gift; the

[4]Text CSEL 60.240; trans. LNPF 5.125
[5]Text: CSEL 42.176; trans. LNPF 5.241

desire is in our will, and the realization is in the result, and both
come from our will and are our proper domain.

> "We distinguish," says he, "three things and arrange them in
> a definite order. We put in the first place *posse* (ability,
> possibility); in the second, *velle* (volition); in the third, *esse*
> (existence, actuality). The *posse* we assign to our nature, the
> *velle* to the will, the *esse* to actual realization. The first of
> these, *posse*, is properly ascribed to God, who conferred it
> on his creatures; while the other two, *velle* and *esse*, are to be
> referred to the human agent, since they have their source in
> his will. Therefore the human agent's praise lies in his willing
> and doing a good work; or rather this praise belongs both to
> the human person and to God who has granted the
> possibility of willing and working, and who by the help of
> this grace assists even this very possibility. That a person has
> this possibility of willing and effecting any good work is due
> to God alone.... Therefore (and this must be often repeated
> because of your calumnies), when we say that it is possible
> for a person to be without sin, we are even then praising
> God by acknowledging the gift of possibility which we have
> received. He is it that bestowed this *posse* on us, and there is
> no occasion for praising the human agent when we are
> treating of God alone; for the question is not about *velle* or
> *esse*, but solely about the possible (*On the Grace of Christ*
> Book I, 4, 5).[6]

Thirdly, Pelagius admits that Adam's sin did harm the whole
human race, and not merely himself, but by example, not by
physical transmission, and that children at birth are not in the
same state as Adam before the fall, because they, unlike him,
are not yet capable of using reason.

> ...Pelagius tells them that "the reason why he condemned
> the points which were objected against him, is that he
> himself maintains that the primary sin was injurious not
> only to the first man, but to the whole human race not by

---

[6]Text: CSEL 42.127; trans. LNPF 5.219

transmission, but by example.... The reason why infants are not in the same state in which Adam was before the transgression, is that they are not yet able to receive the commandment, whereas he was able; and further because they do not yet make use of that choice of rational will which he certainly made use of, since otherwise no commandment would have been given him..." (*On Original Sin,* Book II, 15, 16).[7]

Fourthly, Pelagius argues that if one were to say that sin is unavoidable, one would fall into Manichaeism and deny the goodness of the Creator. If we were driven by necessity to evil, then there would be no justice in our punishment.

In conclusion, it may be helpful to report some of the arguments against the doctrine of original sin that Pelagius presented, not as his own, but as advanced by other people he knew, in his commentary on Rom 5: 12 and which Augustine quoted in his *On the Merits and Forgiveness of Sins,* his first work against Pelagianism. The arguments are as follows:

1. "If Adam's sin injured even those who do not sin, Christ's righteousness ought likewise profit even those who do not believe."

2. "No one can transmit what he has not; and hence, if baptism cleanses from sin, the children of baptized parents ought to be free from sin."

3. "If the soul is not inherited, but only the flesh, then only the latter inherits the sin, and it alone deserves punishment; it would be unjust for the soul, which is now created and does not come out of the lump of Adam, to bear the burden of so old a sin committed by another person."

4. "It cannot be admitted that God, who remits to a person his own sins, should impute to him another's" (*On the Merits and Forgiveness of Sins,* 3.3, 5).[8]

[7]Text: CSEL 42.177; trans. NPNF 5.242
[8]Text: CSEL 60.130, 141, 144; trans. LNPF 5.69, 76, 74

III. Augustine's Writings Against Pelagius and Julian

It was noted above how at first, preoccupied with the Donatist controversy, Augustine did not at once join the struggle against Pelagius when the latter came to Hippo in 411 and later to Carthage. Once he realized the pernicious consequences of Pelagianism, he attacked it vehemently, first against Caelestius and Pelagius himself and later against Julian. He did this in his sermons, letters, and treatises, and through various councils.

Among his sermons (e.g. 151, 152, 155, 156, 170, 174, 175, 176, 293, 294) the last two are probably the most remarkable. They were delivered at Carthage, midsummer of 413; in both of them Augustine dealt with the question of infant baptism. According to Pelagius, infants are not affected by the sin of Adam but only by his bad example; they were baptized, not for salvation, but for the kingdom of God. Augustine argued that there is no eternal life outside the kingdom of God, no middle place between the right and the left hands of the Judge on the last day, and that, therefore, to exclude one from the kingdom of God is to assign him to the pains of eternal hell. Further, Augustine pointed out, no one enters into heaven unless he had been made a member of Christ, and this can only be by faith, which, in the infant's case, is professed by another in his stead. He bolstered up his arguments with a quotation from the letter of Cyprian, the famous third-century bishop of the see of Carthage, to Fidus to the effect that "infants should be baptized at the earliest possible age, lest they should die in their inherited sin, and so pass into eternal punishment" (cfr. *On the Merits and Remission of Sins*, 3, 10).

Among his letters (146, 150, 156, 157, 166, 175, 176, 177, 181, 182, 183, 188, 190, 191, 193, 194, 201, 202) we have already mentioned in passing those he wrote to Proba and her daughter-in-law Juliana, Demetrias' mother, to warn them against the danger of Pelagianism (letters 150 and 188). The most important letter is arguably letter 157, Augustine's long reply to a certain Hilary in Sicily who had written to solicit Augustine's opinion on some doctrines, widespread in his city, which sounded suspiciously like those of Pelagius and Caelestius. Among these are the assertions that humans can

live without sin and can fulfill without difficulty the commandments of God, if they will, and that an infant who dies before
receiving baptism does not deserve to be punished since it is
born without sin. Augustine affirmed that neither the Law nor
free will have of themselves any power to justify us; we are at
every point driven back upon our need for the free grace of
God. Hence, there is the absolute necessity for the prayer of
repentance. Further, on the basis of his reading of Rom 5: 12
("*in quo omnes peccaverunt*") he argued for a physical
transmission of original sin from Adam to his descendants.

Among Augustine's treatises against Pelagius, the following
in their chronological order stand out in importance: *On the
Merits and Remission of Sins* (412), *On the Spirit and the
Letter* (412), *On Nature and Grace* (415), *On the Human
Person's Perfection in Righteousness* (415), *On the Proceedings
of Pelagius* (417), *On the Grace of Christ and On Original Sin*
(418).

In what follows we will give extracts from some of these
works as well as from Augustine's writings against Julian
which have already been mentioned toward the end of the first
section of this chapter.

ON THE MERITS AND REMISSION OF SINS

Augustine wrote his three-volume work at the request of his
friend Flavius Marcellinus who had sought his view on the
doctrines that were being propounded regarding the mortality
of Adam, the relation of our sin to his, and infant baptism. In
the first book Augustine pointed out that death is the
punishment for the sin of Adam, and it has affected his whole
progeny. The practice of infant baptism confirms the existence
of an inherited taint from which infants need redemption. In
the second book, Augustine dealt with the wider issues of
Pelagianism, but he was still unwilling to impugn either
Pelagius or Caelestius by name. He was ready to admit the
abstract possibility of sinlessness in this life, a position he had
once propounded but now rejected. He was now convinced
that no one is wholly without sin, except the one mediator,
Jesus. At this point he had concluded the presentation of his

arguments when he came upon Pelagius' commentary on the letters of Paul, and felt constrained to reject Pelagius' denial of original sin found there.

> 9. You (i.e. Marcellinus) tell me in your letter that they attempt to twist into some new sense the passage of the Apostle in which he says: "By one man sin entered into the world, and death by sin." (Rom 5: 12). You did not, however, inform me what they suppose to be the meaning of these words. So far as I have discovered from others, they think that the death which is mentioned here is not the death of the body, which they will not allow Adam to have deserved by sin, but that of the soul, which takes place in actual sin. Further, they say that this actual sin has not been transmitted from the first man to other persons by natural descent, but by imitation. Hence, likewise, they refuse to believe that in infants original sin is remitted through baptism, for they contend that no such original sin exists at all in people by their birth. But if the Apostle had wished to assert that sin entered into the world, not by natural descent, but by imitation, he would have mentioned as the first offender, not Adam, indeed, but the devil, of whom it is written that "he sinned from the beginning" (1 Jn 3: 8), of whom also we read in the Book of Wisdom: "Nevertheless through the devil's envy death entered into the world" (Wisd 2:24). Now insofar as this death came upon humans from the devil, not because they were propagated by him, but because they imitated his example, it is immediately added: "And those who belong to his side imitate him" (Wisd 2: 25). Accordingly, the Apostle, when mentioning sin and death together, which had passed by natural descent from one upon all others, set him down as the introducer thereof from whom the propagation of the human race took its beginning.
>
> XVI.21. It may therefore be correctly affirmed, that such infants as die without being baptized will be punished with the mildest condemnation of all. That person, therefore, greatly deceives both himself and others, who teaches that they will not be condemned at all. The Apostle, in fact, says: "The sentence followed upon one offense and brought

condemnation" (Rom 5: 16); and again a little after: "A single offense brought condemnation to all" (v. 18). When, indeed, Adam sinned by disobeying God, then his body—although it was a natural and mortal body—lost the grace whereby it used in every part of it to be obedient to the soul. Then there arose in humans affections common to the brutes which produce shame and made them ashamed of their own nakedness. Then also, by a certain disease which occurred in humans as the result of a suddenly injected and pestilential corruption, they lost the stability of life in which they had been created, and, by reason of the changes which they underwent in the stages of life, ended at last in death. However many were the years they lived in their subsequent life, they began to die on the day when they received the law of death, because they kept verging toward old age. . . . As a consequence, then, of this disobedience of the flesh, and this law of sin and death, whoever is born of the flesh has need of spiritual regeneration, not only that he may reach the kingdom of God, but also that he may be freed from the damnation of sin. Just as we, born in the flesh, are subject to sin and death from the first Adam, so too, born again in baptism, are we associated with the righteousness and eternal life of the second Adam. . . .

Book II. Concupiscence, therefore, as the law of sin which remains in the members of this body of death, is born with infants. In baptized infants, it is deprived of guilt and is left for the struggle of life; but it brings no condemnation for those who die before the struggle. Unbaptized children, however, it implicates as guilty and draws them into condemnation as children of wrath, even if they die in infancy. In baptized adults, on the other hand, endowed with reason, whatever consent their mind gives to this concupiscence for the commission of sin, is an act of their own will. After all sins have been blotted out, and that guilt has been cancelled which bound humans from their very birth in a conquered condition, concupiscence still remains, not in order to hurt in any way those who yield no consent to it for unlawful deeds, until it is swallowed up in victory, and, in that perfect peace, nothing is left to be conquered. Those, however, who yield consent to it for the commission

of unlawful deeds, it holds as guilty; and unless they are
healed through the medicine of repentance, and through
works of mercy, by the intercession in our behalf of the
heavenly High Priest, it leads them to the second death and
utter condemnation...(2, 4).[9]

ON THE SPIRIT AND THE LETTER

Marcellinus was troubled by Augustine's affirmation of the
abstract possibility of sinlessness, since no concrete example of
sinless people, except Jesus, could be adduced, and questioned
him further. The result is Augustine's *De Spiritu et Littera.* He
begins by arguing that the impossibility of an event is not
disproved by the absence of actual examples. Then, as he puts
it in his *Retractations,* 2, 37: "As far as God enabled me, I
vigorously disputed with the enemies of that grace of God
which justifies the ungodly." The work contains an exaltation
of God's grace, mediated by the Holy Spirit, as its author
contrasts the Law with the Gospel, bringing out clearly the
inadequacy of the former by itself, and thus gives a beautiful
commentary on 2 Cor 3: 6, the verse from which the treatise
takes its name. In the following extracts Augustine discusses
the relationship between divine grace and human free will.

Do we then by grace make void free will? God forbid! On
the contrary, we establish free will. For even as the Law is
not made void but established by faith, so also free will by
grace. For neither is the Law fulfilled except by free will; but
by the Law is the knowledge of sin, by faith the acquisition
of grace against sin, by grace the healing of the soul from the
disease of sin, by the health of the soul the freedom of the
will, by free will the love of righteousness, by love of
righteousness the fulfillment of the Law. Accordingly, as the
Law is not made void but established by faith, since faith
procures grace whereby the Law is fulfilled, so free will is
not made void but is established by grace, since grace heals
the will whereby righteousness is freely loved....

[9]Text: CSEL 60. 10, 20, 73; trans. NPNF 5.18, 22, 45

It remains for us briefly to inquire whether the will by which we believe is itself the gift of God, or whether it arises from that free will which is naturally implanted in us? If we say that it is not the gift of God, we must then incur the fear of supposing that we have discovered some answer to the Apostle's reproachful question: "What have you that you have not received? If, then, you have received it, why are you boasting as if it were your own?" (I Cor 4: 7)—even some such answer as this: "See, we have the will to believe, which we did not receive!" If, however, we were to say that this kind of will is nothing but the gift of God, we should then have to fear lest unbelieving and ungodly people might not unreasonably seem to have some fair excuse for their unbelief in saying that God has refused to give them this will. Now when the Apostle says: "It is God that works in you both to will and to do of his own good pleasure" (Phil 2: 13), we are already in the sphere of grace, granted to faith, so that we may have the good works, wrought by faith through the love which is poured forth in our hearts by the Holy Spirit which is given to us. But we believe in order that his grace may be granted and our belief is an act of free will. It is concerning this will that we ask where it comes from. If by nature, then why not to all, since the same God is the Creator of all? If by the gift of God, still why not to all, since he wills that all be saved and come to the knowledge of the truth (1 Tim 2: 4)?

Here the first point to be made, as a possible solution of the difficulty, is that free will, which the Creator has assigned to our rational soul, is a neutral power, which can either incline to faith or turn toward unbelief. Accordingly, a person cannot be said to have even that will with which he believes in God without having received it, since it arises at God's call from the free will which he naturally received when he was created. God wills that all be saved and come to the knowledge of the truth; but in such a way as not to deprive them of that free will for the good or evil use of which they are subject to the judgment of absolute justice. By that judgment, unbelievers act against God's will when they disbelieve his Gospel; yet they do not defeat his will but deprive themselves of a supreme good and fall into the distress of punishment and thereby experience the power of him in punishments whose mercy in his gifts they despised. Thus God's will is forever invincible, which would not be had he no way of dealing with his despisers, or were there any escape for them from his sentence upon such.... The despiser of his mercy, which calls for belief, is guilty unto condemnation under God's power. But whosoever shall put his trust in God, and gives himself up to him, for the forgiveness of all his sins, for the healing of all his corruption, and for the kindling and illumination of his soul by his warmth and light, shall have good works by his grace. He shall be even in his body redeemed from the corruption of death, crowned, satisfied with blessings—not temporal, but eternal—above what we can ask or understand (57-58).[10]

ON NATURE AND GRACE

Of this work Augustine says in his *Retractations*, 2, 68: "At that time also there came into my hands a certain book of Pelagius', in which he defends, with all the argumentative skill he could muster, the nature of man, in opposition to the grace of God whereby the unrighteous is justified and we become Christians. The treatise which contains my reply to him, and in which I defend grace, not indeed as opposed to nature, but as that which liberates and governs nature, I have entitled *On Nature and Grace*" (CSEL 36.180).

Human nature, indeed, was created at first faultless and sinless; but that human nature in which every one is born from Adam, now needs the physician, because it is not sound. All good qualities, no doubt, which it still possesses in its constitution, life, senses, and intellect, it has from the Most High God, its Creator and Maker. But the flaw, which darkens and weakens all those natural goods, so that it has need of illumination and healing, it has not contracted from its blameless Creator, but from that original sin, which it committed by free will. Accordingly, animal nature is rightly punished. For, if we are now newly created in Christ, we were, for all that, children of wrath, even as others, "but God, who is rich in mercy, for his great love wherewith he loved us, even when we were dead in sins, has brought us to life with Christ, by whose grace we were saved" (Eph 2: 4). This grace of Christ, without which neither infants nor adults can be saved, is not, however, rendered for any merits, but is given *gratis*, on account of which it is also called *grace*. "We are justified freely through his blood," says the Apostle (Rom 3: 24). Whence, they are indeed justly condemned who are not liberated through grace, either because they are not yet able to hear, or because they are unwilling to obey, or again because they did not receive, at the time when they were unable to hear on account of their youth, that bath of regeneration, which they might have received and through which they might have been saved. The reason is that they are not without sin, either that which they have inherited from their birth, or that which they have added from their own misconduct. "For all have sinned"—whether in Adam or in themselves—"and come short of the glory of God" (Rom 3: 23).

The entire mass, therefore, incurs penalty; and if the deserved punishment of condemnation were rendered to all, it would without doubt be rightly rendered. They, therefore, who are delivered from it by grace are called, not vessels of their own merits, but "vessels of mercy" (Rom 9: 23). But of whose mercy, if not of him who sent Christ Jesus into the world to save sinners, whom he foreknew, and foreordained, and called, and justified, and glorified? (Rom 8: 29-30). Now, who could be so madly insane as to fail to give ineffable thanks to the mercy which liberates whom it would? The person who correctly appreciates the whole subject cannot possibly blame the justice of God in wholly condemning all whatsoever (3-5).[11]

---

[11] Text: CSEL 60.235; trans, LNPF 5.122, 149

ON THE GRACE OF CHRIST AND ON ORIGINAL SIN

After the "great African council" at Carthage in 418 which condemned Pelagianism, Augustine remained in Carthage, and while he was there he received a letter from Pinianus and Melania, who had been married but now lived separately in continence in Bethlehem. They solicited Augustine's opinion on Pelagianism and in reply he wrote two books which are found together in one work, namely *On the Grace of Christ and On Original Sin*. The first book dealt with "the assistance of the divine grace toward our justification, by which God cooperates in all things for good to those who love him, and whom he first loved, giving to them that he may receive from them" and the second book deals with "the sin which by one man has entered the world along with death, and so has passed upon all human beings" (*On the Grace of Christ*, 55).

After quoting Pelagius' distinction between *posse*, *velle* and *esse* and his attributing the *posse* to God and claiming the *velle* and *esse* for us, Augustine affirms that God's grace is needed for all three.

> Let Pelagius, therefore, cease at last to deceive both himself and others by disputing against the grace of God. God's graciousness to us must be proclaimed not only in the case of one of these three, namely the capacity for good willing and doing, but also in the case of good will and operation as well. He specifies that this power is capable of both directions. He wants to attribute our good works to God because they come from this power; yet the sins which come from this same power should not be referred to God. Hence, the help of divine grace is to be recognized not simply because it assists the natural capacity.
> Pelagius must cease to say: "Our ability to do, say, think any good, is from him who has given us this ability, and who also assists this ability; whereas our doing a good deed, or speaking a good word, or thinking a good thought, proceeds from ourselves." He must, I repeat, cease to say this. For God has not only given us the ability and aids it, but he further works in us "to will and to do." It is not because we do not will, or do not do, that we will and do

nothing good, but because we are without his help. How can he say: "Our ability to do good is God's, but our actual doing it is ours," when the Apostle tells us that he "prays to God" on behalf of those to whom he was writing, "that they should do no evil, but that they should do that which is good?" (2 Cor 13: 7). His words are not: "We pray that you be *able* to do nothing evil," but, "that you do no evil." Neither does he say: "that you be *able* to do good"; but, "that you do good." Insofar as it is written: "As many as are led by the Spirit of God, they are children of God" (Rom 8: 14), it follows that in order that they may do that which is good, they must be led by him who is good. How can Pelagius say: "Our ability to make a good use of speech comes from God, but our actual making good use of speech proceeds from ourselves," when the Lord declares: "It is the Spirit of your Father who speaks in you?" (Mt 10: 20). He does not say: "It is not you who have given to yourselves the ability of speaking well"; rather his words are: "It is not you that speak." Nor does he say: "It is the Spirit of your Father who *gives, has given,* you the *power* to speak well"; rather he says: "who speaks in you." He does not mention the actualization of a capacity; he expresses the accomplishment of cooperation. How can this arrogant asserter of free will say: "Our ability to think well is from God, whereas good thinking is our own"? The humbler preacher of grace replies to him: "We are not fit to think anything of ourselves from our own resources. Our competence is from God." (2 Cor 3: 5). He says "to think," not "*to be able to* think."[12]

ON MARRIAGE AND CONCUPISCENCE

Augustine's first book *On Marriage and Concupiscence,* which he addressed to Count Valerius, was read by the Pelagians, especially by Julian, who then wrote four books in opposition to it, charging that Augustine's doctrine of original sin condemns marriage. Various extracts of Julian's books were collected by some interested person and forwarded to

[12]Text: CSEL 42.145-147, 163; trans. LNPF 5.229, 235

Valerius who gave them to Alypius to bring back to Augustine. The latter wasted no time in responding to Julian's attacks in a second book with the same title as before, *On Marriage and Concupiscence.* Augustine maintains that marriage is good and that concupiscence of the flesh, or "the law in our members which wars against the law of our spirit," is not a fault of marriage. Further, he suggests, conjugal chastity makes a good use of the evil of concupiscence in the procreation of children.

> Now this concupiscence, this law of sin which dwells in our members, to which the Law of righteousness forbids allegiance, saying in the words of the Apostle: "Let not sin, therefore, reign in your mortal body and make you obey its lusts; no more shall you offer your members of your body to sin as weapons for evil" (Rom 6: 12-13), this concupiscence, I say, which is cleansed only by the sacrament of rebirth, does undoubtedly, by means of natural birth, pass on the bond of sin to a person's descendants, unless they are themselves loosed from it by rebirth. In the case, however, of the reborn, concupiscence is not itself sin any longer, whenever they do not consent to it for illicit works, and when the members are not applied by the ruling mind to perpetrate such deeds.... In a manner of speech, however, concupiscence is called sin, both because it arose from sin and because it produces sin when it is victorious, and consequently its guilt prevails in the natural person. Nevertheless, this guilt, by Christ's grace through the remission of all sins, is not allowed to prevail in the person who is reborn, if he does not yield obedience to it whenever it urges him to commit evil....
> ...Carnal concupiscence is remitted, indeed, in baptism; not so that it is put out of existence, but so that it is not imputed for sin. Although its guilt is now taken away, it still remains until our entire infirmity is healed by the advancing renewal of our inner self, day by day, when at last our outward self shall be clothed in incorruption. It does not remain, however, substantially, as a body or a spirit; it is nothing more than a certain affection of an evil quality, such as languor, for instance. There is not, to be sure, anything

left which is still to be remitted whenever, as the Scripture says, "The Lord forgives all our iniquities" (Ps: 103, 3). But until that happens which immediately follows in the same passage: "Who heals all your infirmities, who redeems your life from corruption" (Ps 103: 4), there remains this concupiscence of flesh in the body of this death. Now we are admonished not to obey its sinful desires to do evil: "Let not sin reign in your mortal body" (Rom 6: 12). Still this concupiscence is daily lessened in persons of continence and increasing years, and most of all, when old age approaches near. The person, however, who yields to it a wicked service, receives such great energies that, even when all his members are now failing through age, and those special parts of his body are unable to be applied to their proper function, he does not ever cease to revel in a still increasing rage of disgraceful and shameless desire.[13]

IV. *The Teaching of the Sixteenth Council of Carthage*

The Council of Carthage, attended by 214 bishops in 418, formulated eight canons regarding the primitive state of Adam, original sin, infant baptism, and justifying grace.

> This has been decided by all the bishops...gathered together in the holy Synod of the church of Carthage:
> (1) Whoever says that Adam, the first man, was made mortal in the sense that he was to die a bodily death whether he sinned or not, which means that to quit the body would not be a punishment for sin but a necessity of nature, *anathema sit.*
> (2) Likewise it has been decided: If anyone denies that infants newly born from their mothers' wombs are to be baptized, or says that, though they are baptized for the remission of sins, yet they do not contract from Adam any trace of original sin which must be expiated by the bath of regeneration, so that in their case the formula of baptism

[13]Text: CSEL 42.237, 240; trans. NPNF 5.274-275

"for the forgiveness of sins" would no longer be true but would be false, *anathema sit.*

For, what the Apostle says: "Sin came into the world through one man and death through sin, and so death spread to all humans as all sinned in him" (Rom 5: 12, *Vulgate*), should not be understood in another sense than that in which the Catholic Church spread over the whole world has understood it at all times. For, because of this rule of faith, in accordance with apostolic tradition, even children who of themselves cannot have yet committed any sin are truly baptized for the remission of sins, so that by regeneration they may be cleansed from what they contracted through generation.

(3)Likewise it has been decided: Whoever says that the grace by which we are justified through Jesus Christ our Lord serves only for the remission of sins already committed, and is not also a help not to commit them, *anathema sit.*

(4) Likewise it has been decided : Whoever says that this same grace of God through our Lord Jesus Christ solely helps us not to sin because through it an understanding of the commandments is revealed and opened to us that we may know what we should seek and what we should avoid, but not because through it is given to us the love and the strength to do what we have recognized to be in our duty, *anathema sit.*

For since the Apostle says: "Knowledge puffs up, but love builds up" (1 Cor 8:1), it would be very wrong to believe that we have the grace of Christ for knowledge which puffs up and not for love which builds up; for both are the gift of God: the knowledge of what we should do and the love to do it, so that, built up by love, we may not be puffed up by knowledge. Just as it is written: "Love is of God" (1 Jn 4:7).

(5) Likewise it has been decided: Whoever says that the grace of justification is given to us so that we may do more easily with grace what we are ordered to do by our free will, as if even without grace we were able, though without facility, to fulfil the divine commandments, *anathema sit.*

For when the Lord spoke of the fruits of the commandments, He did not say that apart from Him we could do things with greater difficulty, but rather: "Apart from me you can do nothing" (Jn 15:5).

(6) Likewise it has been decided: When St. John the apostle says: "If we say we have no sin we deceive ourselves, and the truth is not in us" (1 Jn 1:8), whoever takes this to mean that we must say we have sin out of humility, not because it is true, *anathema sit.*

For the Apostle continues: "If we confess our sins, He is faithful and just, and will forgive our sins and cleanse us from all unrighteousness" (1 Jn 1:9). From this passage it is quite clear that that is not said only out of humility, but also in truth. For the Apostle could have said: "If we say that we have no sin, we are boasting and humility is not in us." But since he says: "We deceive ourselves and the truth is not in us," he clearly shows that anyone who says he has no sin is not speaking truly but falsely.

(7) Likewise it has been decided: Whoever says that the reason why the saints say in the Lord's prayer: "Forgive us our debts" (Mt 6: 12) is not that they are saying this for themselves—for such a petition is no longer necessary for them—but for others among their people who are sinners, and that this is why none of the saints says: "Forgive me my debts," but: "Forgive us our debts," so that the just person is understood to pray for others rather than for himself, *anathema sit.*

For "We all offend in many things" (James 3: 2 Vulgate). Why was the word "all" added if not to bring the expression into agreement with the Psalm where we read: "Enter not into judgment with your servant, for no living person is righteous before you" (Ps 143 [142]: 2)?

And in the prayer for Solomon, the wise man, (we read): "There is no person who does not sin" (2 Chron 6: 36); and in the book of the holy man Job: "He seals up the hand of every one, that every one may know his weakness' (cf. Job 37: 7, old mistranslation). Even the holy and just Daniel used the plural form in his prayer, when he said: "We have sinned, we have done wickedly" (Dan 9: 5, 15), and other things which he there truly and not humbly confesses. And lest anyone should think, as some do, that he was not speaking of his own sins, but of those of his people, he said further: "While I was . . . praying and confessing my

sins, and the sins of my people to the Lord my God" (Dan
9: 20). He would not say "our sins," but he spoke of the sins
of his people and of his own sins, for as a prophet he foresaw
that in the future there would be some who would badly
misunderstand him.

(8)) Likewise it has been decided: Whoever holds that the
words of the Lord's prayer where we say: "Forgive us our
debts" (Mt 6: 12) are said by the saints out of humility but
not truthfully, *anathema sit.*

For who could tolerate that a person who prays be lying not
to other persons but to the Lord Himself, by saying with his
lips that he wishes to be forgiven while in his heart he denies
that he has any debts to be forgiven?[14]

[14]Text: CCL 149.74-77

10

Augustine, Doctor of Grace

So far we have seen Augustine's theology of grace which he developed in the context of the Pelagian controversies from 411 until his death in 430. In this chapter we shall study his anthropology in the more general framework of his theological development. It is almost trite to say that Augustine is the father of Western theology. There is hardly any aspect of Christian thought to which he has not made an original and lasting contribution. In particular he has been given the title of *doctor gratiae* on account of the sublimity of his theology of grace.

In what follows, we will provide extracts from Augustine's works containing his teachings on the triune God's image in human beings, human freedom, the nature of sanctifying and actual grace, and predestination.

I. Human Beings as The Image of the Trinity

Augustine elaborates his metaphysical and theological doctrine of creation in explicit confrontation with, now as a synthesis of, now as a defense against, the two philosophies of his day, represented pre-eminently by Neoplatonism and Manichaeism. On the one hand, the influence of Neoplatonism (Plotinus and Porphyry) is discernible in Augustine's notion of God as "summa essentia" (*On the Trinity*, 3, 9, 16) and as the "primordial good" (*On the Trinity*, 8, 3, 4) of which all other being and goodness is only a participation. It is also visible in

Augustine's understanding of God's immutability, eternity, and incomprehensibility (*On the Trinity*, 5, 1, 2). Further, of Neoplatonic derivation is also his conception of the universe as a hierarchy of being that starts from the supreme being of God and reaches down to nothingness, which is akin to formless matter (*Unfinished Commentary on Genesis*, 4, 11), the "invisible and formless earth" (*Confessions*, 12, 8, 8). Augustine's concept of formless matter, together with his theory of time (cfr. *Confessions*, Book XI) and the eternal ideas (which, however, like Philo, he roots in the mind of God) is a distinguishing feature of his doctrine of creation.

On the other hand, it is no less clear that Augustine did not simply transfer the Neoplatonic philosophical doctrine into his theology of creation, but transformed and corrected it in light of the biblical teaching on creation. He firmly rejected the idea of emanation and taught the doctrine of *creatio ex nihilo*. Matter, too, is created out of nothing, a truth, he claims, is stated in the first verse of Genesis (*On Genesis Against the Manichaeans*, 1, 7, 12). Further, he rejected both Plato's conception of time (as found in the *Timaios*) and Aristotle's. Creation takes place *in tempore*, or rather, *cum tempore* (*On the City of God*, 11, 6), although the archetypes are eternally present in the mind of God.

It is, however, only when Augustine brings the whole Trinity into the work of creation that the essentially Christian character of his doctrine of creation is made manifest. He understands the *in principio* of Gen 1: 1, not as referring to the beginning of time (though acknowledging the possibility of such an interpretation), but to the Logos, the source and ground of creation. He even attempts to distinguish the functions of the three divine Persons, deriving creation from God the Father through the Word and the divine goodness personified in the Holy Spirit (*On the True Religion*, 7, 13; *On the City of God*, 11, 23).

The involvement of the Trinity in creation means that there is a trinitarian structure, or the vestiges of the Trinity, in created things, especially in humans (*On the City of God* 11, 28; *On the Trinity*, 9, 2, 2; 14, 16, 22). At a very early date in his writings Augustine takes note of the trinitarian reflections in every creature, the *"vestigia"* of the Trinity in the universe, which, he thinks, are intimated by Wis 11: 20: "He has disposed all things in measure, number, and weight."

> When this Trinity is known as far as it can be known in this life, it is perceived, without any doubt, that every creature, intellectual, animal, and corporeal, derives such existence as it has from that same creative Trinity, has its own species, and is subject to the most perfect order. It is not as if the Father were understood to have made one part of creation, the Son another, and the Holy Spirit another, but the Father through the Son in the gift of the Holy Spirit together made all things and each individual thing. For every thing, substance, essence, nature, or whatever better word there may be, possesses at once these three qualities: It is a particular thing; it is distinguished from other things by its own species; and it does not transgress the order of nature (*On True Religion*, 7, 13).[1]

In a passage from a work of Augustine's maturity, the expression *vestiges* of the Trinity appears, and again a distinction among the different general classes of being according to unity, species, and order.

> All these things, therefore, which are made by the divine act, show in themselves a certain unity, and species, and order. For each of them is both one particular thing, as are the natures of bodies and the dispositions of souls; and is formed in some species, as are the figures and qualities of bodies and the learnings or skills of souls; and seeks or maintains some order, as are the weights or combinations of bodies, or the loves and the delights of souls.
> We must then understand as Creator, gathering understanding from the things which have been made, the Trinity of whom there appear vestiges in the creature, as is fitting. For in that Trinity is the supreme origin of all things, and the most perfect beauty, and the most blessed delight (*On the Trinity*, 6, 10, 12).[2]

[1]Text: CCL 32; trans. J. H. Burleigh, *St. Augustine Of True Religion*: Chicago, 1959, 14

[2]Text: CCL 50.242; trans. FOTC 45.214

Augustine plays on the same theme with elaborate variations in Book XI of *On the City of God* which is probably later in composition than most books of *On the Trinity.*

> XI.24...The whole Trinity is made known to us in its works. It is therein that the Holy City has ... its origin, its informing, and its beatitude. Ask what gives it being: we answer, God's act of creation. Ask what gives it wisdom: we answer, God's act of enlightening. Ask what gives it happiness: we answer, the enjoyment of God. In existence it is controlled, in contemplation it is illumined, in union it has delight. It is, it beholds, it loves. In God's eternity it is strong, in God's truth it shines, in God's goodness it rejoices (*On the City of God*, 11, 24).[3]

Among created things, humans, of course, bear the greatest resemblance to the Trinity. Augustine attempts to show that there are Trinitarian vestiges in what he calls the "outer man," that is the bodily senses, external and internal, and the "inner man." In the external vision, Augustine suggests that there are three things involved which coalesce into a close-knit unity: the visible object, the act of vision itself, and the attention of the mind (cfr. *On the Trinity*, 11, 2, 2). In the internal vision, the trinity consists of memory, internal vision, and the will uniting both; these three internal members are, it is to be noted, consubstantial (cfr. *ibid.*, 11, 3, 6). In the "inner man," which is the *mens* and the site of the divine image, Augustine distinguishes between *ratio inferior*, which is the mind's consideration of bodily things and events and by which *scientia* is achieved, and *ratio superior*, which is the mind's contemplation of divine, immutable truths and by which *sapientia* is obtained. Augustine proceeds to point out different trinities in both the *ratio inferior* and the *ratio superior*, insisting, however, that true trinities are found only in the latter: "...not only a trinity may be found, but also an image of God in that alone which pertains to the contemplation of eternal realities; while in this other which is diverted from it in its dealings with

[3]Text: CCL 48.344; trans. LNPF 2.219

temporal things, although there may be a trinity, yet there cannot be found an image of God" (*On the Trinity*, 12, 4, 4). This attempt to discover the "vestiges" of the Trinity in humans was only a first stage in Augustine's full-blown development of what is called the psychological image of the Trinity in the human person. Fourteen years had elapsed after his conversion before mention was made of this psychological trinity, and this appearance was a brief one (*Confessions*, 13, 11). We have to wait for another decade or so before this trinity received its full elaboration in the later parts of *On the Trinity*. Augustine distinguishes three levels of the trinitarian image in the human person. The first is a permanent, ineradicable trinity, which is left in him even after sin; it is the habitual trinity consisting in self-memory, self-knowledge, self-love (*memoria, intelligentia, voluntas sui*). To be associated with this permanent trinity in the human mind is the presence of God common to all human beings, even to sinners, which is the potential basis for the actual remembering, knowing, and loving of God.

The second level is the reformed trinitarian image which presupposes the renewal of the human mind by grace and the accompanying gifts. It consists in the "memory," knowledge, and love of God (*memoria Dei, intelligentia, voluntas*). The *memoria Dei* in the supernatural image is associated with the indwelling of the Trinity and its act of "recollection" of God. The *intelligentia Dei* is knowledge of God, ranging from the gift of faith to perception of God's presence through the gift of Wisdom. The *voluntas Dei* is the love of God which is charity, accompanying and preceding the knowledge of him.

The third level is the fully perfected trinitarian image which is reserved for the blessed in heaven where God is immediately to the mind by means of the beatific vision, where, too, God is known "as he is" in himself, and where, finally, he is loved in fullest measure.

> Who can understand the omnipotent Trinity? We all speak of it, though we may not speak of it as it truly is, for rarely does a soul know what it is saying when it speaks of the Trinity. People quarrel and dispute about it, but it is a vision that is given to none unless he is at peace.

There are three things, all found in humans themselves,
which I should like to consider. They are far different from
the Trinity, but I suggest them as a subject for reflection by
which we can test ourselves and realize how great this
difference is. The three things are: existence, knowledge,
and will; for I am, I know, and I will. I am a knowing and
willing being; I know that I am and that I will, and I will
both to be and to know. In these three—being, knowledge,
and will—there is one inseparable life, one life, one mind,
one essence; and therefore, although they are distinct from
one another, the distinction does not separate them. This
must be plain to anyone who has the ability to understand it.
In fact he need not look beyond himself. Let him examine
closely, take stock, and tell me what he finds ...
(*Confessions*, 13, 11).[4]

In his *On the Trinity*, the triad of existence, knowledge, and
will is substituted by that of memory, understanding, and will.
The second and third members of this triadic pattern (i.e.
understanding and will) are retained throughout the search for
the image of the Trinity in the soul. The first member,
however, i.e. being, existence, or life does not appear in any of
the psychological triads which Augustine studies in detail. The
reason for this is that Augustine needs three terms that imply
relations, whereas being, existence or life is not relative and
cannot serve as distinctive analogue for any one Person in the
Trinity. It is also for this reason that in *On the Trinity* the first
triad of mind, knowledge, and love is replaced by the second
triad of memory, understanding, and will, mind being an
absolute and not a relative term.

Now this triad of memory, understanding, and will, are not
three lives, but one; nor three minds, but one; it follows that
they are not three substances, but one substance. Memory,
regarded as life, mind, or substance, is an absolute term;
regarded as memory, it is relative. The same may be said of
understanding and of will; for both terms can be used

[4]Text: CCL 27.247; trans. LNPF 1.193

relatively. But life, mind, and essence are always things existing absolutely in themselves. Therefore the three activities named are one, inasmuch as they constitute one life, one mind, one essence; and whatever else can be predicated of each singly in itself, is predicated of them all together in a singular and not in the plural.

But they are three inasmuch as they are related to one another; and if they were not equal, not only each to each but each to all, they could not comprehend or take in one another as they do. For in fact they are comprehended, not only each by each but all by each. I remember that I possess memory and understanding and will; I understand that I understand, will and remember; I will my own willing and remembering and understanding. And I remember at the same time the whole of my memory, understanding, and will. Whatever I do not remember as part of my memory, is not in my memory; and nothing can be more fully in my memory than the memory itself. Therefore I remember the whole of it.

Again, whatever I understand, I know that I understand, and I know that I will whatever I will; but whatever I know, I remember. Therefore I remember the whole of my understanding and the whole of my will. Similarly, when I understand these three, I understand all three as a whole. For there is nothing open to understanding that I do not understand except that of which I am ignorant; and that of which I am ignorant I neither remember nor will. It follows that anything open to understanding that I do not understand, I neither remember nor will, whereas anything open to understanding that I remember and will, I understand. Finally, when I use the whole content of my understanding and memory, my will covers the whole of my understanding and the whole of my memory. Therefore, since all are comprehended by one another singly and as wholes, the whole of each is equal to the whole of each, and the whole of each to the whole of all together. And these three constitute one thing, one life, one mind, one essence (*On the Trinity*, 10, 11, 18).[5]

[5]Text: CCL 50.330; cf. FOTC 45.311-312

This trinitarian image belongs to the human nature and cannot be lost, even in sin. It is defaced but remains in us as the basis for a possible restoration by grace.

> Now we have reached the point in our discussion at which we have undertaken to consider that highest element in the human mind whereby it knows or can know God, with a view to our finding therein the image of God. Although the human mind is not of that nature which belongs to God, yet the image of that nature, which transcends every other in excellence, is to be sought and found in the element which in our own nature is the most excellent.
>
> But first we have to consider the mind in itself, before it has participation in God, and discover his image there. We have said that it still remains an image of God, even if it has become an image faded and defaced by the loss of that participation. It is in virtue of the fact that it has a capacity for God and the ability to participate in God, that it is his image; only because it is his image can so high a destiny be conceived for it.
>
> Here then is the mind, remembering itself, understanding itself, loving itself. Perceiving this, we perceive a trinity—a trinity still less than God, but already an image of God. In this trinity, the memory has not imported from outside what it should retain, nor has the understanding discovered in the outer world the object for its beholding, like the body's eye. Nor has the will made an outward union of these two, as it joins the form of the body and that which was wrought from it in the eye of the beholder. An image of the external object seen, taken up, as it were, and stored in the memory, has not been discovered by thought directed towards it, and from which the gaze of the one recollecting has been formed, while the two are united by the further activity of will. This was the system displayed in those trinities which we found to exist in material processes, or to pass somehow into our inward experience from the external body through the bodily sense (*On the Trinity*, 14, 8, 11).[6]

[6]Text: CCL 50A.435; cf. FOTC 45.425-426

But it is only by remembering, understanding and loving God, its Maker, that the soul attains wisdom.

> Now this trinity of mind is God's image, not because the mind remembers, understands and loves itself, but because it has the power also to remember, understand and love its Maker. And it is in so doing that it attains wisdom. If it does not do so, the memory, understanding and love of itself is no more than act of folly. Let the mind then remember its God, in whose image it was made, let it understand him and love him. In a word, let it worship the uncreated God who created it with the capacity for himself, and in whom it is able to be made partaker. For this cause it is written: "Behold, the worship of God is wisdom" (Job 28:28). Wisdom will be the mind's, not by its own illumination, but by partaking in that supreme Light: and only when it enters eternity will it reign in bliss. But to say that a person may possess such wisdom is not to deny that it is the property of God. God's is the only true wisdom; were it human, it would be vain. Yet when we call it the wisdom of God, we do not mean the wisdom wherewith God is wise; he is not wise by partaking in God. It is rather as we speak of the righteousness of God, not only in the sense of that whereby God is righteous, but of that which he gives to humanity when he "justifies the ungodly." To this the Apostle refers when he speaks of those who "being ignorant of God's righteousness, and willing to establish their own righteousness, were not subject to the righteousness of God" (Rom 4:5; 10:3). In the same way we might speak of some who, being ignorant of the wisdom of God, and willing to establish their own, were not subject to the wisdom of God (*On the Trinity* 14, 12, 15).[7]

II. Human Freedom: Liberum Arbitrium and Libertas

As we have seen in chapter nine, at the heart of the debate between Augustine and Pelagius is the concept of freedom.

[7]Text: CCL 50A.442; cf. FOTC 45.432

Whereas Pelagius claims the *velle* (to will) as ours, Augustine attributes it to God. Does the Doctor of Grace then deny human freedom? Augustine carefully distinguishes free choice (*liberum arbitrium*) and a higher freedom (*libertas*). The former is a part of the human created nature: the soul as will is endowed at birth with the ability to turn toward or away from its supreme good. *Liberum arbitrium* implies a choice of alternatives: to do what is good or what is evil. On the other hand, God may so dispose the human will that it inclines only toward its true good. This divine disposition would *liberate* the will from its tendency toward evil. Such liberated freedom is *libertas*, which is the result of grace.

Shortly after his conversion and on the way back to Thagaste, Augustine wrote, during his delay in Rome, a work against Manichaeism, entitled *On Free Will* (388) in which he explained the origin of evil as the result of a bad choice. Later, Pelagius would make use of this text to defend his teaching on human freedom. In his *Retractations* Augustine contends that such use is a distortion of the text and clarifies his meaning.

> In these books (i.e. *On Free Will*), many things were discussed. Several questions arose which I could not solve or which required lengthy treatment. They were so broadly handled in their pros and cons that, either way, even when it was not quite clear where the truth lay, our reasoning led to this conclusion: Whatever be true in these difficult matters, it is to be believed, or at least made clear, that God is to be praised. The disputation was undertaken on account of those who deny that evil derives its origin from the free choice of the will and who contend accordingly that God the Creator of all things is to be blamed. In this way, following their impious error (for they are Manichees), they seek to introduce an evil nature, unchangeable and coeternal with God. Because this was the subject we proposed to debate, there is no discussion in these books of the grace of God whereby he has predestined his elect and himself prepares the wills of those among them who make use of their freedom of choice. But wherever an occasion occurs to make mention of this grace it is mentioned in passing, not laboriously defended as if it were in question. It is one thing

to inquire into the origin of evil, and another to seek the means of returning to humanity's original good estate or even to a better one.

Wherefore, do not let the Pelagians exult as if I had been pleading their cause, because in these books I said much in favor of free will, which was necessary for the purpose I had in view in that discussion. For the Pelagians are a new brand of heretics who assert the freedom of the will in such a way as to leave no room for the grace of God, since they say it is given to us according to our merits. I have said, it is true, in the First Book, that evil-doing is punished by God. And I added: "It would not be justly punished unless it were done voluntarily."

Again, when I was showing that a good will is so great a good that it should deservedly be preferred to all material and external goods, I said: "You see now, I believe, that it lies with our will whether we enjoy or lack so great and so true a good. For what is more in the power of the will than the will itself?" (He quotes a large number of similar passages to the effect that a person can live aright if he will, concluding with this from Book III, xviii, 50.) "Who commits sin by an act which he could by no means avoid? If sin has been committed, therefore it could have been avoided." Pelagius has made use of this quotation in one of his books; and when I had written a book in reply to his I chose as its title *De Natura et Gratia.*

In these and similar words of mine no mention is made of the grace of God, because it was not under discussion. Hence the Pelagians think, or may think, that I once held their opinion. But that is a vain thought. Certainly, the will is that by which a person sins or lives righteously, as I argued in these works. But mortals cannot live righteously and piously unless the will itself is liberated by the grace of God from the servitude to sin into which it has fallen, and is aided to overcome its vices. Unless this divine liberating gift preceded the good will, it would be the reward of its merits and would not be grace, which is grace precisely because it is freely given... (*Retractations* 1, 9, 2-4).[8]

[8]Text: CSEL 36.36; trans. FOTC 60.32

In sum, for Augustine to be free is to love the good, to delight in justice, to order all one's actions to the pursuit of eternal life. In other words, it is to be able to love God above all things by preferring him to all finite goods. It is this freedom that we have lost by our fall. The sinner is a slave to sin; captive of concupiscence, his will is no longer capable of desiring the good. To have the freedom to do the good, to be able to accomplish justice, to have the power to observe God's commandments, fallen humanity must first be justified by grace.

> But that part of the human race to which God had promised release and the eternal kingdom, could it be restored through the merits of its own works? God forbid. What good can a condemned person do except as he has been released from his condemnation? Can he by the free decision of his own will? Here again, God forbid. People misusing their free will destroy both themselves and it. A person who kills himself no longer lives and cannot restore himself to life. Also, when he has sinned through free will, sin is victorious and his free will is lost; "for by whatever a person is overcome, of this also he is the slave" (2 Pet 2: 19.) The sentence quoted is from the Apostle Peter. Since it is surely true, what liberty, I ask, can a slave have except when it pleases him to sin. For that service is liberty which freely does the will of the master. Accordingly, he is free to sin who is the servant of sin. Wherefore, no one is free to do right who has not been free from sin and begins to be the servant of justice. And such is true of liberty because he has the joy of right-doing, and at the same time dutiful servitude because he obeys the precept. But, for the person sold into the bondage of sin, where will that freedom of right-doing come from unless he be redeemed by him who said: "If the Son makes you free, you will be free indeed" (Jn 8: 36). If this operation has not begun in a person and he is not yet free to do right, how can he glory in free will and in good works, unless he puffs himself up with foolish pride? And it was this the Apostle spoke against when he said: "By grace you have been saved through faith" (Eph 2: 8). And, lest his hearers should claim that faith itself for themselves, not

understanding it to be given of God—as elsewhere the same Apostle says that he has obtained mercy in order to be faithful—in this place also he adds: "And that not from yourselves, for it is the gift of God; not as the outcome of works, lest anyone may boast" (Eph 2: 8-9). And, lest it might be thought that good works will fail in those who believe, he adds this also: "For his workmanship we are, created in Christ Jesus in good works, which God has made ready beforehand that we may walk in them" (Eph 2: 10). We shall be made truly free, then, when God fashions, that is, forms and creates us, not as people—for that he has already done—but to be good people, which he now accomplishes by his grace; that we may be in Christ a new creature, according as it is written: "Create a *clean* heart in me, O God" (Ps 50: 12)... (*Enchiridion*, 9, 30-31).[9]

III. Divinizing Grace

Divine grace, for Augustine, is not only healing or liberating grace (*gratia sanans*), although because of the Pelagian error he was forced to emphasize this aspect of grace; it is also divinizing grace (*gratia elevans*). The grace of Christ not only destroys sins and restores true freedom to us but also renews us ontologically. It creates us in the image of God, makes us adoptive children of God, and partakers of the divine nature. In his letter to Dardanus on the presence of God (letter 187), he repeatedly asserts: "God who is everywhere present...does not dwell in all, but only in those whom he has made his most blessed temple" (187, 35). Again: "We say that the Holy Spirit dwells in baptized children even though they do not know it" (187, 17). Elsewhere he says: "He descended that we might ascend. Keeping his own nature, he shared our nature so that we, while keeping our nature, might share his" (Letter, 140).

Augustine sometimes uses the word *gratia* to designate the Holy Spirit himself (Sermon 144, 1). More often, however, he uses this word to refer to the effect produced in our souls, the created gift and the absolute gratuitousness of this gift (cfr. *On the Spirit and the Letter*, 29, 51). The gift of the Holy Spirit and that of charity are inseparable, though Augustine would lay the emphasis on the latter.

In a beautiful passage from *On the City of God,* Augustine describes the work of sanctifying grace.

> Nevertheless, in the "heavy yoke that is laid upon the children of Adam, from the day that they go out of their mother's womb to the day that they return to the mother of all things," there is found an admirable though painful monitor teaching us to be sober-minded, and convincing us that this life has become penal in consequence of that outrageous wickedness which was perpetrated in Paradise, and that all to which the New Testament invites belongs to that future inheritance which awaits us in the world to come, and is offered for our acceptance, as the guarantee that we may, in its own due time, obtain that of which it is the pledge. Now, therefore, let us walk in hope, and let us by the spirit mortify the deeds of the flesh, and so make progress from day to day. For "the Lord knows them that are his" (2 Tim 2:19) and "as many as are led by the Spirit of God, they are children of God" (Rom 8:14), but by grace, not by nature. For there is but one Son of God by nature, who in his compassion became Son of humanity for our sakes, that we, by nature children of humanity, might by grace become through him children of God. For he, abiding, unchangeable, took upon him our nature, that thereby he might take us to himself; and, holding fast his own divinity, he became partaker of our infirmity, that we, being changed into some better thing, might, by participating in his righteousness and immortality, lose our own properties of sin and mortality, and preserve whatever good quality he had implanted in our nature, perfected now by sharing in the goodness of His nature. For, as by the sin of one man we have fallen into a misery so deplorable, so by the righteousness of one Man, who is also God, shall we come to a blessedness inconceivably exalted. Nor ought any one to trust that he has passed from the one man to the other until he shall have reached that place where there is no temptation,

and have entered into the peace which he seeks in the many and various conflicts of this way, in which "the flesh lusts against the spirit, and the spirit against the flesh" (Gal 5:17)...(*On the City of God*, 21, 15).[10]

IV. The Necessity of Actual Grace

Augustine affirms, against the Pelagians, the existence of both exterior and interior graces. Exterior graces consist mainly of the Law and the Gospels, as well as the example of Jesus. Interior graces are of two kinds: those that illuminate our soul regarding our duty, and those that affect our will and move it to act.

As Augustine himself tells us (cfr. *Retractations*, 22, 3), he had at first thought that the beginning of conversion and the first step toward salvation could be left to the human person. Thus, in his first commentaries on Saint Paul, written in 394, he states: "It is up to us to believe or will, and it is up to God to give those believing and willing the power of good action through the Holy Spirit" (*Exposition of 84 Propositions Concerning the Epistle to the Romans*, 61). But in 397, encouraged by his friend Simplician, Augustine re-examined more carefully the letters of Paul and came to the realization that preaching and good will are not sufficient to bring us to justification. What is further needed is an interior activity of God preceding the consent of the will and moving the will to respond to his call. In what follows we will give extracts from four of Augustine's works which illustrate the principal stages of the development of his thought on the necessity of operative grace.

RESPONSE TO VARIOUS QUESTIONS FROM SIMPLICIAN (396-397)

Simplician, whom Augustine had come to know before his conversion in Milan, succeeded Ambrose as bishop there in 397. He wrote to Augustine soliciting his opinions on certain

---

[10]Text: CCL 48.780-783, trans. LNPF 2.464-466

Scriptural texts. The latter replied in two books the first of which is of immediate interest to us. In it Augustine explains the meaning of Rom 7: 7-25 and Rom 9: 10-29. Regarding the first text, he interprets Paul to be describing the situation of the person still under the Law and not yet under grace. Controversy with the Pelagians forced him later to abandon this view (cfr. *Against Two Letters of the Pelagians*, 1, 8). He came to understand that baptized Christians and even apostles could not in this life attain a state of perfect peace and righteousness without further assistance from God. The justified person is like a convalescent. He needs to rely on God's help so as not to fall again (cfr. *On Grace and Free Will* , 6, 13). There remains in him a certain inability to persevere in the good. First of all, he cannot avoid all venial sins (cfr. *On the Spirit and the Letter*, 36, 65). He is still subject to the unruly inclinations of concupiscence. He can overcome them only by God's grace which he must pray for (cfr. *On Nature and Grace* , 43, 50). God remedies the justified person's relative inability to persevere in the good by giving him not only the power to do good but also the act of doing good (cfr. *On Grace and Free Will*, 16, 32).

These are the doctrines which Augustine later developed and defended against Pelagianism. Meanwhile, in his reply to Simplician, Augustine corrected his earlier interpretation of Paul in his *Responses to Various Questions,* written from 389-396, and in his *Exposition of 84 Propositions Concerning the Epistle to the Romans.* On the basis of Rom 9: 10-29 he now recognizes for the first time the existence of a divine working which achieves its purpose without independent consent of the human will, a grace which causes the will's assent and cooperation, an operative grace. Now he teaches that God must himself graciously prepare the human heart or faith, so that faith itself is regarded as the gift of grace, no less than the power to do good. Human salvation is, therefore, wholly the work of God. To illustrate his point, Augustine gives a commentary on God's preference of Jacob over Esau.

> This is the truth the Apostle wanted to urge; just as in
> another passage he says, "By the grace of God we are saved,
> and that, not of ourselves. It is the gift of God. It is not of

works, lest any human being should boast" (Eph 2:8, 9) And so he gave a proof from the case of those who had not yet been born. No one could say that Jacob had conciliated God by meritorious works before he was born, so that God should say of him, "The elder shall serve the younger." So "Not only so," he says, was Isaac promised in the words, "At this time I will come, and Sarah shall have a son" (Rom 9:9). Now Isaac had not conciliated God by any previous meritorious works so that his birth should have been promised, and that in Isaac "Abraham's seed should be called " (Gen 21:12). That means that those are to belong to the lot of the saints in Christ who know that they are the children of promise; who do not wax proud of their merits but account themselves co-heirs with Christ by the grace of their calling. When the promise was made that they should be this they did not as yet exist and so could have merited nothing. "Rebecca also having conceived by one, even by our father Isaac. . . . " He is most careful to note that it was by one act of intercourse that twins were conceived so that nothing could be attributed to the merits of the father, as if someone might say the son was born such as he was because his father had such or such a disposition when he lay with his wife; or that his mother was disposed in such a way when she conceived a son. Both were begotten and conceived at one and the same time. . .

These things are related to break and cast down the pride of people who are not grateful for the grace of God but dare to glory in their own merits. "For the children being not yet born, and having done nothing either good or evil, not of works but of him that calls, it was said to her, 'The elder shall serve the younger.'" Grace is therefore of him who calls, and the consequent good works are of him who receives grace. Good works do not produce grace but are produced by grace. Fire is not hot in order that it may burn, but because it burns. A wheel does not run nicely in order that it may be round, but because it is round. So no one does good works in order that he may receive grace, but because he has received grace. How can a person live justly who has not been justified? How can he live in his holiness who has not been sanctified? Or, indeed, how can a person live at all

who has not been vivified? Grace justifies so that he who is
justified may live justly. Grace, therefore, comes first, then
good works...
Unless, therefore, the mercy of God in calling precedes, no
one can even believe, and so begin to be justified and to
receive power to do good works. So grace comes before all
merits. Christ died for the ungodly. The younger received
the promise that the elder should serve him from him that
calls and not from any meritorious works of his own. So the
Scripture "Jacob have I loved" is true, but it was of God
who called and not of Jacob's righteous works (*Response
to Various Questions from Simplician*, 2, 3-7).[11]

If faith is gratuitous and not a reward for good deeds, what
about those to whom it is not given? Is God unjust? Augustine
replies that there is no injustice with God; he has the right to
treat human beings differently "as he wills." A creditor may
exact or remit a debt, and in neither case can he be accused of
injustice. Like the potter with the clay, God makes vessels,
some to honor, others to dishonor. All human beings are
sinners, made of a *massa peccati*; and some are to be saved,
others are to be lost. To these whom he wills to save, God
provides a motive adequate to win them to faith and
obedience. Some are simply called, others are elected. To the
latter, God gives the efficacious grace that brings about the
desired result of salvation. Justification, therefore, precedes
election and, without previous election, there can be neither
faith nor obedience.

The Apostle, therefore, and all those who have been
justified and have demonstrated for us the understanding of
grace, have no other intention than to show that he that
glories should glory in the Lord. Who will call in question
the works of the Lord who out of one lump damns one and
justifies another? Free will is most important. It exists,
indeed, but of what value is it in those who are sold under
sin? "The flesh," says he, "lusts against the spirit and the
spirit against the flesh so that you may not do the things that

---

[11]Text: CCL 44.25-; trans. J.H.S. Burleigh, *Augustine's Earlier Writings*. 370-371

you would" (Gal 5: 17). We are commanded to live righteously, and the reward is set before us that we shall merit to live happily for ever. But who can live righteously and do good works unless he has been justified by faith? We are commanded to believe that we may receive the gift of the Holy Spirit and become able to do good works by love. But who can believe unless he is reached by some calling, by some testimony borne to the truth? Who has it in his power to have such a motive present to his mind that his will shall be influenced to believe? Who can welcome in his mind something which does not give him delight? But who has it in his power to ensure that something that will delight him will turn up, or that he will take delight in what turns up? If those things delight us which serve our advancement towards God, that is due not to our own whim, or industry, or meritorious works, but to the inspiration of God and to the grace which he bestows. He freely bestows upon us voluntary assent, earnest effort, and the power to perform works of fervent charity. We are bidden to ask that we may receive, to seek that we may find, and to knock that it may be opened unto us. Is not our prayer sometimes tepid or rather cold? Does it not sometimes cease altogether, so that we are not even grieved to notice this condition in us. For if we are grieved that it should be so, that is already a prayer. What does this prove except that the one who commands us to ask, seek and knock, himself gives us the will to obey? "It is not of him that wills, nor of him that runs, but of God that has mercy." We could neither will nor run unless he stirred us and put the motive-power in us (*Response to Various Questions of Simplician*, 1, 2, 21).[12]

LETTER TO SIXTUS (418)

Twenty years after his reply to Simplician, Augustine developed in his letter to Sixtus of Rome (letter 194) a further explanation of the relationship between divine grace and human free will. In 396 the grace of faith was conceived as a congruous vocation by which the elect receive a call which is adapted to their particular dispositions and thereby provokes the acceptance which God intends. In this letter Augustine presents the grace of faith as an interior movement of the elect's will by grace which adapts their dispositions to the preaching of the gospel and thereby produces the positive response God intends. No external grace, therefore, is effective unless God gives such interior grace to those he chooses. Hence, strictly speaking, there is no merit on the human person's part, or, as Augustine puts it in this letter: "In crowning our merit, God is only crowning his own gifts" (5, 19).

> If we say that prayer produces antecedent merit so that the gift of grace may follow, it is true that prayer, by asking and obtaining whatever it does obtain, shows clearly that it is God's gift when a person does not think that he has grace of himself, because, if it were in his own power, he would assuredly not ask for it. But, lest we should think that even the merit of prayer is antecedent to grace, in which case it would not be a free gift—and then it would not be grace because it would be the reward which was due—our very prayer itself is counted among the gifts of grace. As the Doctor of the Gentiles says: "We know not what we should pray for as we ought, but the Spirit himself asks for us with unspeakable groanings" (Rom 8: 26). And what does "ask for us" mean but that he makes us ask? It is a very sure sign of one in need to ask with groaning, but it would be monstrous for us to think that the Holy Spirit is in need of anything. So, then, the word "ask" is used because he makes us ask, and inspires us with the sentiment of asking and groaning, according to that passage in the Gospel: "For it is not you that speak, but the Spirit of your Father that speaks to you (Mt 10: 20). However, this is not accomplished in us without any action on our part, and therefore the help of the Holy Spirit is described by saying that he does what he makes us do.
>
> The Apostle himself makes it quite clear that our spirit is not meant when he says it "asks with unspeakable groanings," but the Holy Spirit by whom our infirmity is helped. He

begins by saying: "The Spirit helps our infirmity"; then he goes on: "For we know not what we should pray for as we ought," and the rest (Rom 8: 26). And indeed he speaks even more plainly of this Spirit in another place: "For you have not received the spirit of bondage again in fear, but you have received the spirit of adoption of sons, whereby we cry: "Abba, Father" (Rom 8: 15). Notice that he does not here say that the Spirit himself cries in his prayer, but he says: "Whereby we cry: 'Abba, Father.'" However, in another passage he says: "Because you are children, God has sent the Spirit of his Son into your hearts, crying: 'Abba. Father'" (Gal 4: 6). Here he does not say "whereby we cry," but he preferred to represent the Spirit himself as crying, which has the effect of making us cry, as in the other two passages: "The Spirit himself asks with unspeakable groanings," and "The Spirit of your Father that speaks in you."

Therefore, as no one has true wisdom, true understanding; no one is truly eminent in counsel and fortitude; no one has a pious knowledge or a knowledgeable piety; no one fears God with a chaste fear unless he has received "the spirit of wisdom and understanding, of counsel and fortitude, of knowledge and piety and fear of God" (Is 11: 2, 3); and as no one has true power, sincere love, and religious sobriety except through "the spirit of power and love and sobriety" (2 Tim 1: 7), so also without the spirit of faith no one will rightly believe, without the spirit of prayer no one will profitably pray; not that there are so many spirits, "but all these things one and the same Spirit works dividing to every one according as he will" (1 Cor 12: 11), because "the Spirit breaths where he will" (Jn 3: 8). But it must be admitted that his help is given differently before and after his indwelling, for before his indwelling he helps people to believe, but after his indwelling he helps them as believers.

What merit, then, has a person before grace which could make it possible for him to receive grace, when nothing but grace produces good merit in us; and what else but his gifts does God crown when he crowns our merits? For, just as in the beginning we obtained the mercy of faith, not because we were faithful but that we might become so, in like

manner he will crown us at the end with eternal life, as it
says, "with mercy and compassion"(Ps 102: 4). Not in vain,
therefore, do we sing to God: "His mercy shall precede me,"
and "His mercy shall follow me"(Ps 58: 11). Consequently,
eternal life itself, which will certainly be possessed at the end
without end, is in a sense awarded to antecedent merits, yet,
because the same merits for which it is awarded are not
effected by us through our sufficiency but are effected in us
by grace, even this very grace is so called for no other reason
than that it is given freely; not, indeed, that it is not given for
merit, but because the merits themselves are given for which
it is given. And when we find eternal life itself called grace,
we have in the same Apostle Paul a magnificent defender of
grace: "The wages of sin," he says, "is death. But the grace of
God life everlasting in Christ Jesus our Lord" (Rom
6: 23).[13]

ON GRACE AND FREE WILL (427)

Augustine's letter to Sixtus on gratuitous and prevenient
grace, which Florus discovered and sent to his fellow monks at
the monastery at Adrumentum, was found scandalous. The
monks thought that grace could not be defended without
denying free will. After sending them letters to clarify his
teaching, Augustine composed a treatise entitled *On Grace
and Free Will* to give a fuller exposition. Augustine begins by
asserting and proving the two propositions in which Scripture
teaches that humans have free will (2-5) and that grace is
necessary for doing any good (6-9). Further he shows that both
free will and grace are implicated in the heart's conversion
(31-32), and that love is the spring of all good in us (33-40),
which, however, we have only because God first loves us.

Whoever, therefore, has the will to keep God's commandment, but lacks the power, already possesses a good will, but
one that is still small and feeble. But once he comes to have a
great and robust will, he will have this power. When the

[13]Text: CSEL 57.187-191; trans. FOTC 30.310-313, Sr. W. Parsons

martyrs, for example, carried out those great commandments, they did so with a great will, namely, with that great
love whereof the Lord Himself says: "Greater love than this
no one has, that lay down his life for his friends" (Jn 15: 13).
This is also the reason why the Apostle says: "For he who
loves his neighbor has fulfilled the law. For 'Thou shalt not
commit adultery; Thou shalt not kill; Thou shalt not steal;
Thou shalt not covet'; and if there is any other commandment, it is summed up in the saying, 'Thou shalt love thy
neighbor as thyself.' Love does no evil to a neighbor. Love
therefore is the fulfillment of the Law" (Rom 13: 8, 10).
When the Apostle Peter thrice denied the Lord out of fear,
he did not yet have this love, for, as John the Evangelist says
in his Epistle: "There is no fear in love, but perfect love casts
out fear" (1 Jn 4: 18). Yet, though it was not great or perfect,
love was not wanting in Peter when he declared: "I will lay
down my life for you" (Jn 14: 37), inasmuch as he fancied he
could do what he had the will to do. And who was it that
had begun to impart to him this love, however small, but
God who prepares our will and brings to perfection through
his cooperation the work which his operation begins in us?
For he who first works in us the power to will is the same
who cooperates in bringing this work to perfection in those
who will it. Accordingly, the Apostle says: "I am convinced
of this, that he who has begun a good work in you will bring
it to perfection until the day of Christ Jesus" (Phil 1: 6).
God, then, works in us, without our cooperation, the power
to will, but once we begin to will, and do so in a way that
brings us to act, then it is that he cooperates with us. But if
he does not work in us the power to will or does not
cooperate in our act of willing, we are powerless to perform
good works of a salutary nature. With reference to his
working in us the power to will, it is said: "For it is God who
works also in you to will" (Phil 2: 13), whereas, concerning
his cooperation in us, once we begin to will so that our
volition brings us to act, the Apostle says: "Now we know
that for those who love God all things work together unto
good" (Rom 8: 28) (*On Grace and Free Will,* 33).[14]

[14]Text: PL 44.901; trans. FOTC 59.288, R.P. Russell

It is of interest to note that in quoting Rom 8: 20 Augustine adopts the reading *cooperatur* instead of the Vulgate reading of *cooperantur*. Taken in conjunction with the previous text from Philippians 2: 13, "For it is God who wakes also in you to will," the reading *cooperatur* enables Augustine to draw a distinction between *gratia operans* and *gratia cooperans,* which will occur again in his later work *On Admonition and Grace* under the form of *adjutorium sine quo non* and *adjutorium quo,* respectively. The *gratia operans* gives a beginning of charity which enables the will to receive still more by its docile correspondence to these first graces. Here the word "charity" indicates all supernatural love of good, even in its lowest forms. In the *gratia cooperans,* this same charity, together with the action of the will, is in a sense perfect in relation to the act in question, since this act is actually produced. There are here, therefore, two operations which are coordinated: the human persons indeed will and act, but are moved by the divine operation which penetrates their will. All the acts they perform are properly theirs and are rightly attributed to them; but inasmuch as they are meritorious they are properly to be attributed to God, since they derive all their supernatural goodness wholly from grace.

ON ADMONITION AND GRACE (427)

Augustine's treatise *On Grace and Free Will* only partially resolved the difficulties of the monks. Some of them objected that if all good was, in the last resort, from God's grace, people ought not to be blamed for not doing what they could not do, but God ought to be besought to do for them what he alone could do. In other words, fraternal correction would not be necessary; rather we ought to apply directly to the source of power, namely God.

This occasioned the composition of yet another treatise, *On Admonition and Grace,* the object of which was to explain the relationship between grace and human conduct, and especially to make it plain that the sovereignty of God's grace does not annul our duty to ourselves and our neighbors. It is in this work that we find Augustine's celebrated distinction between the grace of Adam (grace before the fall) and our grace (grace after the fall), the *adjutorium sine quo non* and the *adjutorium quo,* respectively. For Augustine, a justified person has need of a more powerful grace than Adam before his fall. Since he had received the supernatural gift of grace and a righteous will, Adam needed only the *"adjutorium sine quo non"* to do good; this grace, which gave him the *posse* (ability), was enough; the *agere* (act) and consequently perseverance, remained in the power of his free will. On the other hand, the justified person, on account of his concupiscence, has need of a more efficacious aid, which gives him the justice, righteousness and good will, the *posse,* and what is more, the *velle* (the *auxilium quo*) or the very act of willing, and finally, perseverance which can be obtained only by means of similar aid *(auxilium quo).*

> 29. What is the conclusion? That Adam did not have the grace of God? On the contrary, he had a great grace, but one different from ours. He had gifts, which he had received from the goodness of his Creator (he had not garnered them by his own merits), and in their midst he experienced no evil. But the saints in this life, who are the subjects of this grace of liberation, are in the midst of evils, out of which they cry to God: "Deliver us from evil." Adam in the midst of his gifts did not need the death of Christ; but the blood of the Lamb absolves the saints from a guilt which is both hereditary and their own. Adam had no need of that help for which the saints beg when they say: "I see another law in my members, warring against the law of my mind, and making me prisoner to the law of sin that is in my members. Unhappy man that I am! Who will deliver me from the body of this death? The grace of God through Jesus Christ our Lord" (Rom 7: 23-25). In the saints, the flesh is at war with the spirit and the spirit with the flesh. Struggling in this conflict, and in danger, they ask that the power to fight and conquer be given to them through the grace of Christ. Adam, however, was not tempted and troubled by any such conflict between the two selves in him; and in that place of blessedness he enjoyed interior peace with himself.
>
> 30. The result is that the saints in this present life need a grace, not richer indeed, but more powerful. And what

more powerful grace is there than the only-begotten Son of God, equal to, and co-eternal with, the Father; who was made man for them, and crucified by sinful humanity, he in whom there was neither original nor personal sin? Although he rose on the third day, never to die again, he first bore death for mortal people; to those who were dead he gave life, in order that, redeemed by his Blood and possessed of this secure guaranty, they might say: "If God is for us, who is against us? He who has not spared even his own Son but has delivered him for us all, how can he fail to grant us also all things with him?" (Rom 8: 31-32). God therefore took our nature—that is, the rational soul and the flesh of the man Christ—in a manner uniquely wonderful and wonderfully unique; in such wise that, through no preceding merits of his own justice, he was the Son of God at the first instant that he began to be man—he and the Word which had no beginning were one person. . . .

The grace which the first man had was not one whereby he would never will to be evil. But his grace was such that, if he willed to abide in it, he never would be evil; and such, too, that without it he could not be good, even with all his freedom. But he could, nevertheless, freely abandon it. God, you see, did not wish Adam to be without his grace, which he left under the power of Adam's free will; for the power of free choice is sufficient in the matter of evil, but of little avail in that of good, unless it is aided by omnipotent Goodness. And if Adam had not freely and deliberately abandoned the aid which he had, he would have always been good; but he did abandon it, and was abandoned.

His aid was such that he could abandon it, when he willed; or, if he willed, he could hold on to it; but it was not such as to make him will. This was the first grace, that was given to the first Adam; but more powerful than it is the grace in the second Adam. The effect of the first grace was that a man might have justice, if he willed; the second grace, therefore, is more powerful, because it effects the will itself, a strong will, a burning charity, so that by a contrary will the spirit overcomes the conflicting will of the flesh. Not that the first grace, whereby the power of free will was displayed, was a small grace; for its help was such that without this aid the man would not continue in good; but he could, if he willed, abandon this aid. However, the second grace is so much the greater in this, that it is not enough for it to repair humanity's lost liberty, nor again enough that without it a person could neither lay hold of good nor abide in good even though he willed; actually, by it a person is also brought to will. . . .

At present, however, it is a punishment of sin on those to whom this aid is lacking; and to those to whom it is given, it is given by way of grace, not by way of merit. And to those to whom God pleases to give it, through Jesus Christ our Lord, it is given in so much the greater measure, that we have not only that without which we could not continue, even if we willed, but also something of such a kind that we do will. Actually, the effect of this grace of God in us is that, in recovering and holding on to good, we not only are able to do what we will, but we also will to do what we are able to do. This was not the case with the first man; he had one of these things, not the other. You see, he did not need grace in order to recover good, because he had not yet lost it. But for perseverance in it he did need the aid of a grace, without which he was powerless to persevere. He had received the power to persevere, if he willed, but he had not the will to use his power of perseverance; for, had he had that will, he would have persevered. He could have persevered, if he had willed to; and the fact that he did not will goes back to his free choice, which at the time was free in the sense that he could will either good or evil. However, what will be more free than the free will, when it shall have no power to serve sin? This was to have been for humanity, as it was for the holy angels, the reward of merit. As things are, however, now that our merit is all lost through sin, those who are freed receive as the gift of grace that which was to have been the reward of merit.

We must have a careful and attentive look at the difference between these two sets of things: to be able not to sin, and not to be able to sin; to be able not to die, and not to be able to die; to be able not to forsake good, and not to be able to forsake good. The first man was able not to sin, he was able not to die, he was able not to forsake good. Are we to say that he was not able to sin, having this kind of free will? Or that he was not able to die, seeing that it was said to him: "If you sin, you shall die?" Or that he was not able to forsake good, when he did forsake it by sin, and for that reason died? As I say, the first freedom of the will was in being able not to sin; the final freedom will be much greater—in not being able to sin. The first immortality was in being able not to die; the final immortality will be much greater—in not being able to die. The first power of perseverance was in being able not to forsake good; the final power will be the blessedness of perseverance—in not being able to forsake good. Because these latter gifts are better and more desirable, the former gifts are not therefore of no account or of small account.

In the same fashion, the aids themselves are to be distinguished. One is an aid without which something is not done; the other, by which something is done. For instance, we cannot live without food, but even when one has food, it does not make him live, if he wishes to die. Food, therefore, is an aid without which there is no living, not an aid by which one is made to live. On the other hand, take beatitude; when it is given to a person who did not have it, immediately he becomes blessed. It is, therefore, an aid not only without which that does not come to pass for which it is given, but also by which it does come to pass. You see, then, how this is an aid both by which something is done, and without which it is not done; first, because a person immediately becomes blessed, if beatitude is given to him, and secondly, he never becomes blessed, if it is not given to him. On the other hand, food does not inevitably make a person live, and still he cannot live without it.

To the first man, then, who was created just and who received the power not to sin, the power not to die, and the power not to forsake good, there was given an aid to perseverance, not by which he would be made to persevere, but without which he could not of his own free will persevere. At the present time, however, this sort of aid is not given to the saints predestined by grace for the kingdom of God; but an aid is given of such a kind that perseverance itself is given them. The result is that not only are they unable to persevere without this gift, but also by reason of this gift they cannot fail to persevere.…

In view of the fact that the first man did not receive this gift of God (that is, perseverance in good), but perseverance or non-perseverance was left to his power of choice, he had such energies of will—a will that was made without sin and met no resistance from any interior conflict—that the power of perseverance might fittingly be entrusted to it, considering its goodness and the ease with which it could live well. God, it is true, foresaw the evil that humans would do (foreseeing it, of course, he did not force them to it), but at the same time he knew the good that he would himself make come out of it. As things are now, after the loss of that great liberty in consequence of sin, a weakness remains that must be aided by still greater gifts. It has pleased God completely to extinguish the pride of human presumption, "lest any flesh should pride itself before him" (1 Cor 1: 29). In what respect may flesh not pride itself before him, save in respect of its merits? It could indeed have had merits, but it lost them; and it lost them by the very thing through which it might have had them—its free will.

Clearly, then, even in the matter of perseverance in good, God did not want his saints to take pride in their own strength, but in him; for he not only gives them an aid of the kind given to the first man, without which they are not able to persevere, if they will; but he also effects in them the will itself. The result is that, since there is no perseverance without the power and the will to persevere, both the possibility and the will to persevere are given them by the bounty of divine grace. Their will is so roused by the Holy Spirit that they are able to persevere, because they will to do so; and they will to do so, because God effects this will. If in the weakness of this life (in which, however, strength is to be perfected, that pride may be curbed), their will were to be left to itself, to keep faithful, if it wished, to that aid of God without which they could not persevere, and if God did not effect in them the will itself, their will would, in its weakness, be overcome amid life's many and severe temptations. They would not be able to persevere, because they would fail in their weakness and not will (to persevere); or at least, by reason of the will's weakness they would not so will as to be able to persevere (*On Admonition and Grace,* 29-38).[15]

V. Predestination and the Universal Saving Will of God

Augustine does not limit himself to considering the order of grace in itself; he also examines it inasmuch as it is eternally prepared by God. The word he uses for this eternal preparation is predestination insofar as it affects those elected for salvation. This teaching is found chiefly in the writings of his last years, e.g. *On Admonition and Grace,* 39-48; and the two-part work *On the Predestination of the Saints* and *On the Gift of Perseverance* (428-429). However, its essential outline is already present at the beginning of his episcopate, and, as he himself says (cfr. *On the Gift of Perseverance,* 53), it is implicity contained in the famous expression in the *Confessions,* 10, 37, 60: "Give what you command, and command what you will."

For Augustine, predestination is not merely God's foreknowledge but also his firm and efficacious will to sanctify and save all the elect gratuitously. It is "the foreknowledge and the preparation of God's kindnesses, whereby they are most certainly saved, whoever they are that are saved" (*On the Gift of Perseverance,* 35). The number of the elect is fixed once and for all (*On Admonition and Grace,* 39; *On the City of God,* 14, 26; *On the Predestination of the Saints,* 34). God knows them individually; he has prepared infallible means to lead each one to grace; he wills that they shall accomplish the meritorious works which are the condition for gaining heaven, although not the condition of the divine election. Lastly, he wills to vouchsafe perseverance to them so that they may be glorified. Hence, perseverance is a gift and cannot be merited (*On the Gift of Perseverance,* 10). However, we can dispose ourselves to it through prayer and keep on praying until the day when God in crowning our merits will crown his own gifts.

As to the text regarding the universal saving will of God (cfr.

[15]Text: PL 44.933-940; cf.FOTC 2.280-293, trans. J. Courtney Murray

1 Tim 2: 4), Augustine, in his *Enchiridion,* 27, takes *all* (*omnes*) as meaning that Christ is the salvation of all those who in actual fact are saved, or as meaning that there will be many saved from all classes of society. Elsewhere he translates *omnes* by *multi* (many) [*Against Julian,* 4, 44] or explains wills (*vult*) in the sense that God gives to the predestined the will to be saved (*On Admonition and Grace,* 47).

> Will anyone dare to say that God did not foreknow those to whom he would give to believe, or whom he would give to his Son, that of them he should lose none (Jn 18: 9)? And certainly, if he foreknew these things, he equally certainly foreknew his own kindnesses, by means of which he condescends to save us. This is the predestination of the saints, nothing else: the foreknowledge and the preparation of God's kindnesses, whereby they are most certainly saved, whoever they are that are saved. But where are the rest left by the righteous divine judgment except in the mass of ruin, where the Tyrians and the Sidonians were left? These would have believed if they had seen Christ's wonderful miracles. But since it was not given them to believe, the means of believing also were denied them. Hence it is clear that some have in their understanding itself a naturally divine gift of intelligence, by which they may be moved to the faith, if they either hear the words or behold the signs congruous to their minds. Yet if, in the higher judgement of God, they are not by the predestination of grace separated from the mass of perdition, neither those very divine words nor deeds are applied to them by which they might believe if they only heard or saw such things. Moreover, the Jews were left in the same mass of ruin because they could not believe such great and eminent mighty works as were done in their sight. . . .
> Therefore, the eyes of the Tyrians and Sidonians were not so blinded nor was their heart so hardened, since they would have believed if they had seen such mighty works as the Jews saw. But it did not profit them that they were able to believe, because they were not predestinated by him whose judgments are inscrutable and whose ways beyond discovery. Neither would inability to believe have been a

hindrance to them, if they had been so predestinated as to have their blind eyes illuminated by God, or their stony hearts taken away from those hardened ones. But what the Lord said of the Tyrians and Sidonians may perhaps be understood in light of the sayings that no one comes to Christ unless it were given him, and that it is given to those who are chosen in him before the foundation of the world. This must be confessed beyond a doubt by anyone who hears the divine utterance, not with the deaf ears of the flesh, but with the ears of the heart. This predestination, which is plainly unfolded even by the words of the gospels, applies the Lord's saying ("Believe in God; believe also in me"), as I have suggested before, to the beginning of faith as well as to perseverance in it ("A person ought always to pray, and not to faint"). For they hear these things and act upon them to whom it is given; but they do not act upon them, whether they hear or not, to whom it is not given. . . . Because, "To you," said he, "it is given to know the mystery of the kingdom of heaven, but to them it is not given" (Mt 13: 11). Of these, the one refers to mercy, the other to the judgment of him to whom our soul cries: "I will sing of mercy and judgment unto you, Lord" (Ps 101: 1 [*On the Gift of Perseverance*, 35]).[16]

[16]Text: PL 45.1014; trans. NPNF 5.539

11

Semipelagianism and
the Synod of Orange (529)

Augustine's teachings on grace, in particular on interior grace, the *adjutorium quo,* predestination, and final perseverance, did not meet with universal approval, even in his lifetime. As we have seen, the African monks at Adrumentum raised objections against them. Augustine attempted to solve these difficulties in his last works *On Admonition and Grace, On the Predestination of the Saints* and *On the Gift of Perseverance.* His replies, however, did not appease another group of critics, this time the monks of southern Gaul in the two monasteries of Saint Victor and Lerins.

The controversy began even during Augustine's lifetime, but intensified after his death between 432 and 529. The monks of Provence who opposed Augustine were given the name of Semi-Pelagians in the seventeenth century during the controversies *de auxiliis.* Contrary to Pelagius they admitted the need for baptism and for the grace given at baptism; on the other hand they rejected Augustine's predestinationism, or more precisely, they only partially accepted this determinism of grace. They allowed that there might be cases where grace triumphs over freedom (e. g. Paul's conversion), but these are exceptions; most people, like Zacchaeus and Cornelius, come to baptism after they have asked, knocked, and searched. God desires the salvation of all humans, and he offers his grace to all. It is up to them to choose freely, and it is they who entirely determine their destiny. Of course God's grace is necessary for salvation, but the first steps toward salvation—the *"initium fidei"*—that is, the devout sentiments, the good desires, the sorrow over one's sinful past and the beginning of faith, are within human power and are taken by the human will. God's predestination amounts to his foreknowledge of the merits of those he has predestined. Perseverance is not a grace different from that of baptism.

These "Semi-Pelagian" teachings were first developed by John Cassian, who founded in about 410 the monastery of Saint-Victor of Marseilles. In about 425, he composed his famous *Thirteenth Conference* in which he defended the two ways in which a person may receive the beginnings of a devoted will, *ortus bonae voluntatis,* as described above (cfr. *ibid.,* 8, 3). For Cassian, the fall has not caused total depravity in humankind; the human will is not dead, as Augustine thinks; of course it is not healthy, but Cassian holds that, though it is sick, it is not incapable at times of willing the good, even if not of performing it (cfr. *ibid.,* 11, 4). Cassian treats grace, not so much as a divine gift recreating the whole human nature, but as an indispensable aid, a supporting rather than a transforming force. Finally, he rejects Augustine's restrictive interpretation of God's universal salvific will, for grace, according to him, is granted to all indifferently and is neither irresistible nor indefectible.

These teachings were reported to Augustine by Prosper of Aquitaine and Hilary of Arles in letters 225 and 226, respectively, in the corpus of Augustine's letters, sometime between 427 and 429. Augustine answered by sending his treatises *On the Predestination of the Saints* and *On the Gift of Perseverance.* These works, however, brought no appeasement to the controversy; rather they added fuel to the fire. The person of Augustine became the object of false insinuations and his ideas were travestied in anonymous writings in an effort to discredit them in the eyes of educated Catholics. The best known of these are the *Quindecim capitula Gallorum* (PL 51, 157-170), and the *Praedestinatus* (PL 53, 583-586, 621-628). Augustine is made to say, among other things, that Christ did not die for all, that God does not will the salvation of all, that he creates the largest part of humanity for damnation, that he wills the apostasy of a great number of souls, and that God is the author of sin because he predestines people to damnation.

In defense of Augustine, Prosper published a one thousand-verse poem, *Carmen de ingratis* (PL 51, 91-148), and refuted the monks' attack in his *Pro Augustino responsiones ad capitula objectionum Gallorum calumniantium* (PL 51, 155-175). Further he went to Rome to request Pope Celestine to send a letter to the Gallic bishops vindicating Augustine, but Celestine refused to get too involved and contented himself with general formulas. The papal letter did little to allay the controversy; and upon his return to Gaul, Prosper had to refute another attack made by a work edited by Vincent of Lerins, the *Capitula objectionum Vincentianarum* (PL 51, 177-186). Vincent was already an ardent adversary of Augustine; it is quite probable that the *"privatae opiniunculae"* mentioned in Chapters 26 and 28 of his famous *Commonitorium* refer to the teachings of Augustine. Prosper also composed a work, *Liber contra Collatorem* (PL 51, 213-276), to refute the teaching of Cassian on grace and free will. In particular he frequently attacks the distinction between two classes of people, with one group attaining salvation through natural powers alone, and the other through overpowering grace.

Toward the year 435 the controversy quieted down. Cassian died in 435 and Prosper went to Rome to work for the new Pope Leo I. He composed several works, in particular a collection of Augustine's sentences (PL 51, 427-496) and, in all likelihood, the *De vocatione omnium Gentium* (PL 51, 647-722). Also between 435-443, an important document on grace was composed in Roman circles, which was later attached to the letter of Pope Celestine mentioned above. This work came to be known as the *Indiculus Caelestini,* but its author was either Leo or Prosper of Aquitaine. The text will be given below with some background comments.

The controversy against Augustianism flared up again some forty years later with the condemnation of the predestinarian theses taught by the priest Lucidus who held that Christ did not die for all and that some are predestined to eternal life and others to eternal death. His bishop, Faustus of Riez (c. 408-490), persuaded him to retract his errors, and when his exhortations proved futile, he had him condemned by the council of Arles (473) and later by the council of Lyons (475) where Lucidus had to sign a confession of faith. On the request of the council of Arles, Faustus composed a work entitled *De gratia* in which he rejected both Pelagianism and predestinarianism. For him, predestination consists only in divine foreknowledge which foresees what will be accomplished by human free will. Free will can desire and take the initiative for grace which does no more than cooperate with it (cfr. *De gratia,* 2, 2).

Faustus' work was not attacked in his lifetime, but in c. 517 it fell into the hands of the Scythian monks in Constantinople who found it offensive and asked Rome, through the intermediary of the African bishop Possessor, what authority it attached to Faustus' writings. Pope Hormisdas replied that Faustus had no authority and that the doctrine on grace was to be found in the works of Augustine, in particular in the *On the Predestination of the Saints* and *On the Gift of Perseverance,* and in the *capitula* of the *Indiculus.* Not satisfied with the Pope's answer, the monks turned toward the African bishops whom the Vandal persecution had forced into exile in Sardinia, among whom the most noteworthy was Fulgentius of Ruspe. In reply Fulgentius wrote, besides a christological treatise entitled *Liber de incarnatione et gratia Domini nostri Jesu Christi* (PL 65, 451-493), a work named *Contra Faustum,* which is no longer extant. After his return to Africa, he wrote still more treatises on grace and predestination. Fulgentius was a thoroughgoing follower of Augustine, subscribing to all the latter's teaching on grace.

The solution to the whole conflict was finally reached through the work of Caesarius of Arles, who, though a monk of Lerins, accepted the teaching of Augustine. Elected bishop of Arles in 503, he governed his see for forty years. To combat serious Pelagianism, Caesarius asked Pope Felix IV to approve nineteen doctrinal assertions taken from Augustine's works. This is probably the *Capitula sancti Augustini in urbe Romae transmissa* discovered at Trier in the seventeenth century. The Pope retained but eight of the original *capitula;* the others were replaced by sixteen propositions extracted from Prosper's collection of Augustine's three hundred and ninety-two sayings, the *Sententiarum ex op. S. Aug. delibatarum liber* (PL 51, 427-496).

Caesarius came to the council of Orange, which was attended by 14 bishops, in July 529. He brought with him Pope Felix's document to which he added another canon of his own and a conclusion in the form of a rule of faith. The document was approved by the council and was sent to Rome. Pope Boniface II (530-532) approved by letter the decisions of the synod.

In what follows we will give the text of the *Indiculus* and the document approved by the council of Orange.

I. The Indiculus

The Roman document, which embodies much of Augustine's theology of grace, gives excerpts from Innocent I with his approval of the councils of Carthage and Milevis (chapters 1-4), from Zozimus' *Tractoria* (chapters 5-6), and from the council of Carthage of 418 (chapter 7). The *Indiculus* teaches that grace is necessary for fallen humanity (chapter 1), that everything good comes from God (chapter 2), that the justified person still needs grace at every moment in order to overcome temptation and persevere (chapter 3), that God acts in our hearts with his inspirations (chapter 5). Thus, every good thought and plan and every good movement of the will comes from God (chapter 6). Not just the beginning, but also the continuation of our good works and our final perseverance are the effects of Christ's grace (chapter 8). From start to finish, everything in our salvation is the work of Christ's grace (chapter 9).

> Some who pride themselves on having the name of Catholics are, either through malice or inexperience, spending their time on the condemned propositions of the heretics, and they have the presumption to contradict very faithful writers. Although these people do not hesitate to heap anathemas upon Pelagius and Coelestius, still they find fault with our own teachers for being extremists. They say that they follow and approve only what, through the ministry of its bishops, the holy see of the apostle St. Peter had taught and approved against the enemies of the grace of

God. For this reason it has been necessary to make a diligent investigation as to what judgment the rulers of the Roman Church made about heresy that arose during their time, and what opinion they thought should be held about the grace of God against the dangerous upholders of "free will." We are also attaching some statements of the councils of Africa, which the apostolic bishops certainly adopted as their own when they gave them their approval.

Therefore, to instruct more fully those who are doubtful about some point, we promulgate the doctrine of the holy Fathers in this brief catalogue. Thus, if a person is not too contentious, he may see that the conclusion of all these disputes is contained in the following brief summary, and that there is no ground left him for asserting the contrary if only he believes and professes his faith with the Catholics as follows:

Chapter 1. In Adam's sin all humans lost their natural power for good and their innocence. No one can of his own free will rise out of the depths of this fall if he is not lifted up by the grace of the merciful God. This is the pronouncement by Pope Innocent I of blessed memory in his letter to the Council of Carthage: "He (Adam) acted out of his free will when he used his gifts thoughtlessly; he fell into the abyss of sin and sank and found no means to rise again. Betrayed by his freedom for ever, he would have remained weighed down by his fall had not later the advent of Christ raised him up by his grace when through the cleansing of a new regeneration he washed away all previous guilt in the bath of his baptism."

Chapter 2. Unless he who alone is good grants a participation in his being, no one had goodness within himself. This truth is proclaimed by that pontiff (St. Innocent I) in the following sentence of the same letter: "For the future, can we expect anything good from those whose mentality is such that they think they are the cause of their goodness and do not take into account him whose grace they obtain each day, and who hope to accomplish so much without him?"

Chapter 3. No one, not even he who has been renewed by the grace of baptism, has sufficient strength to overcome the snares of the devil, and to vanquish the concupiscence of the flesh, unless he obtains help from God each day to persevere in a good life. And the truth of this statement is confirmed by the same pope's teaching in the letter cited above: "For although he redeemed humans from their past sins, still, since he knew they could sin again, he had at hand many things whereby he could restore them and set them straight even after they sinned, offering those daily remedies upon which we must rely and trust in our struggle; for by no other means would we be able to overcome our human mistakes."

Chapter 4. No one, except through Christ, can make a good use of his freedom. This truth is proclaimed by the same pope in his letter to the council of Milevis where it is taught: "Let those wicked minds corrupted by perverse doctrines take note that the first man was so deceived by his freedom that while making indulgent use of its restraints he fell into sin by his presumption. Nor could he be rescued from it except through the coming of our Lord Jesus Christ who restored the state of his pristine freedom by means of regeneration."

Chapter 5. All the efforts, and all the works and merits of the saints must be attributed to the praise and glory of God, because no one can please God with anything that is not his very own gift. It is the directive authority of Pope Zosimus of happy memory that leads us to this conclusion; for, when writing to the bishops of the whole world, he says: "But We, inspired by God (for all good things must be attributed to the source from which they proceed), have committed the entire matter to the consideration of our brothers and co-bishops."

This letter shone with the light of purest truth, and the bishops of Africa held it in such esteem that they wrote the following reply to Zosimus: "We considered the contents of the letter which you made sure was sent to all the provinces—the letter in which you said, 'But We, inspired by God . . .'—as a swift thrust of the naked sword of truth with which you dispatch those who exalt human freedom above God's grace. What have you ever done with greater freedom of choice than to commit this entire matter to our humble consideration? And, nevertheless, with sincerity and wisdom you knew that your decision to commit the matter to us was inspired by God, and you truthfully and courageously proclaimed that it was. Without doubt, you did so because the will is prepared by the Lord (Prov 8: 35 Septg), and he himself as a father touches the hearts of his children with inspirations that they may do good of any sort. For as many as are led by the Spirit of God, they are the children of God (Rom 8: 14). Thus we do not judge that we are without freedom of choice nor do we entertain any doubt that God's grace plays an even more predominant role in each and every good impulse of the person's will."

Chapter 6. God so works in the hearts of humans and in free will itself that the holy thought, the gentle counsel, and every movement of a good will are from God, because it is through him that we can do any good, and without him we can do nothing (Jn 15: 5). The same teacher Zosimus instructed us to acknowledge this truth when, speaking to the bishops of the world about the assistance of divine grace, he said: "Is there ever a time when we do not need his help? Therefore, in every action and situation, in every thought and movement, we must pray to him as to our helper and protector. For whatever human nature presumes to do by itself manifests pride, since the Apostle warns: 'Our wrestling is not against flesh and blood, but against the principalities and the powers of this darkness, against the spiritual forces of wickedness on high' (Eph 6: 12). And as he says on another occasion: 'Unhappy man that I am! Who will deliver me from the body of this death? The grace of God through Jesus Christ our Lord' (Rom 7: 24 f). And again: 'By the grace of God I am what I am, and his grace in me has not been fruitless; in fact I labored more than any of them, yet not I, but the grace of God with me'" (1 Cor 15: 10).

Chapter 7. We likewise uphold as the personal teaching of the apostolic see what was set down in the decrees of the Council of Carthage and defined in the third chapter: "Whoever says that God's grace, which justifies humankind through our Lord Jesus Christ, has the power only for the remission of those sins already committed, and is not also a help to prevent sins from being committed: let him be anathema."

We uphold also what was defined in the fourth chapter: "Whoever says that God's grace through Jesus Christ our Lord helps us avoid sin solely because it gives us a very clear knowledge and understanding of the positive and negative commandments, but denies that through this grace there is given to us an ability and a love of doing what we know should be done: let him be anathema. For since the Apostle says: "Knowledge puffs up, but charity edifies" (1 Cor 8: 1), it would be very wrong to believe that we have Christ's grace for knowledge, which puffs up, and not for charity, which edifies. Knowledge of what we ought to do and love of doing it are both gifts of God. Thus knowledge working with charity cannot make us puffed up. For it is also written: "Love is from God" (1 Jn 4: 7).

We uphold also what was defined in the fifth chapter: "Whoever says that grace of justification was given us so that grace could facilitate our fulfilling what our free will is ordered to do, as if to say that, if grace were not given, it would be possible but not easy to obey God's commandments without that grace: let him be anathema. For the Lord was speaking of the observance of the commandments when he said: 'Without me you can do nothing' (Jn 15: 5). He did not say: 'Without me it will be more difficult for you to do anything.'"

Chapter 8. The preceding chapters are the inviolable decrees of the most holy and apostolic see, the decrees by which our Fathers, suppressing the spread of a dangerous novelty, taught us to attribute to the grace of Christ both the initial impulses of a good will and the increase of praiseworthy efforts as well as final perseverance in them. Besides these decrees, let us also examine the sacred words of prayers the priests say. Let us examine these sacred words which were handed down from the apostles throughout the world and which are uniformly used in every Catholic Church, and thus find in the prayers of the liturgy confirmation for the Law of our faith.

For when the leaders of the holy people perform the functions of the office entrusted to them, they plead the cause of the human race before the tribunal of divine mercy. And with the whole Church earnestly praying along with them, they beg and entreat that the faith be given to infidels, that idolators be freed from the errors of their ungodliness, that the veil be removed from the hearts of the Jews so that the light of truth may shine upon them, that heretics may come to their senses and accept the Catholic faith, that schismatics may receive the spirit of charity that restores life, that sinners be given the healing powers of repentance, and finally, that catechumens may be brought to the sacrament of regeneration and that the heavenly court of mercy may be opened to them.

That these requests from the Lord are not just a matter of form is shown by the actual course of events. For God, indeed, deigns to draw many people from errors of every description—people whom he has rescued from the power of darkness and transferred into the kingdom of his beloved Son (Col 1: 13), and whom he has changed from vessels of wrath into vessels of mercy (Rom 9: 22 f). And this is felt to be so exclusively a divine operation, that thanksgiving and praise are being constantly given to God, who brings about the enlightenment and correction of such persons.

Chapter 9. By these ecclesiastical norms and these documents derived from divine authority, we are so strengthened with the help of the Lord, that we profess that God is the author of all good desires and deeds, of all efforts and virtues, with which from the beginning of faith we tend to God. And we do not doubt that his grace anticipates every one of our merits, and that it is through him that we begin both the will and the performance (Phil 2: 13) of any good work.

To be sure, free will is not destroyed by this help and strength from God, but it is freed; so that from darkness it is brought to light, from evil to good, from sickness to health, from ignorance to prudence. For such is God's goodness to us that he wills that his gifts be our merits, and that he will grant us an eternal reward for what he has given us. Indeed, God so acts in us that we both will and do what he wills; he does not allow to lie idle in us what he bestowed upon us to be employed, not neglected. And he acts in this manner in us so that we are cooperators with his grace. And if we notice that there is some weakness in us because of our own negligence, we should with all care hasten to him who heals all our diseases and redeems our lives from destruction (Ps 102: 3 f), and to whom we say each day, "Lead us not into temptation but deliver us from evil" (Mt 6: 13).[1]

II. The Council of Orange (529)

Among the definitions of Orange (Arausica), one may distinguish between the canons properly so called (n. 1-8), the propositions (9-25) and the profession of faith which crowns the document. In general, the document reflects a moderate Augustinianism, without upholding each one of Augustine's propositions.

> By the mercy of God, at the invitation of Liberius we had gathered together to dedicate the basilica which this most honorable prefect, our noble son, had with faithful devotion constructed in the city of Orange. A spiritual conference took place among us on matters regarding the faith of the Church. We realized then that there are some who, through simplicity and without thinking, wish to hold opinions on grace and free choice which are not in accord with the role of the Catholic faith. Thus it seemed reasonable and right to us, in accord with the advice and authority of the apostolic see, that we should instruct these people, who are not thinking as they should, by publishing for everyone's observance and undersigning with our own hands a few articles sent to us by the apostolic see that had been gathered from the books of the Holy Scriptures by the ancient fathers on this particular question. Once he has read these articles, anyone who up until now has not believed as he ought about grace and free choice should not hesitate to direct his mind to those things which are proper to the Catholic faith.

[1]Text: PL 50; trans. *The Church Teaches: Documents of the Church in English Translation* (St. Louis: B. Herder, 1955)

THE CANONS

(1) If anyone says that the whole person, that is, in both body and soul, was not changed for the worse through the offense of Adam's transgression, but that only the body became subject to corruption while the liberty of the soul remains unharmed, then he has been deceived by Pelagius' error and opposes the Scripture which says, "The soul which sins shall die" (Ezek 18:20) and "Do you not know that if you show yourselves ready to obey anyone, you are the slaves of the one you obey?" (Rom 6:16) and "A person is judged the slave of the one who conquers him" (2 Pet 2:19).

(2) If anyone asserts that the transgression of Adam harmed him alone and not his descendants, or that the damage is only by the death of the body which is a punishment for sin, and thus does not confess that the sin itself, which is the death of the soul, also passed through one person into the whole human race, then he does injustice to God, contradicting the Apostle who says, "Through one person sin entered the world and through sin death, and thus it passed to all humans, in whom all have sinned" (Rom 5:12).

(3) If anyone says that God's grace can be acquired by human prayer but not that grace itself makes us pray, he contradicts the prophet Isaiah or the Apostle who says the same thing, "I was found by those who did not seek me; I showed myself plainly to those who did not ask for me" (Isa 65:1; Rom 10:20).

(4) If anyone maintains that God awaits our will before cleansing us from sin, but does not profess that even the desire to be cleansed is accomplished through the infusion and the interior working of the Holy Spirit, he opposes the Holy Spirit speaking through Solomon: "The will is prepared by the Lord" (Prov 8: 35 Septg). And he opposes the Apostle's salutary message: "It is God who of his good pleasure works in you both the will and the performance" (Phil 2: 13).

(5) He is an adversary of the apostolic teaching who says that the increase of faith as well as the beginning of faith and the very desire of faith—by which we believe in him who

justifies the unjustified, and by which we come to the regeneration of sacred baptism—inheres in us naturally and not by a gift of grace. This grace is the inspiration of the Holy Spirit, guiding our will away from infidelity to faith, from godlessness to piety. For St. Paul says: "We are convinced of this, that he who has begun a good work in you will bring it to perfection until the day of Christ Jesus" (Phil 1: 6). And he says: "You have been given the favor on Christ's behalf—not only to believe in him but also to suffer for him" (Phil 1: 29). And again: "By grace you have been saved through faith; and that not from yourselves, for it is the gift of God" (Eph 2: 8). For those who say that it is a natural faith by which we believe in God teach that all those who are separated from the Church of Christ are, in a certain sense, believers.

(6) If anyone says that mercy is divinely bestowed on us when without God's grace we believe, will, desire, try, labor, pray, watch, apply ourselves, ask, seek, and knock, but does not confess that the bestowal and inspiration of the Holy Spirit brings us the strength to believe, to will, or to do all these things as we ought; and if he thus subordinates the help of grace to either human humility or obedience, and does not admit that our being humble and obedient is itself a gift of grace, then he opposes the Apostle who says, "What do you have that you have not received?" (1 Cor 4:7) and "By the grace of God I am what I am" (1 Cor 15:10).

(7) If anyone affirms that by his natural strength he is able to think as is required or choose anything good pertaining to his eternal salvation, or to assent to the saving message of the Gospel without the illumination and inspiration of the Holy Spirit who gives everyone delight in consenting to the truth, then he is deceived by an heretical spirit and does not understand God's voice speaking in the Gospel, "Without me you can do nothing" (Jn 15:5) and the statement of the Apostle: "We are not capable of thinking anything by ourselves from our own resources; our adequacy is from God" (2 Cor 3:5).

(8) If anyone maintains that some come to the grace of baptism by mercy but others can attain it through free choice, which is wounded in everyone born of the transgres-

sion of the first human being, he shows that he has departed from the true faith. In saying this, he either asserts that not everyone's free choice is weakened through the first person's sin, or he obviously thinks it is wounded but only in a way that still allows them the strength to search out the mystery of eternal salvation by themselves without God's revelation. The Lord himself showed how false this is in testifying that, not certain ones, but no one at all, could come to him unless the Father had drawn him (Jn 6:44). Thus he said to Peter, "Blessed are you, Simon, son of Jonah, because flesh and blood did not reveal this to you but my Father who is in heaven" (Mt 16:17). Similarly the Apostle says, "No one can proclaim Jesus Lord except in the Holy Spirit" (1 Cor 12:3).

THE PROPOSITIONS

(9) The help of God. It is God's gift for us to think properly and to avoid falsehood and injustice. Whenever we do good, God works in us and with us to make us work.

(10) The help of God. Those who are reborn and have been healed should always implore the help of God, so that they may be able to attain the good end and persevere in good work.

(11) The making of vows. No one properly consecrates anything to God unless he promises something received from him, as we read, "And we give to you what we have received from your hand" (1 Chron 29:14).

(12) How God loves us. God loves us as we will be by his own gift, not as we are by our merits.

(13) The restoration of free choice. The choice of the will which was weakened in the first human being can be restored only through the grace of baptism. Once something is lost, it can be returned only by someone who could give it in the first place. Thus Truth himself says, "If the Son sets you free, then you will be free indeed" (Jn 8:36).

(14) No one in trouble is freed from any kind of difficulty unless God's mercy intervenes for him. Thus the Psalmist says, "Your mercy goes quickly before us, Lord" (Ps 79:8) and "My God will go before me with his mercy" (Ps 59:10).

(15) Through his own iniquity, Adam was changed for the worse from what God had made him. Through God's grace the one who is faithful is also changed, but for the better, from what iniquity has done to him. That change was of the first transgressor; this one, according to the Psalmist, "is the change of the right hand of the Most High" (Ps 77:10).

(16) No one should glory in what he seems to possess as though he had not received it, or as though he could receive it because the letter outwardly either appeared so that he could read or sounded so that he could hear. For, as the Apostle says, "If justice comes through the Law, then Christ died in vain" (Gal 2:21) and "Ascending on high, he took captivity captive; he bestowed gifts on humans" (Eph 4:8). Whoever possesses anything has it from him. Anyone who denies he has it from him either does not really possess it or will be deprived of what he does have.

(17) Christian courage. Worldly desire makes the Gentiles brave, but the charity of God makes Christians courageous. This charity is poured into our hearts not through our own choice of will, but through the Holy Spirit who is given to us (Rom 5:5).

(18) No merits precede grace. Rewards are due for good works if they are performed; grace, which is not owed, precedes so that they will be performed.

(19) No one is saved without God's mercy. Human nature, even had it remained in the integrity in which it was created, could by no means have saved itself without the assistance of its Creator. Thus, since without God's grace it could not retain the salvation it had received, without God's grace how will it be able to gain the salvation it has lost?

(20) A person can do nothing good without God. God does many good things in a person which the person himself does not do, but the person does no good thing which God does not provide that the person do.

(21) Nature and grace. As the Apostle truly says to those who wanted to be justified in the Law and thus abandon grace, "If justice is from the Law, then Christ died in vain" (Gal 2:21), so those who think the grace which the faith in Christ receives and praises is actually nature itself are rightly addressed: "If justice is through nature, then Christ died in

vain." The Law had already been given, and it did not justify. Nature as well had already been given, and it did not justify. Thus Christ did not die in vain, so that the Law might be fulfilled through him who said, "I did not come to abolish the Law but to fulfill it" (Mt 5:17). So, too, nature, which was ruined through Adam, was restored through him who said he had come to seek and to save what had perished (Lk 19:10).

(22) The things which are proper to humans. Of himself, one has nothing but lies and sin. If anyone has any truth and justice, this comes from that spring for which we should thirst in this desert, so that by being moistened by a few drops from it we may not fail in the way.

(23) The divine and human wills. When people do what displeases God, they do their own will, not God's. When, however, they serve the divine will in doing what they will, although they perform their actions voluntarily, what they do is actually the will of him who prepares and commands what they will (Prov 8:35).

(24) The vine and the branches. Branches are in a vine not by giving anything to the vine but by receiving their life from it. A vine is in its branches by supplying them with life-giving nourishment, not by receiving it from them. Thus for Christ to remain in them and for them to remain in Christ are both profitable for his disciples, but not for Christ. If one branch is cut off, another can spring up from the living stock; but the branch which is cut off cannot live without the stock.

(25) The love by which we love God. To love God is certainly a gift of God. His own gift makes us love him; he loves before he is loved. We were loved even when we displeased him, so that we might be changed to please him. The Spirit of the Father and the Son, whom we love along with the Father and the Son, has poured forth charity into our hearts (Rom 5:15).

THE DEFINITION OF FAITH

And thus, according to the passages of Holy Scripture and according to the explanations of the ancient Fathers, quoted above, we, with God's help, must believe and preach the following: Human free will was made so weak and unsteady through the sin of the first man that, after the Fall, no one could love God as was required, or believe in God, or perform good works for God, unless the grace of divine mercy anticipated him. Therefore, we believe that the renowned faith which was given to the just Abel, to Noe, to Abraham, to Isaac and Jacob, and to that vast number of the saints of old, was given through the grace of God and not through natural goodness, which had first been given to Adam. This faith of theirs the apostle Paul has praised in his preaching.

And we know and believe that even after the coming of Christ this grace of faith is not found in the free will of all who desire to be baptized, but is conferred through the generosity of Christ, according to what has already been said and according to what Paul preaches: "You have been given the favor on Christ's behalf—not only to believe in him, but also to suffer for him" (Phil 1: 29). And also: "God who has begun a good work in you will bring it to perfection until the day of our Lord" (Phil 1: 6). And again: "By grace you have been saved, through faith; and that not from yourselves, for it is the gift of God" (Eph 2: 8). And the Apostle says of himself: "I have obtained mercy that I might be faithful" (1 Cor 7: 25; 1 Tim 1: 13). He does not say, "because I was faithful," but he says, "that I might be faithful." And Scripture says further: "What have you that you have not received?" (1 Cor 4: 7). And again: "Every good gift, and every perfect gift is from above, coming down from the Father of lights" (Jas 1: 17). And again: "No one has anything unless it is given him from above" (Jn 3: 27). There are innumerable passages of Sacred Scripture that can be cited to bear witness to grace, but they have been omitted for the sake of brevity. And, indeed, more texts would not help a person for whom these few are not sufficient.

According to Catholic faith we also believe that after grace has been received through baptism, all the baptized, if they are willing to labor faithfully, can and ought to accomplish with Christ's help and cooperation what pertains to the salvation of their souls. We do not believe that some are predestined to evil by the divine power; and, furthermore, if there are those who wish to believe in such an enormity, with great abhorrence we anathematize them.

We also believe and profess for our salvation that in every good work it is not that we make a beginning and afterwards are helped through God's mercy, but rather, that without any previous good merits on our part, God himself first inspires us with faith in him and love of him so that we may faithfully seek the sacrament of baptism, and so that after baptism, with his help we may be able to accomplish what is pleasing to him. Therefore, we evidently must believe that the remarkable faith of the thief whom the Lord called to his home in paradise (Lk 23: 43), the faith of Cornelius the centurion to whom an angel of the Lord was sent (Acts 10: 3), and the faith of Zacchaeus who merited to receive the Lord himself (Lk 19: 6), was not a gift of nature but a gift of God's generosity.[2]

---

[2]Text: Mansi, 8. 711-718; trans. J.P. Burns (ed.), *Theological Anthropology,* 112-128

Epilogue

Chronologically, the council of Orange was the last most important event in the development of patristic anthropology. In one sense it marked the end of a theological era; it settled the semi-Pelagian controversy that had been going on for nearly a hundred years in the West by adopting a moderate form of Augustinianism, especially in the question of predestination. In another sense, it opened up a new phase of theological discussion insofar as the Augustinian heritage, particularly as embodied in Augustine's last writings, contained unresolved issues concerning the relationship between divine grace and human freedom and therefore unavoidably provoked further debates.

Indeed, it may be argued that post-Patristic theology of grace, at least in the West, is largely a series of footnotes to Augustine. The Carolingian period was marked by the condemnation of Gottschalk's theory of double predestination and the two opposing councils, that of Quiercy-sur-Oise (853) supported by Charles the Bald and Hincmar, archbishop of Reims, who opposed double predestination, and that of Valence (855), endorsed by right-wing Augustinians such as Ratramnus, Lupus Servatus and Prudentius, who championed the doctrine of double predestination.

Augustinianism is also evident in Anselm of Canterbury who, in his famous *Monologium,* takes inspiration from Augustine and whose *Cur Deus Homo* presupposes the Bishop of Hippo's teaching on original sin. In his reflections on freedom Anselm is closer to the Augustine of the anti-Manichaean writings than to the author of *On Admonition and Grace.* But he remains fully Augustinian in attributing the whole human process of conversion and salvation to grace. Through the *Sentences* of Peter Lombard, many quotations from Augustine became a permanent heritage of the Middle Ages and beyond. Augustinian anthropology is also preserved in Thomas Aquinas' doctrines of the turning to faith, conversion, merit and predestination. On all of these questions, Aquinas scarcely departs from basic Augustinian teaching, even though in formulating his theology of grace the Angelic Doctor makes a greater use of Aristotelian categories and thought forms.

Over against the Pelagianizing tendencies of nominalism, particularly in William of Ockham and Gabriel Biel, rigorist Augustinians such as Gregory of Rimini (+ 1357) and Thomas Bradwardine (+ 1349) reacted by reaffirming, at times too slavishly, the theses of Augustine, especially regarding predestination. Both nominalism and rigorist Augustinianism influenced Luther and Calvin in their understanding of justification, grace, and predestination. The decree on justification of the Council of Trent, especially in its description of the way in which sinners dispose themselves for justification and in its teaching on final perseverance and merit, reveals a profound influence of Augustinianism.

Despite the real achievement of the Council of Trent, disputes regarding the human condition and divine grace did not fail to crop up soon after, first with Baius who taught a form of Pelagianism regarding the primitive state of humanity and a mitigated Protestant doctrine regarding the total corruption of human nature and freedom. Shortly after the condemnation of Baius by Pius V (1567) and Gregory XIII (1580), another series of controversies, the famous *De Auxiliis*, with Molina emphasizing human freedom and Bañez divine grace, broke out first in Spain, then continued in Rome for nine years and finally ended with Paul V imposing silence on the two parties in 1607 without settling anything at all regarding whether God's grace moves the human will physically (as the Dominicans held) or morally (as the Jesuits contended). The unresolved issues were brought to the surface again by Cornelius Jansenius whose *Augustinus,* published in 1640, rejects sufficient grace and defends the *delectatio victrix* of

Christ's grace. The sinner sins freely, though necessarily, because he loves sin, whereas the just person accomplishes the works of the Law with the spontaneity caused by divine delectation. In 1653, thirteen years after the appearance of *Augustinus* and fifteen years after the author's death, Innocent X solemnly condemned the doctrine of Jansenius. Despite the condemnation, the Jansenist party became a subject of debate for more than a hundred years, complicated by the errors of Quesnel (1634-1719), the writings of Henry Noris (1631-1704), and the synod of Pistoia (1786).

From this brief overview of the development of the doctrine of grace it is clear that Western theology was for a long time obsessed with certain aspects of the reality of grace: grace and freedom, grace and merit, justification and predestination. Heresies—Pelagianism, Protestantism, Baianism, and Jansenism—were allowed to dictate the terms of the theology of grace. Even though these aspects are important, they should not occupy the central stage and overshadow the heart of Christian life, namely, humans as image and likeness of God, the divinization of the Christian, adoptive sonship, the mystery of our union with Christ, and the indwelling of the Holy Spirit. Contemporary renewal of theological anthropology, with its remote roots in the works of Petavius (1582-1652) and of Sheeben (1835-1888), and its more recent "resourcement" movement, attempts to retrieve the rich Christian tradition on grace. It is only natural that a careful study of the writings of the early Greek and Latin Christian writers should be an essential part of this ongoing enterprise.

Select Bibliography

Bernard, R., *L'Image de Dieu d'après saint Athanase* (Paris: Aubier, 1952).

Brückner, A., *Quellen zur Geschichte des Pelagianischen Streits* (Tübingen: Verlag von J.C.B. Mohr, 1906).

Burghardt, W.J., *The Image of God in Man According to Cyril of Alexandria* (Woodstock, Maryland: Woodstock College Press, 1957).

Burns, J.P., *The Development of Augustine's Doctrine of Operative Grace* (Paris: Etudes augustiniennes, 1980).

Burns, J.P. (ed.), *Theological Anthropology* (Philadelphia: Fortress Press, 1985).

Chéné, J., *La théologie de s. Augustin. Grâce et prédestination* (Le Puy/Lyon, 1961).

Crouzel, H., *Théologie de l'image de Dieu chez Origene* (Toulouse: Aubier, 1955).

Daniélou, J., *Gospel Message and Hellenistic Culture,* translated and edited by John A. Baker (Philadelphia: The Westminister Press, 1973).

Evans, R., *Pelagius. Inquiries and Reappraisals* (New York: The Seabury Press, 1968).

Ferguson, J., *Pelagius* (Cambridge, The University Press, 1956).

Gross, J., *La divinisation du chrétien d'après les Pères grecs* (Paris: Gabalda, 1938).

Kelly, J.N.D., *Early Christian Doctrines* (New York: Harper and Row, 1960).

Leys, R., *L'Image de Dieu chez saint Grégoire de Nysse* (Brussels and Paris: Desclée de Brouwer, 1951).

Maloney, G.A., *Man. The Divine Icon* (Pecos, New Mexico: Dove Publications, 1973).

Perrin, M., *L'homme antique et chrétien. L'anthropologie de Lactance,* 250-325 (Paris: Beauchesne, 1981).

Rondet, H., *The Grace of Christ,* translated and edited by Tad W. Guzie (New York: Newman Press, 1966).

Rondet, H., *Original Sin. The Patristic and Theological Background,* translated by Cajetan Finegan (Shannon, Ireland:Ecclesia Press, 1969).

Sullivan, J.E., *The Image of God. The Doctrine of St. Augustine and Its Influence* (Dubuque, Iowa: The Priory Press, 1963).

TeSelle, E., *Augustine the Theologian* (New York: Herder and Herder, 1970).

Van der Meer, F., *Augustine the Bishop. Church and Society at the Dawn of the Middle Ages,* translated by Brian Battershaw and G.R. Lamb (London: Sheed and Ward, 1961).

INDEX